IMAGES
of Modern America

Grove City

ON THE FRONT COVER: Clockwise from top left: Beulah Park Racetrack's finish line; Grove City Bowling sign; Society for the Preservation and Encouragement of Barbershop Quartet Singing in America; Faultless, the Grove City High School greyhound; and Hot-air balloon during Balloons Off Broadway. (All Attics to Archives Collection.)

ON THE BACK COVER: From left to right: Opening day of the Super Duper grocery store on October 13, 1960; the Grove City High School Marching Band at the Arts in the Alley Parade; and Endres' Saloon discovers a mail pouch sign under old siding. (All Attics to Archives Collection.)

IMAGES
of Modern America

GROVE CITY

Laura Lanese, Janet Shailer, and Kelli Milligan Stammen

ARCADIA
PUBLISHING

ISBN 978-1-4671-1437-0

Published by Arcadia Publishing
Charleston, South Carolina

Printed in the United States of America

Library of Congress Control Number: 2015931277

For all general information, please contact Arcadia Publishing:
Telephone 843-853-2070
Fax 843-853-0044
E-mail sales@arcadiapublishing.com
For customer service and orders:
Toll-Free 1-888-313-2665

Visit us on the Internet at www.arcadiapublishing.com

Contents

ACKNOWLEDGMENTS

This book is dedicated to all the people—past, present, and future—of Grove City. The authors would like to note that this book would not be possible without the tireless efforts of the Southwest Public Libraries, particularly the Grove City Library's reference staff, in particular Karen Lane. Unless otherwise noted, all images used in the production of this book are from the library's Attics to Archives Collection. In addition, this book would not have been possible without the support of the Southwest Franklin County Historical Society.

Other people who have been most helpful in the completion of this project include Mike Boso, Christina Edwards, Emily Castle, Linda Litzinger, Gillian Nance, Emma Trudeau, Lois Gibboney, Bethanne Gibboney Johnson, Jim and Maria Sigman, Mark Valentine, Les Bostic, Roger Burket, Karen Fahy, the *Southwest Messenger*, Mayor Richard "Ike" Stage, Rosemary Turnbull, state representative Cheryl Grossman, Jim Norris, Don Washburn, Jim Hale, Our Lady of Perpetual Help Church, Jack and Betty Seese, Aneda White, Marilyn Gibboney, the *Grove City Record*, the City of Grove City, Columbus Metropolitan Library, Dave Dildine, Mike Lilly, Gary Rugh, Jackson Township, Sue Zeszotek, Jan Noltemeyer, Gary Buckingham, Andy Furr, Harrison College's Lenee Pezzano, Ben Brace, Amanda Davis, Jason Kaufman, Sue Ruoff Zeszotek, Steven Walters, Bev Babbert, Gary Shyu, Diane and Dave Crosby, James McDonald, Jack Middendorf, South-Western City Schools, Grove City YMCA, Jane Mixer, Sharon Thomas Downs, Sean Hannon family, Chuck Boso, Bill Ferguson, Jr., Ed Reeves, Denise Corkwell, Maria Pontones, Nona Shea, Greg Hritz, Leroy Geyer, and Kim Conrad. The authors would like to apologize for any errors or omissions in this book.

Lastly, we would like to thank our families. Laura Lanese thanks her husband, Mike, and children Michael, Camille, and Francesca. Janet Shailer thanks Jack, Jay, Allison, Annie, Alexander, Evan, and Nathan Shailer. Kelli Milligan Stammen thanks her husband, Ken, and children Ava and Aidan.

INTRODUCTION

The state of Ohio was conceived in the throes of the American Revolution, born out of a wilderness in 1803 and raised in infancy along primitive transportation routes. Such was Grove City, a village founded along a stagecoach line in 1852 by entrepreneur William F. Breck on land once owned by two Revolutionary War soldiers, Gen. Daniel Morgan and Col. William Washington.

The village quickly prospered with an influx of German immigrants and others from the Eastern United States looking for opportunities in the burgeoning new frontier of the American Midwest.

Grove City began to flourish in 1884 with the arrival of the railroad and the addition of the Grove City & Green Lawn Avenue Railroad, known as the interurban, in 1898. The town became a major agricultural hub with a large grain elevator and farmers' exchange. While the elevators were demolished in 2007, the farmers' exchange building still stands and currently houses several retail stores.

This book begins in 1952, Grove City's centennial year, and picks up where the previous book (Arcadia's Images of America: *Grove City*) leaves off. World War II had just ended, and GIs were looking for jobs and places to raise their families. Being a mere five miles from the state capital of Columbus, Grove City attracted new homeowners who wanted the quiet of suburbia with the amenities of a bustling Franklin County.

By the mid-1950s, so many children were pouring into area schools that a better path for educating them was needed. On January 1, 1956, South-Western Local Schools was brought together from five local schools and one exempted village school system scattered throughout four contiguous townships. Today, the school district is the sixth largest in the state, with approximately 20,000 students.

The 1950s saw the extension of Kingston Avenue east to Hoover Road, opening up opportunities for several subdivisions and the First Baptist Church to be built. As new residents arrived, more churches were built, including Our Lady of Perpetual Help on Broadway in 1959. The complexion of Columbus Street began to change as Grove City United Methodist Church, the "Purple Door" church, moved from Park Street east to Columbus Street. Soon it was joined by a new neighbor across the street, the Grove City Church of Christ (now Victorious Living Church).

In the late 1950s, the Women's Juvenile Service Board, a small volunteer group led by Anne Hayes, also known as "Mrs. Woody," identified the need for a residential home for disadvantaged boys with school, home, and community problems. The board raised funds to purchase property in Grove City, and the legacy of Buckeye Boys Ranch began in 1961. During the 1970s and 1980s, the ranch hosted world-class tennis tournaments, which attracted celebrities such as Jack Nicklaus, Arthur Ashe, and Jimmy Connors. Today it is a coed facility known as the Buckeye Ranch and a national leader in the treatment of emotionally, mentally, and behaviorally troubled youth.

By 1962, the interstate highway system had carved I-71 along Grove City's eastern border, followed a few years later by I-270, running along the city's northern border, connecting the city to I-70, which stretches from Baltimore, Maryland, to Cove Fort, Utah, paralleling US 40, the old National Road. This strategic location became a major asset, as businesses found Grove City the perfect place to prosper between these two major highway systems.

The 1960s brought changes to Hoover Road, a major artery running north and south through Grove City. Hoover Road, once a path to shuttle cattle between farm fields, became the location of Jackson Township Fire Station 202 and Grove City High School, south of White Road on the site of the old Milligan turkey farm, a harbinger of the growth that would follow in the decades to come.

By the 1970s, city government began serious discussions about the need for Grove City to expand its tax base. Plans for future industrial parks formed. These became a reality as Southwest Boulevard was extended in 1980 from Broadway west to Demorest Road. On the southern edge of town, a business park on Seeds Road opened. It was during this decade that resident Steve Carr began what is now known as the world's largest high school–alumni softball tournament, which brings thousands of former Grove City High School graduates back to their hometown for a weekend of reunions.

The 1980s saw the first Arts in the Alley event, which has grown into a major draw for artists and tourists every September. After years of planning, a large Wal-Mart Distribution center opened on the west side of town in 1991, while industrial parks sprang up on the east side with the extension of Gantz Road. Tosoh SMD, which began in Grove City in 1975 with two part-time employees, has grown into a world-class specialized-metals company at its Gantz Road facility.

The 1990s began with the grand opening of the Capital City Music Center in June 1990 at Beulah Park. Baptizing the concert series was "Ol' Blue Eyes," Frank Sinatra. He was followed by many others, including Billy Idol, Steve Miller Band, and Guns N' Roses. The transformation of Grove City continued with the new municipal building, dedicated on July 27, 1990. In 1996, the city annexed the land south of Orders Road into the city to expand the parkland available to residents. That land was developed into Fryer Park and today holds eight softball fields, a new YMCA, a wooded preserve, a year-round shelter house, a fishing pond, a sledding hill, and an all-accessible playground for kids of all abilities, as well as Century Village, a historical park within a park.

In 2002, Grove City saw the opening of the second public high school within its borders. Central Crossing High School opened on August 28, 2002, and the school colors of royal blue and silver were soon scattered across town with the crimson and blue of Grove City High School. Upscale housing sprouted along the new extension of Buckeye Parkway with the opening of the Pinnacle Golf Club in 2006 and the BIA Parade of Homes in 2007. In 2009, the Parkway Centre Shopping Center opened on the east side of I-71 along Stringtown Road.

The year 2014 brought excitement with the grand opening of the new Mount Carmel Grove City Emergency facility and the end of an era in the closing of Beulah Park Racetrack. Beulah Park was Ohio's first Thoroughbred racetrack, opening in 1923 on Grove City's west side. During the 1950s, the sport of kings attracted celebrities and professional baseball players from across the country and became the place to be seen. The racetrack served as a major employer in the area for 91 years. It closed for good on May 3, 2014, when the track's license was moved to Austintown, Ohio.

Today, the city has grown to a population of over 37,000 residents and by approximately 4,000 acres, yet it has retained its small-town feel. The once-dusty stagecoach route has turned into a modern-technology, logistics, and shopping hub. It is still a stagecoach stop, too, with more than 700,000 visitors staying in town as they visit Grove City and Columbus. All the hustle and bustle give the city its ever-growing momentum, while its colorful past and solid foundation enable the community to go boldly into a bright future.

One

Historic Town Center

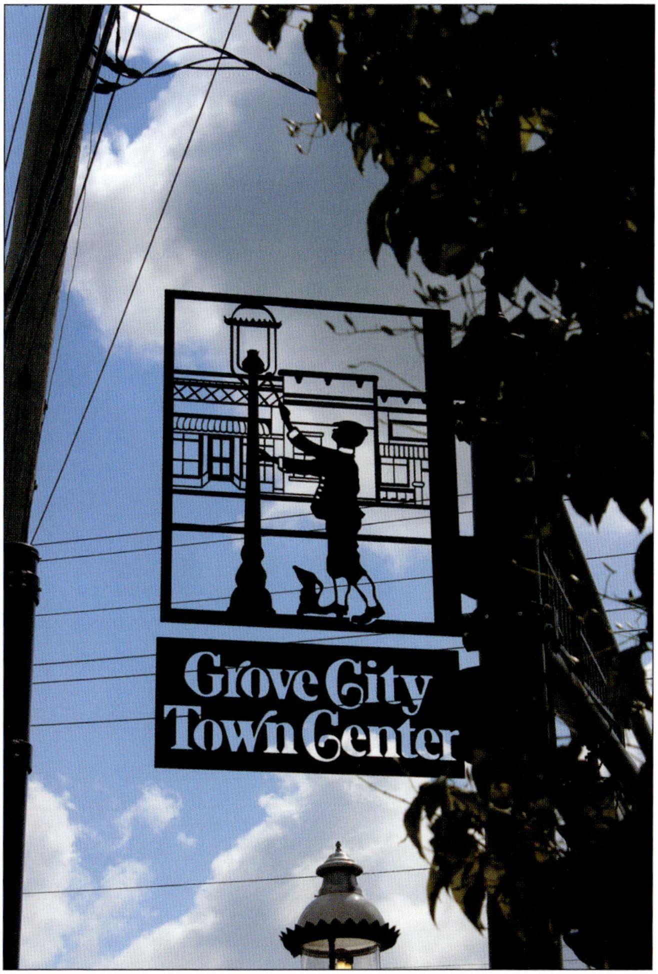

The lamplighter has become the new symbol of Grove City's town center and is used in various depictions in the heart of the city. The lamplighter is a boy in knickers lighting the gas lamps the way it was done in downtown Grove City in 1900. The lamplighter symbol was designed by local artist and longtime resident Earl Nicholson.

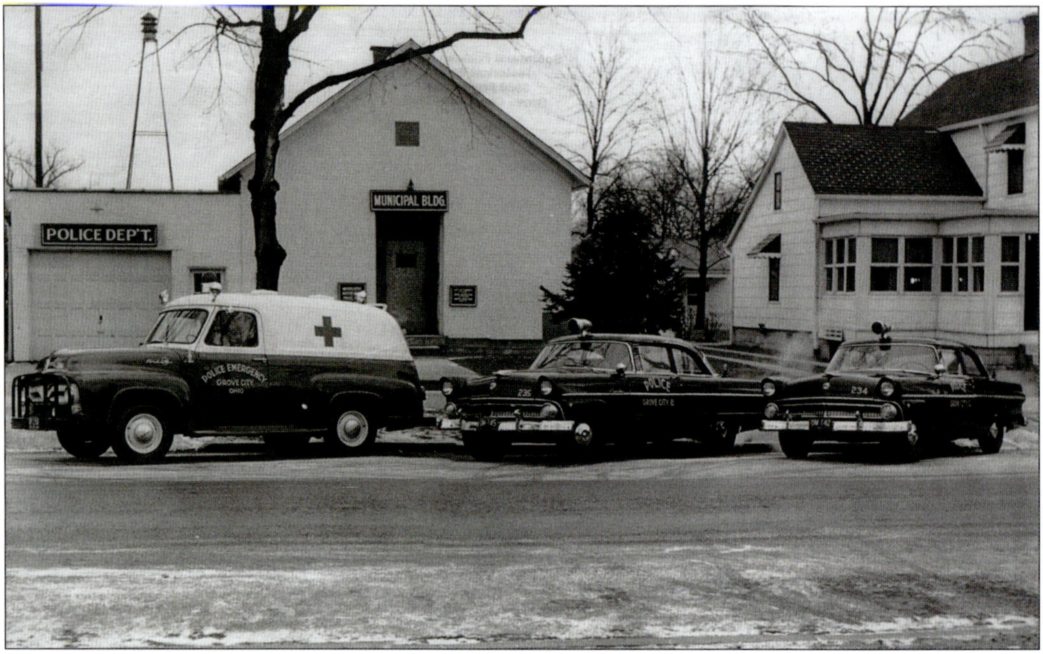

An ambulance and two Grove City patrol cars sit outside the police department and jail at 3435 Park Street. The city began a new era in government facilities when city hall was moved from the cramped quarters of this tiny municipal complex to the current city hall on Broadway. This site still serves as the safety complex and houses the city's division of police and mayor's court.

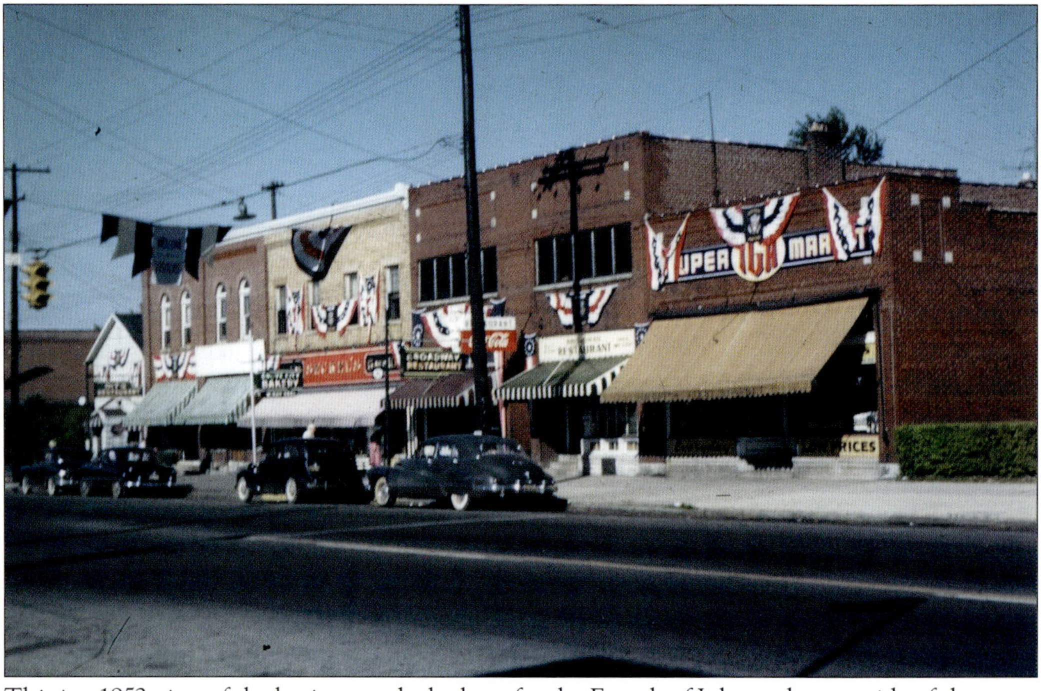

This is a 1952 view of the businesses decked out for the Fourth of July on the east side of the town center, from Park Street to Grove City Road, including a bakery, restaurant, and the IGA grocery store. The buildings, with new awnings and tenants, are still full of thriving businesses today.

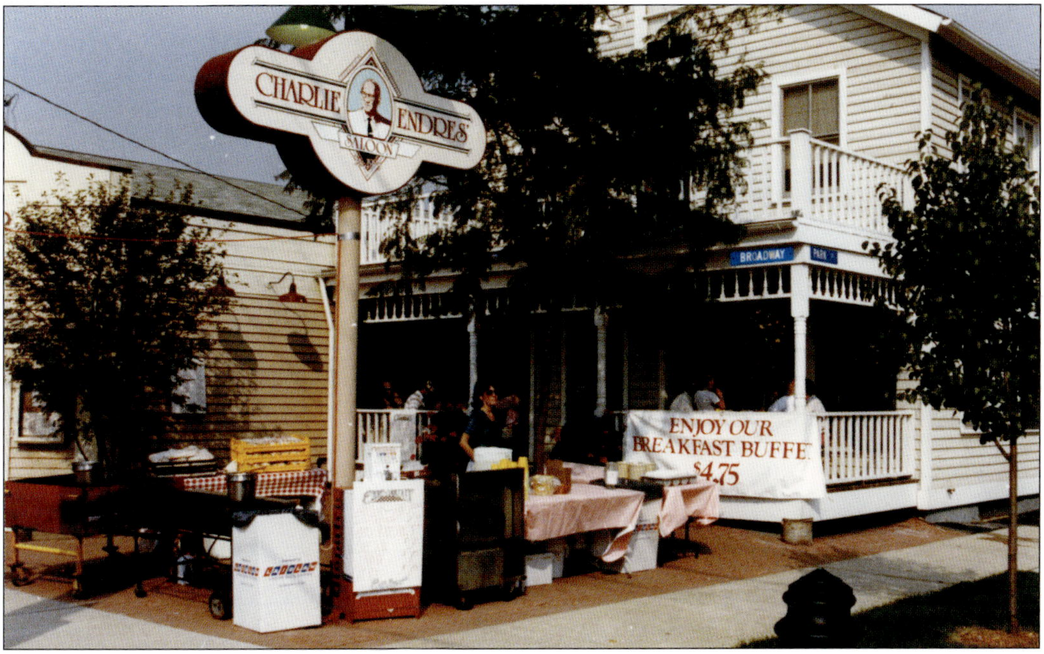

Charlie Endres' Saloon is the oldest continuous business in Jackson Township, beginning in 1854. In the early years, it served as a stagecoach stop and hotel. A German *biergarten* was once located directly to the north. Today, it is Plank's on Broadway and still serves an array of German and American food and plenty of beer.

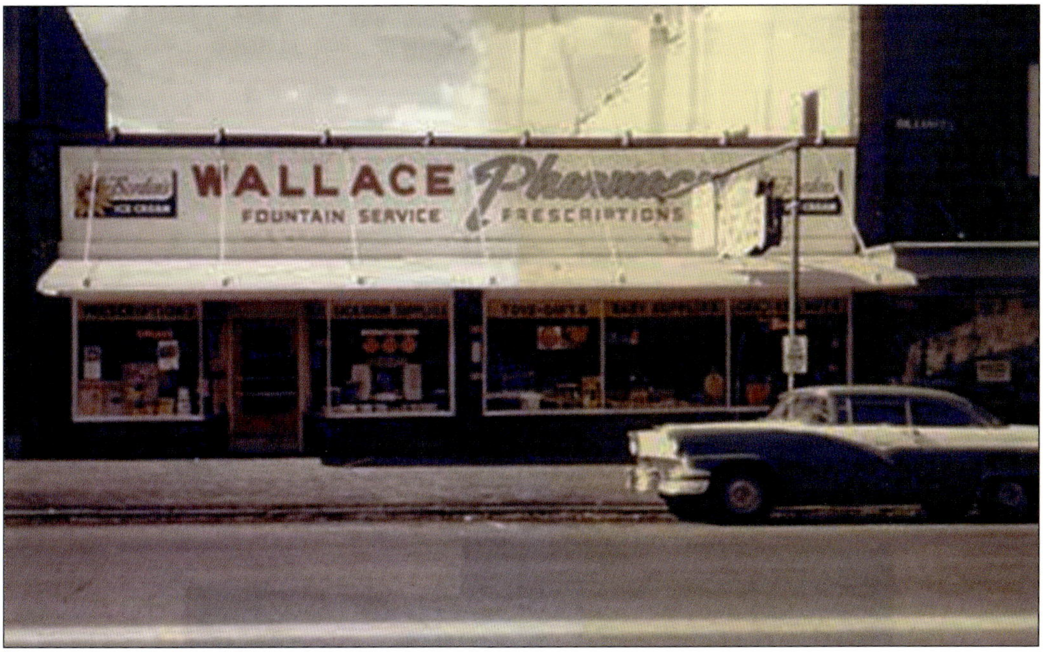

In 1945, pharmacist Fred Wallace purchased a drugstore from Doug Hanna and opened Wallace Drugs. In 1953, Wallace bought Wade's grocery store next door and expanded the business. In 1962, it became Kenstar Pharmacy, which was in business until 2009. Today, it is the location of Venue 62, a boutique social-event site.

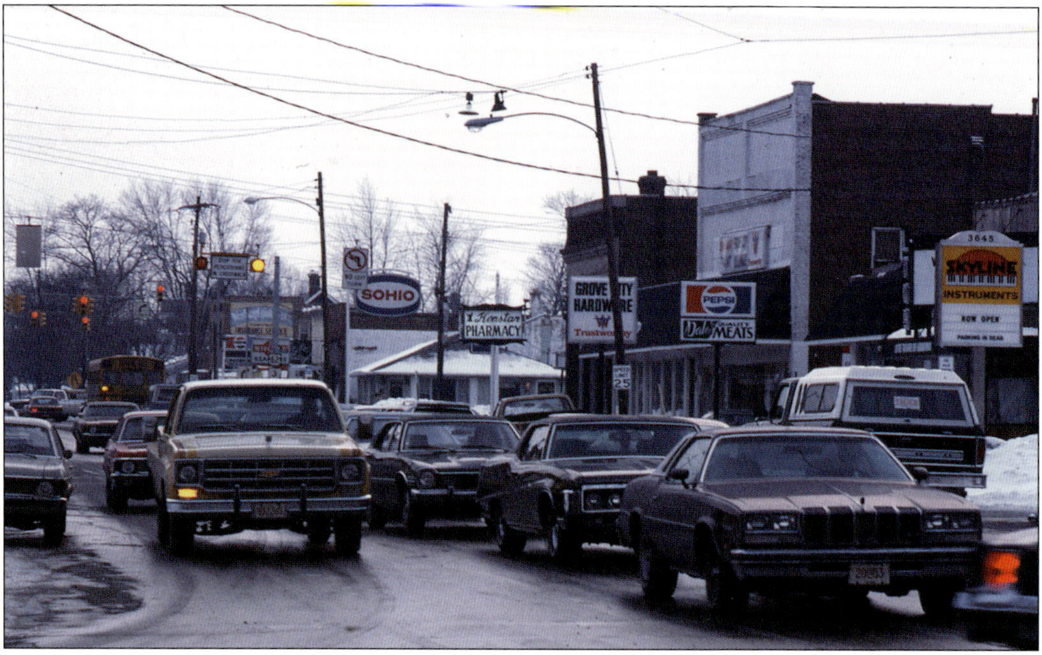

Traffic and congestion began to build up in and around Grove City as the migration into the community increased and the city began a transition from farming town to Columbus suburb. A steady stream of cars and buses slowly makes its way north and south on Broadway in this 1978 photograph taken from the southeast corner of Columbus Street and Broadway.

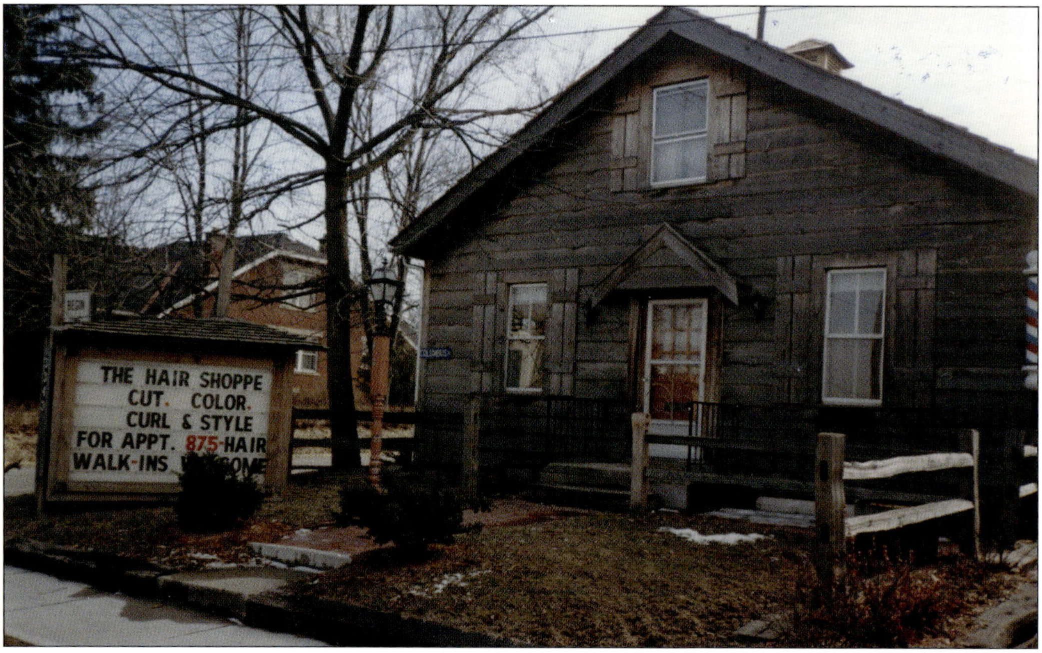

The Hair Shoppe, at 3343 Columbus Street, has been in operation for 36 years and is considered a newcomer among barbershops in the historic town center; however, it is believed that the building was constructed as either a residence or a barn in the 1850s. The present owner is Bob "Steve" Stevenson. There are 13 licensed barbershops in Grove City.

The new Grove City Library opened on March 10, 1954, at the southeast corner of Park Street and First Street at a cost of $81,119. At the time, the library's collection numbered 15,000 books. In 1974, the library, now part of Southwest Public Libraries, expanded to the east at a cost of $350,000. The total collection of items available at the Grove City Library in early 2015 numbered 153,737.

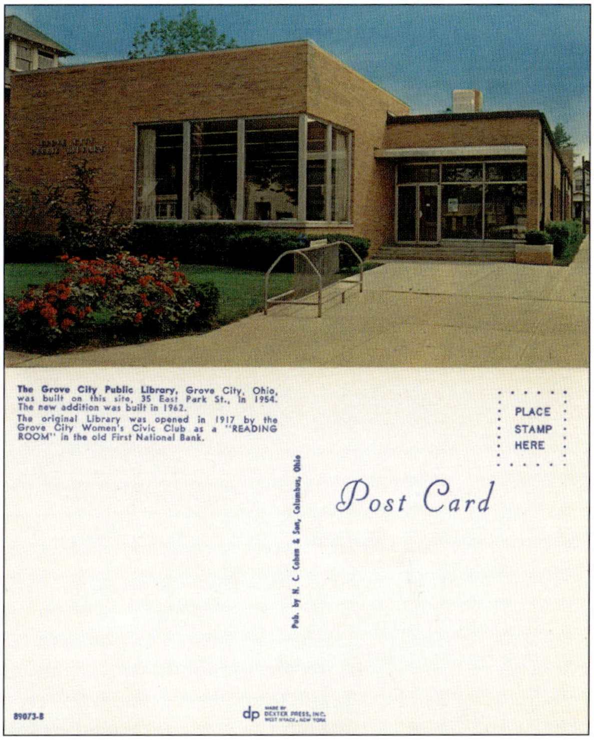

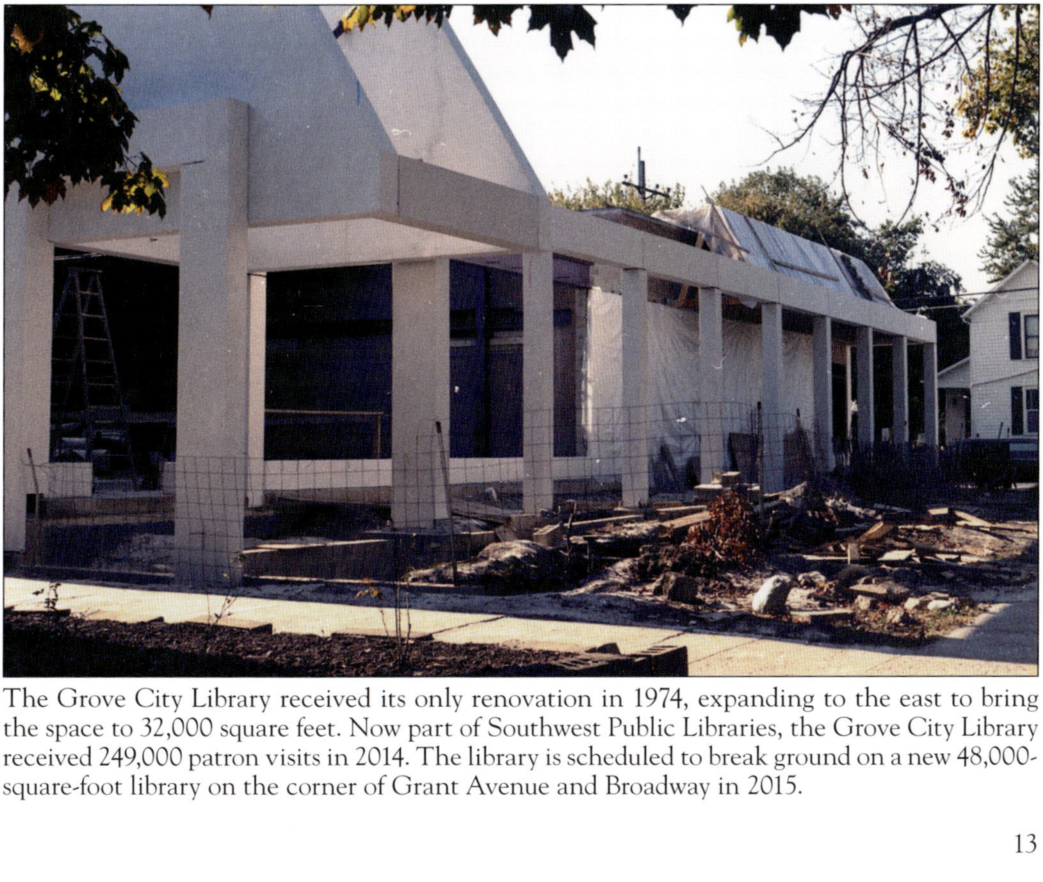

The Grove City Library received its only renovation in 1974, expanding to the east to bring the space to 32,000 square feet. Now part of Southwest Public Libraries, the Grove City Library received 249,000 patron visits in 2014. The library is scheduled to break ground on a new 48,000-square-foot library on the corner of Grant Avenue and Broadway in 2015.

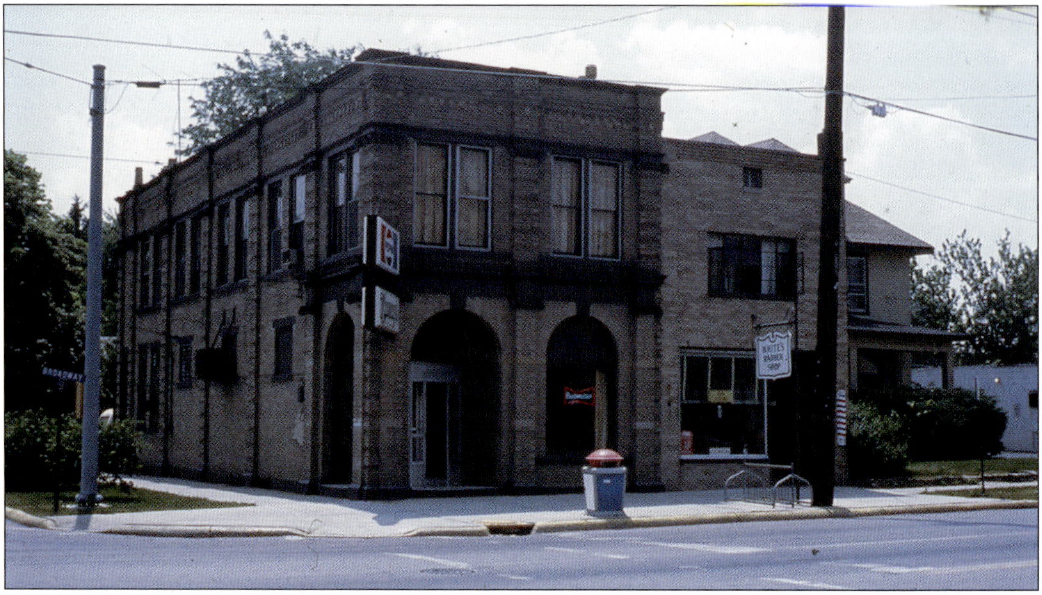

Located on the corner of Broadway and Columbus Street, the old First National Bank began operations in 1903. Hometown bank notes, or national currency, were printed here until 1935. First National merged with Huntington Bank in 1962. The Dreaming Tree Galleries, named after lyrics from a Dave Matthews Band tune, now showcases contemporary art at this site.

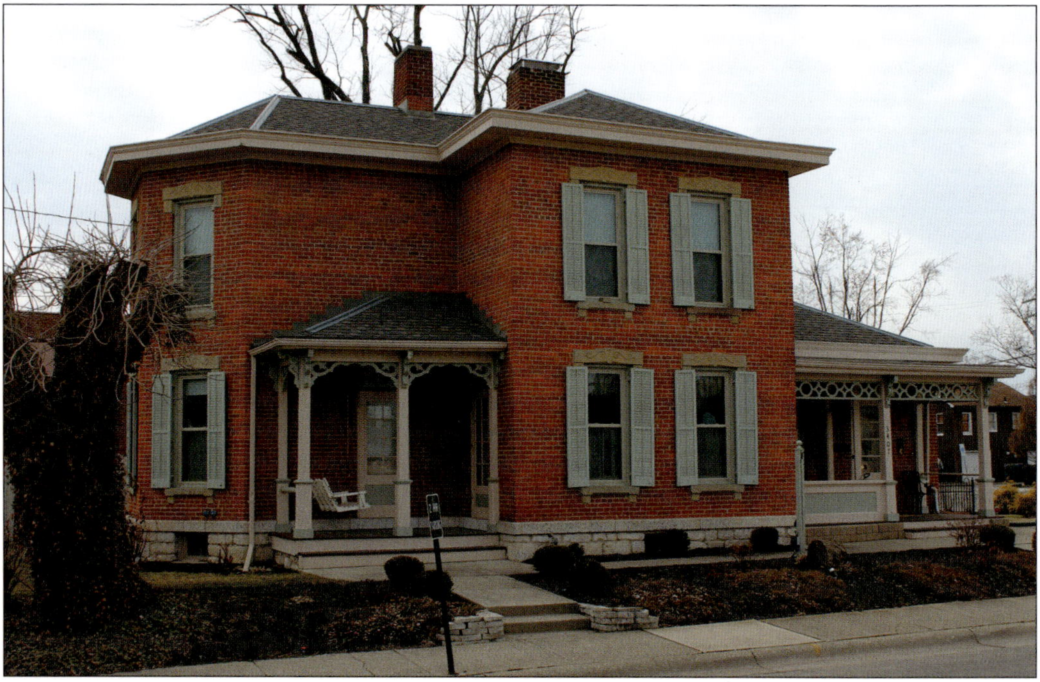

The Corzilius House at 3407 Grant Avenue is believed to date from the 1870s and is located near the original site of Grove City founder William Breck's steam sawmill. For many years, the house was the residence of John Leach and Flora Corzilius Leach. In the early years, the structure had furnished rooms for rent along the interurban electric street railway line. Over the last 20 years, the structure has been occupied by several companies, including a landscaping business.

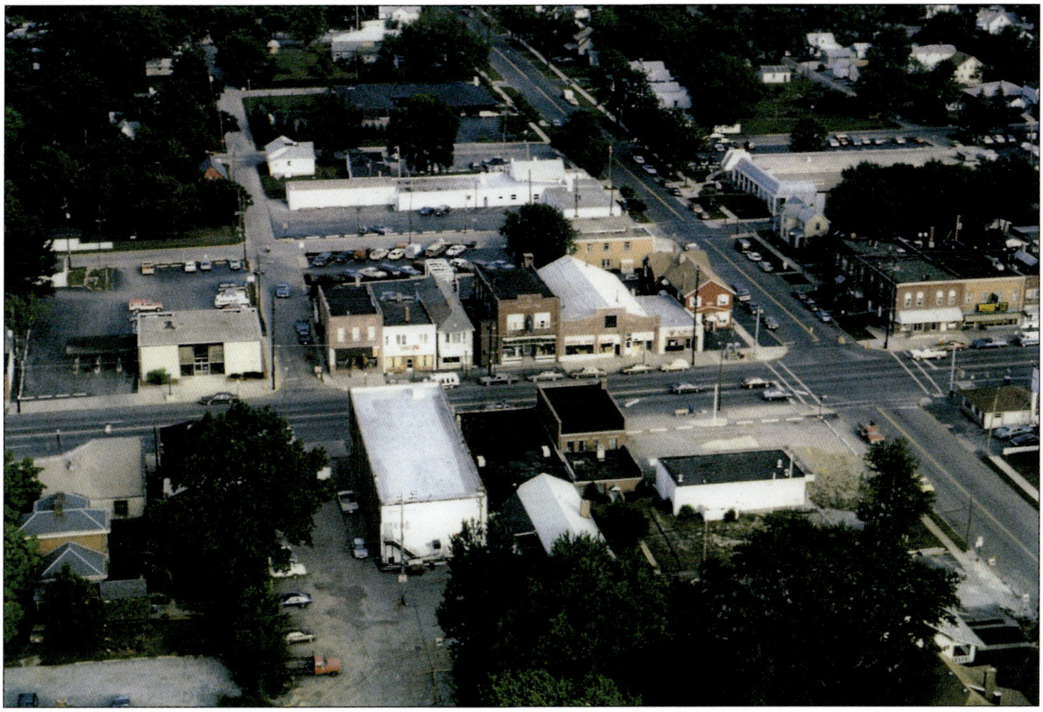

This aerial view of the town center shows the intersection of Broadway and Park Street on the right as it looked in the mid-1980s. At the top of the photograph lies the old Grove City Municipal Building across from the Grove City Library. The municipal building, which also held the jail, was demolished in the late 1980s to make way for a new safety building.

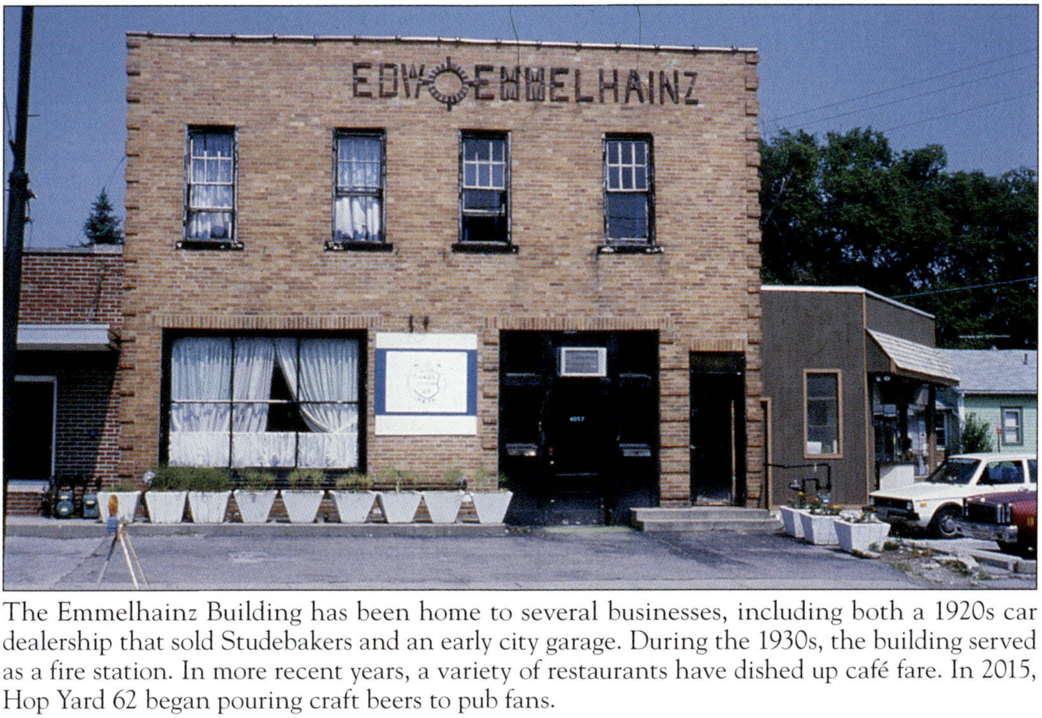

The Emmelhainz Building has been home to several businesses, including both a 1920s car dealership that sold Studebakers and an early city garage. During the 1930s, the building served as a fire station. In more recent years, a variety of restaurants have dished up café fare. In 2015, Hop Yard 62 began pouring craft beers to pub fans.

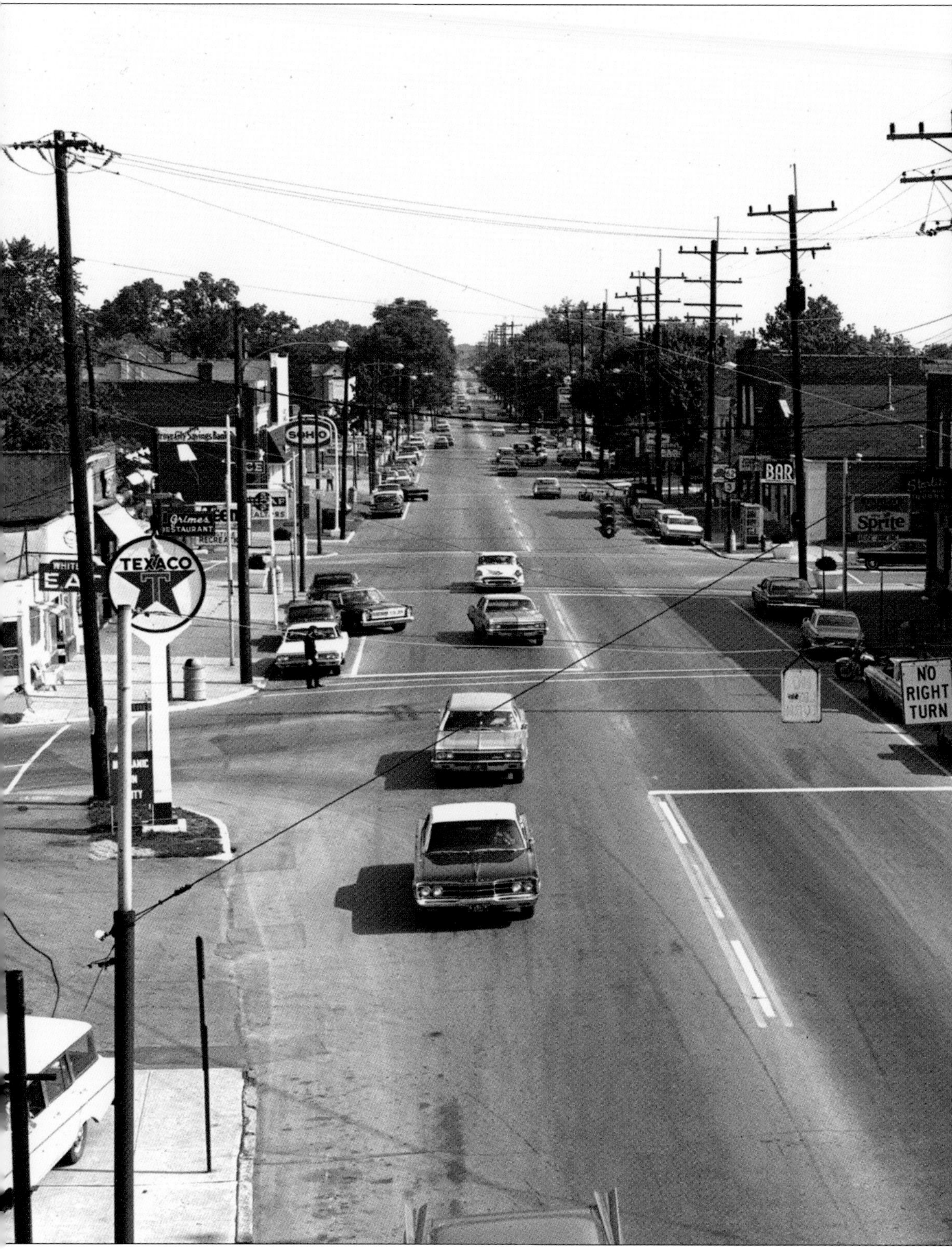
SOHIO
Grimes
RESTAURANT
TEXACO
BAR
Sprite
NO
RIGHT
TURN

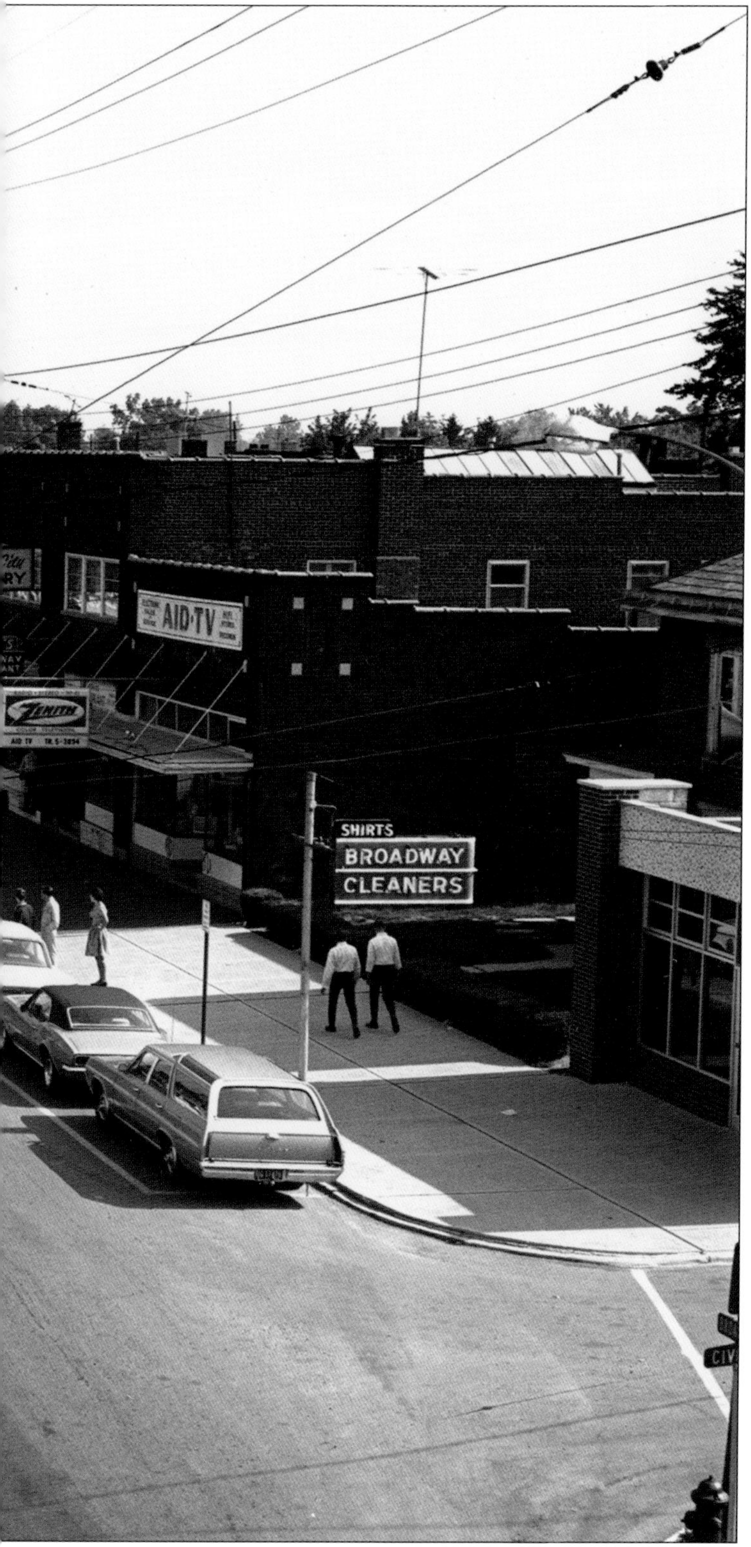

Grove City had a population of about 11,000 residents in the mid-1960s and served as an agricultural hub for area farmers. The largest source of employment in town was Beulah Park—Ohio's first Thoroughbred race track—which opened in 1923. Pictured here is the old Sohio gas station on the northwest corner of Broadway and Park Street. The Standard Oil Company erected a gas station on that corner before 1921. Another gas station, Texaco, is seen at the southwest corner of Broadway and Grove City Road. It is now the site of the town center gazebo. Also on the left are Whitey's Eats, Grimes Restaurant, Shoaf Realtors, Grove City Savings Bank, and Kenstar Pharmacy. On the east side, the businesses include Broadway Cleaners, AID-TV, Grove City Bakery, Gene Edgington's Restaurant, Starlight Lounge, Endres' Saloon, and Murph's Bar.

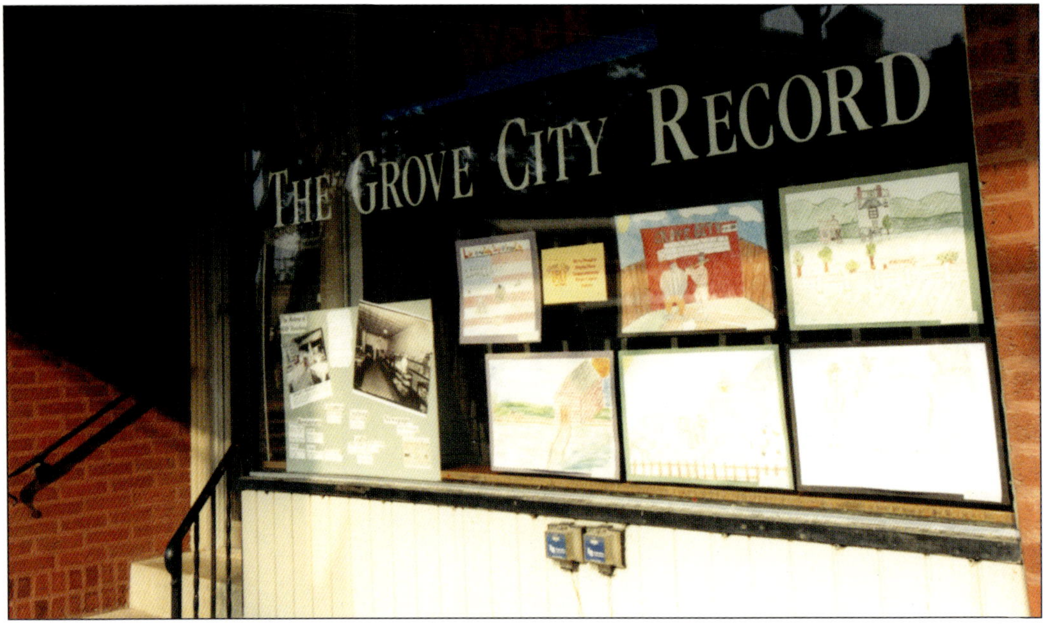

A mainstay in the town center, the offices of the *Grove City Record* moved into 4048 Broadway in January 1991, just over a year after the weekly community newspaper was purchased by the Dispatch Printing Company. For more than 80 years, the *Record* and another newspaper, the *Southwest Columbus Messenger*, have covered all aspects of Grove City life. The Dispatch Company relocated the office outside of Grove City in May 2008.

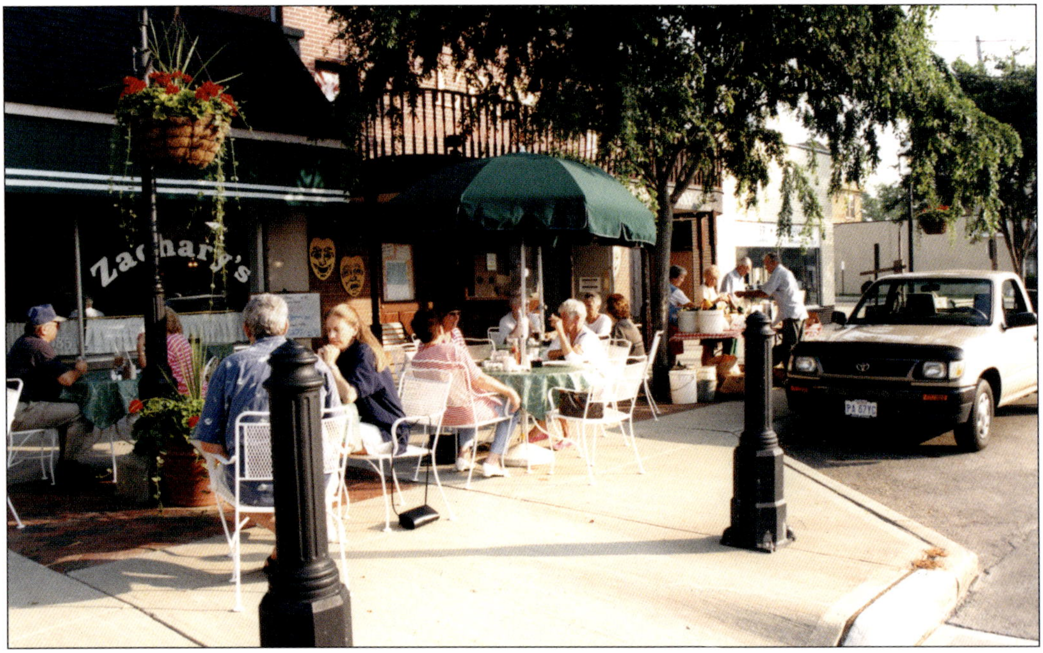

On any sunny, warm day, patrons of the town center restaurants can be seen enjoying the weather and local cuisine at Zachary's. The restaurant next to Little Theatre Off Broadway is always a popular spot, as are local favorites Lilly's and Grandstand Pizza. Today, it is a restaurant called Tossed & Grilled.

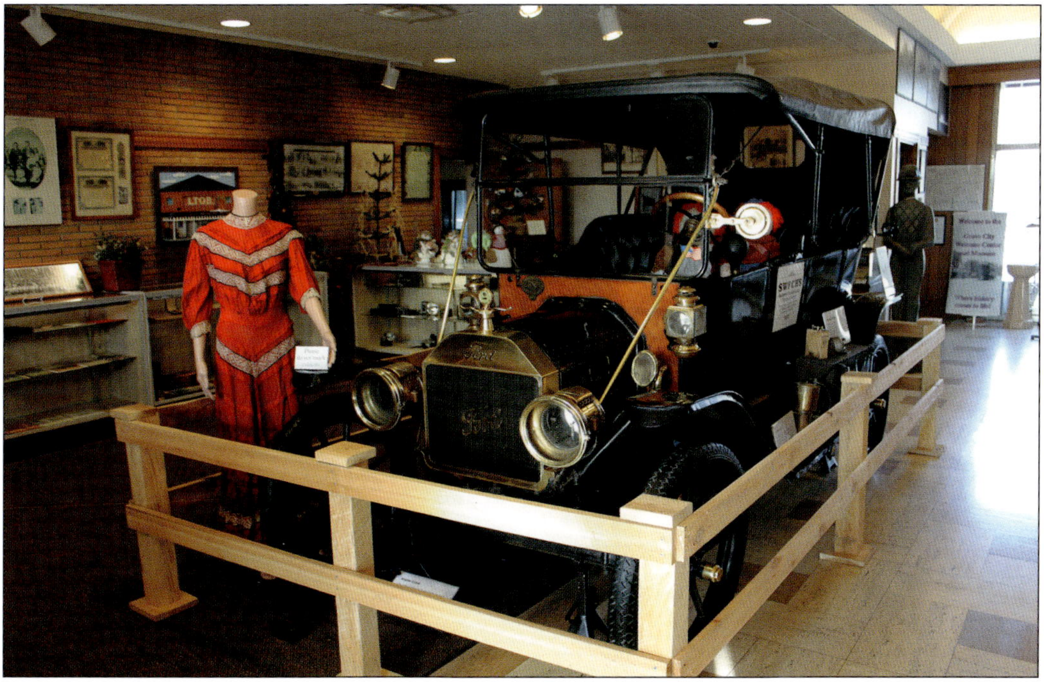

This 1912 Model T Ford is one of the last automobiles made by hand before the assembly line took over production of the cars in Detroit, Michigan. The classic automobile and other displays can be seen in the Grove City Welcome Center and Museum at 3378 Park Street. The purchase price of the car in 1912 was $690. Volunteers from the Southwest Franklin County Historical Society assist in providing new displays of local history.

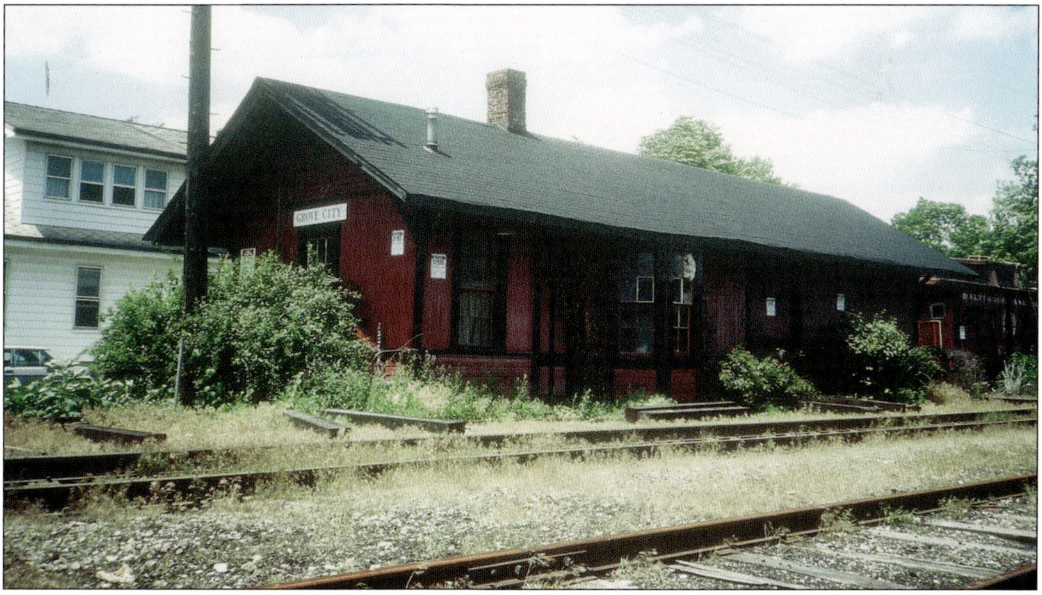

Efforts to save the former B&O Railroad Depot, on the west side of the tracks along Front Street, began in 1972. The depot, which has been part of Grove City history since it was built in 1884, is still sitting next to the tracks. Many are hopeful that it can be moved to Century Village on Orders Road, which has several historic structures on display open for tours.

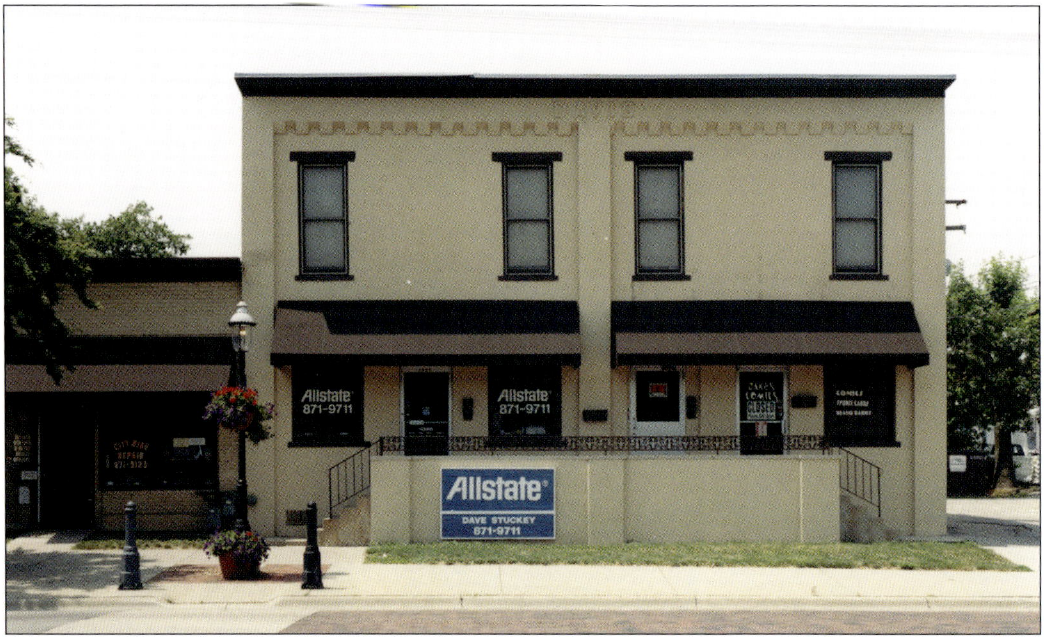

The Davis Building was the site of various businesses over its 128-year history, including a comic-book store and bike-repair shop. In May 2013, Southwest Public Libraries and the City of Grove City formally agreed to build a new $18-million library on that site. To make way for the new structure, the Davis Building was demolished.

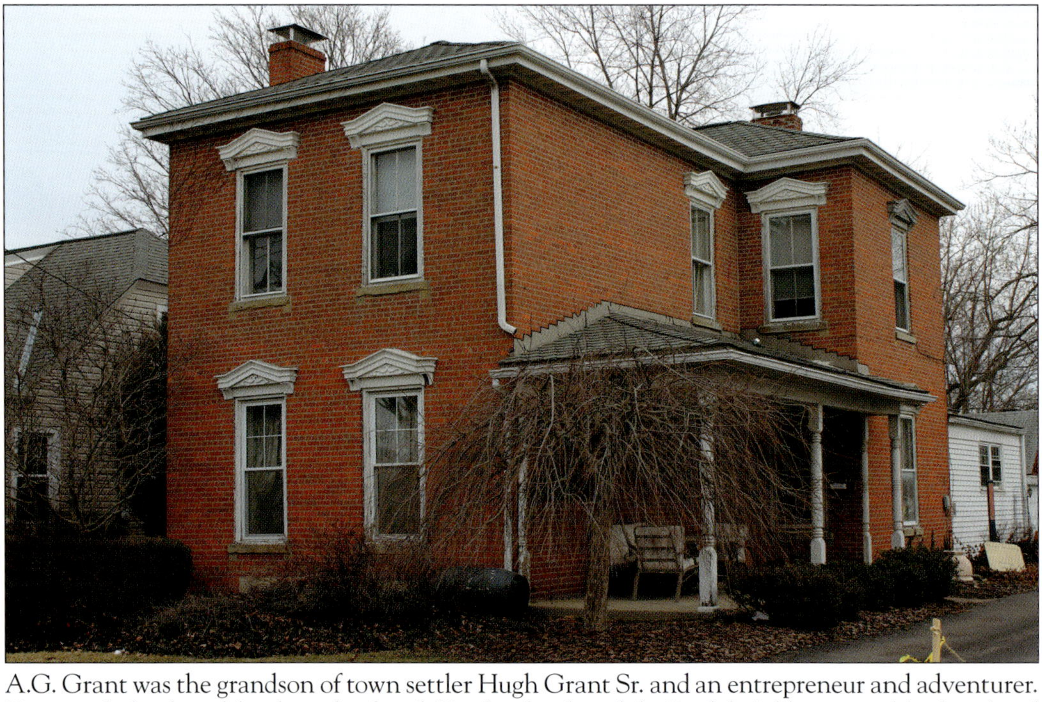

A.G. Grant was the grandson of town settler Hugh Grant Sr. and an entrepreneur and adventurer. He owned a brickyard, bank, and railroad. He also developed the Beulah Addition neighborhood and Beulah Park, naming both sites after his daughter. This building at 4086 Broadway was his home and has housed a scrapbooking store and a tearoom and is currently a wholesale gluten-free bakery.

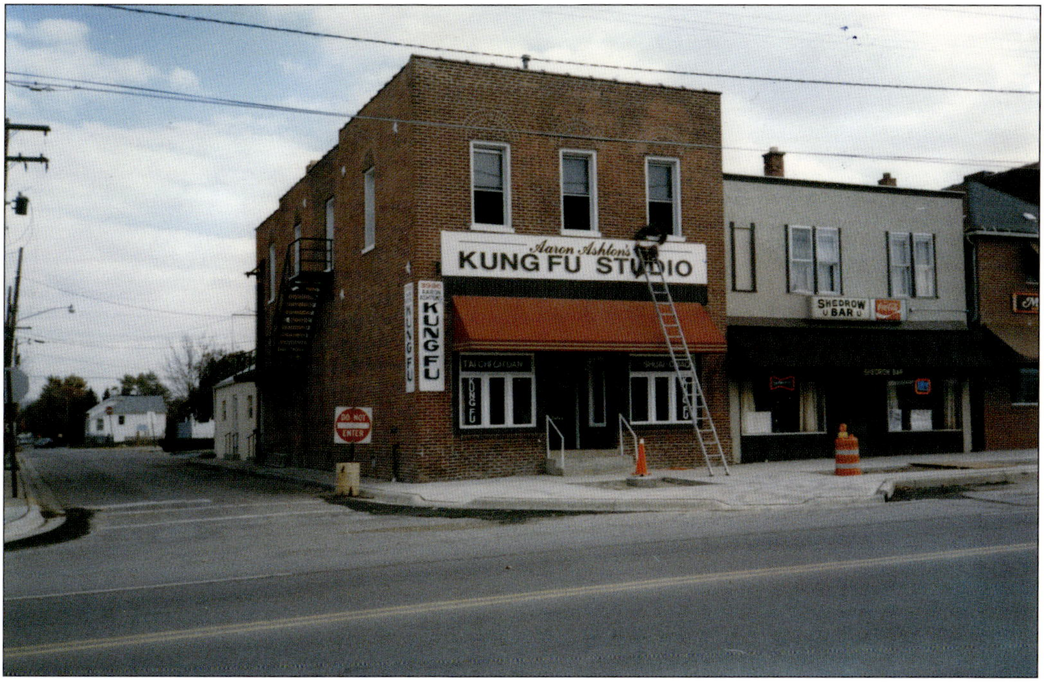

Aaron Ashton Kung Fu studio stood at the southeast corner of Broadway and Jackson Street until a devastating fire destroyed the building on November 26, 1991. Ashton had earned his black belt in kung fu in 1981 and opened his business in 1985. His business and his apartment in the building were completely destroyed, as was the Shedrow Tavern next door. The site is now open space with picnic tables, next to the Jackson Street mural.

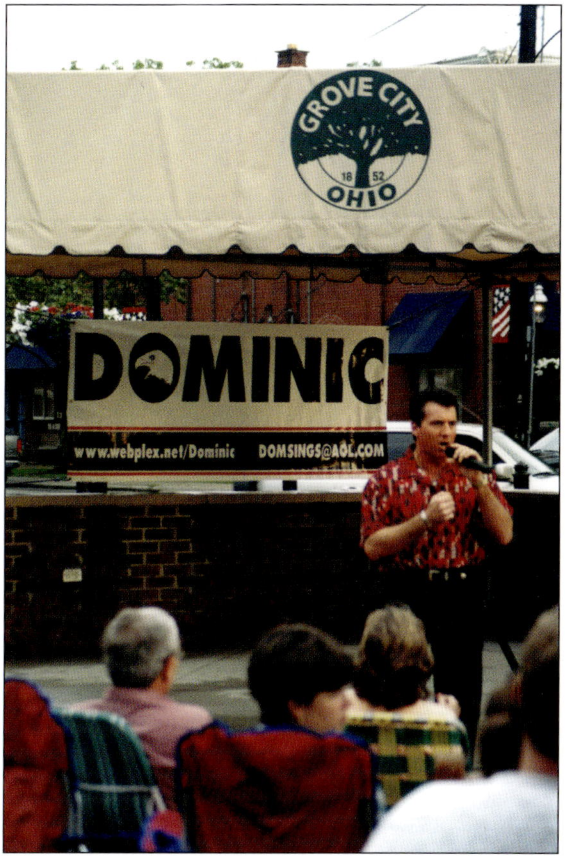

On most Friday and Saturday nights from June through August, the city hosts the Summer Sizzle concert series in the George Edge Music Plaza on the corner of Park Street and Broadway. Each night, a different group performs music from jazz and gospel to brass and rock 'n' roll. Stephen "Dominic" Carter (pictured), a fan favorite, serenaded swooning crowds with tunes from Sinatra to the Backstreet Boys.

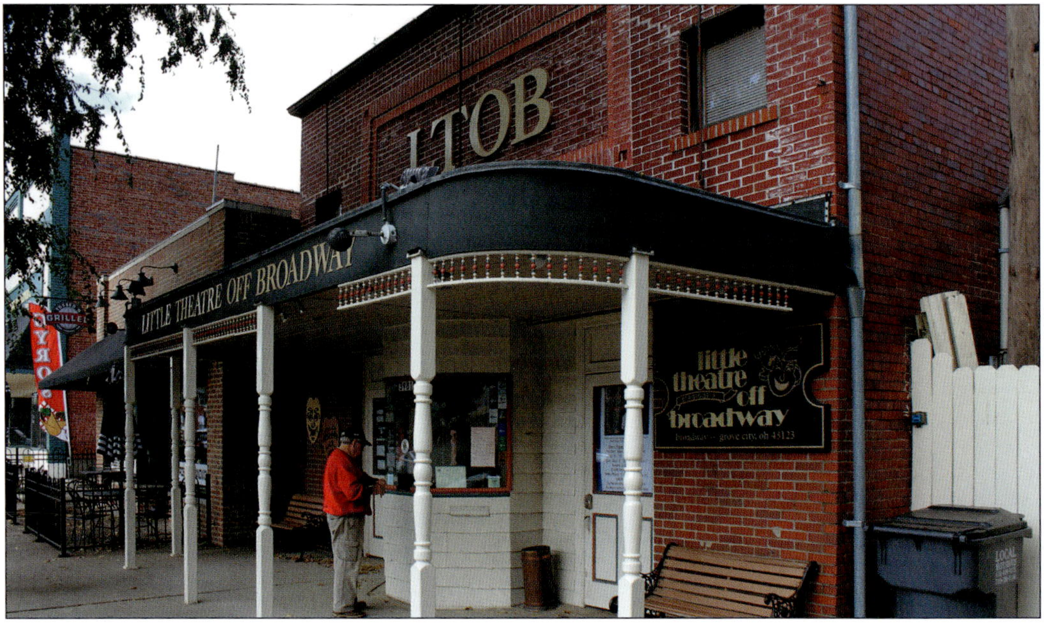

The former Kingdom Theatre, which housed both silent movies and talkies and served as an early home for Our Lady of Perpetual Help Church, became the Little Theatre Off Broadway when it was purchased in 1968. What began as a play-reading group at Richard Avenue School evolved into a community theatre troupe, putting on several live shows per season. The organization also has a very active children's theatre program.

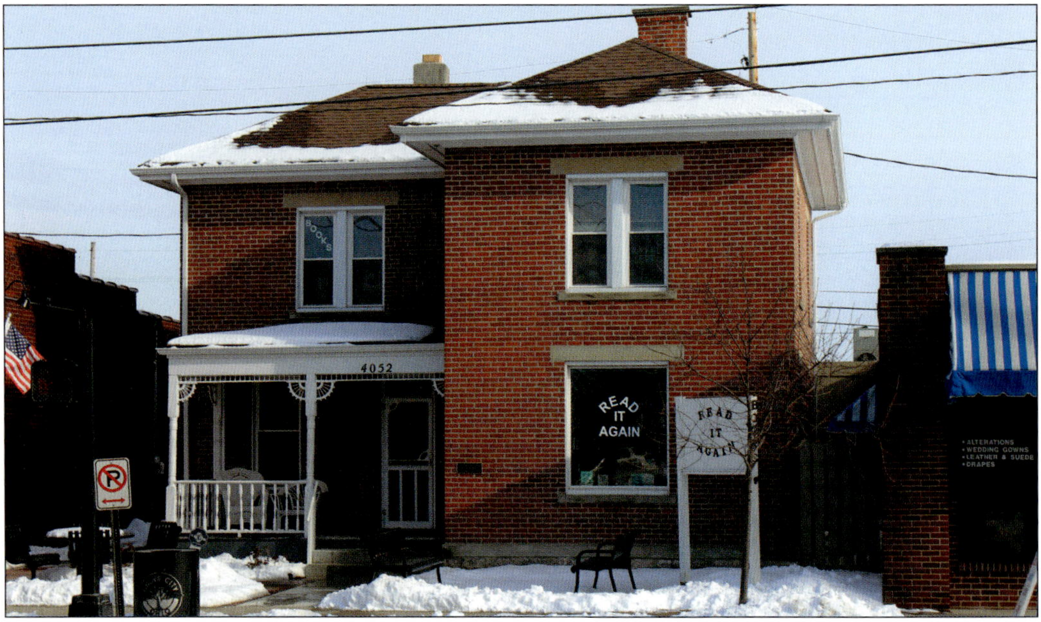

This brick home is known as the Elias White/Edward Schirner House and is located on Broadway. Elias White was a Civil War soldier from Grove City who became an entrepreneur after serving in uniform. The house was constructed by Edward Schirner in the 1870s. Schirner and his wife both drowned in 1875, when the ship SS *Schiller* was lost in fog on its way to Germany and ran onto rocks. The building is now Read It Again Books.

Two

LANDMARKS

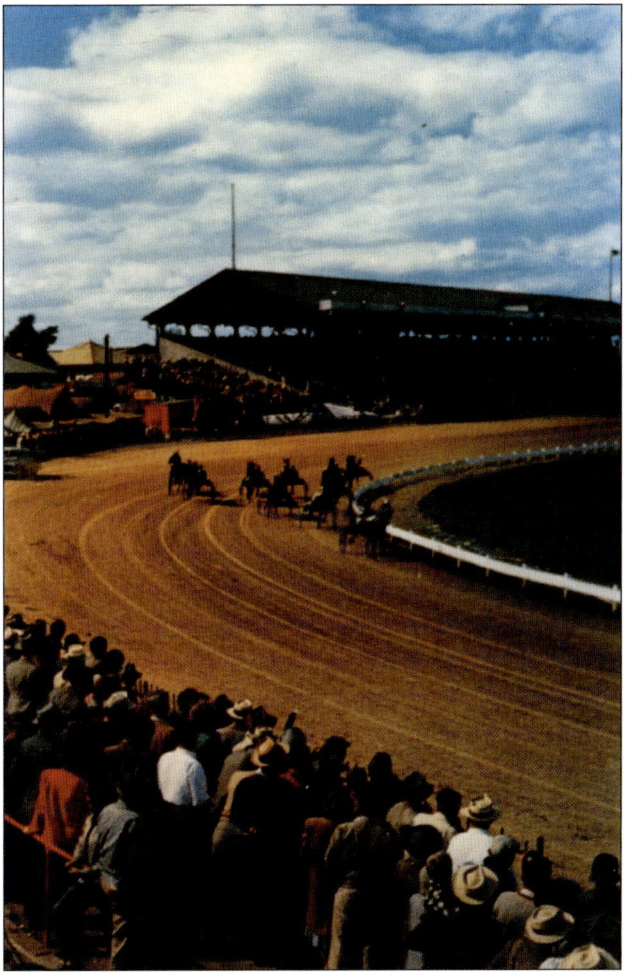

In 1889, A.G. Grant created the Beulah Addition on farmland owned by town founder William F. Breck. Grant added a recreational park and a small track where the Franklin County Fair was held intermittently until 1918. In 1923, it became Beulah Park Race Track, Ohio's first Thoroughbred track. After a 91-year history, it closed in May 2014.

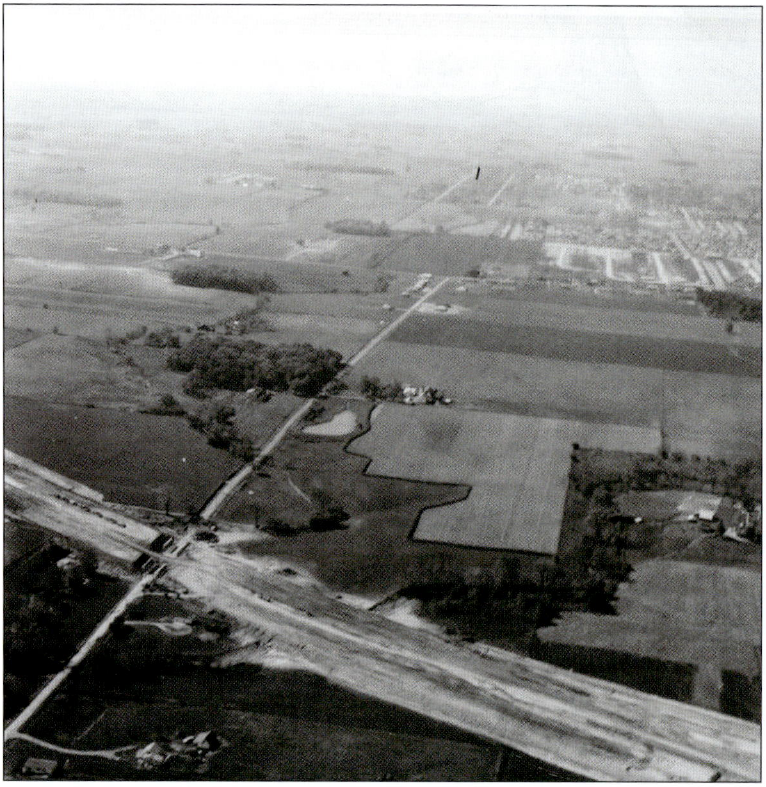

This 1959 photograph shows I-71 being constructed east of Grove City over White Road. I-71 was built in sections, and this portion ended at Miller's Station at US Route 62/State Route 3. In 1964, the South Freeway section was connected in Madison County. Nearly 60 years later, a third lane is now being added.

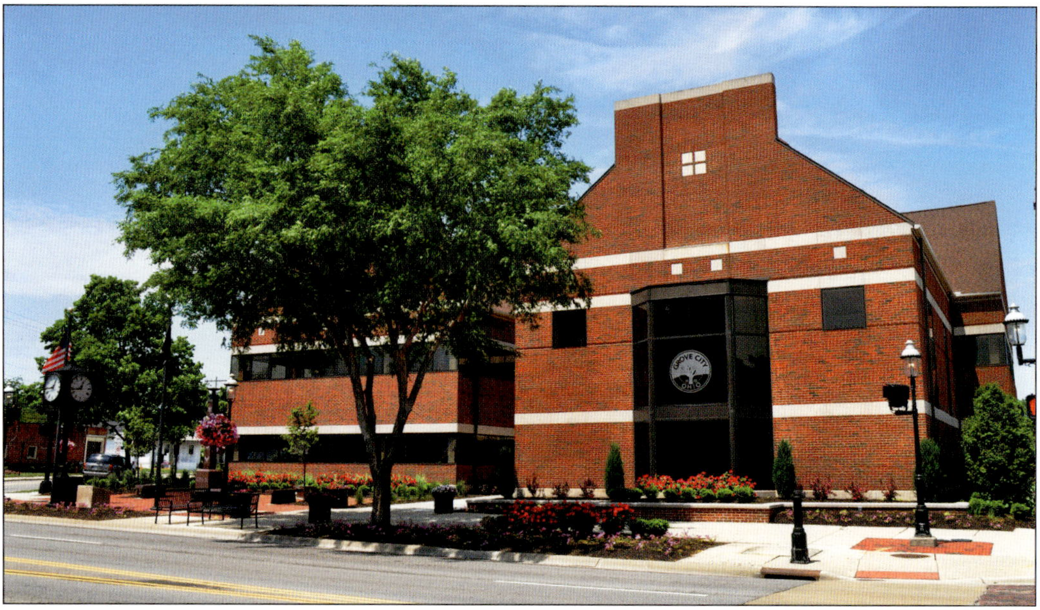

Shortly after the completion of the safety building in 1989, the city dedicated the $1.8-million city hall building on July 27, 1990. The new 15,000-square-foot structure was designed to anchor the southern end of the town center–revitalization project. The dedication ceremony was a highlight of the summer and included a Coney dog–eating competition between the police force and the firefighters, as well as a street dance party with the Danger Brothers Band.

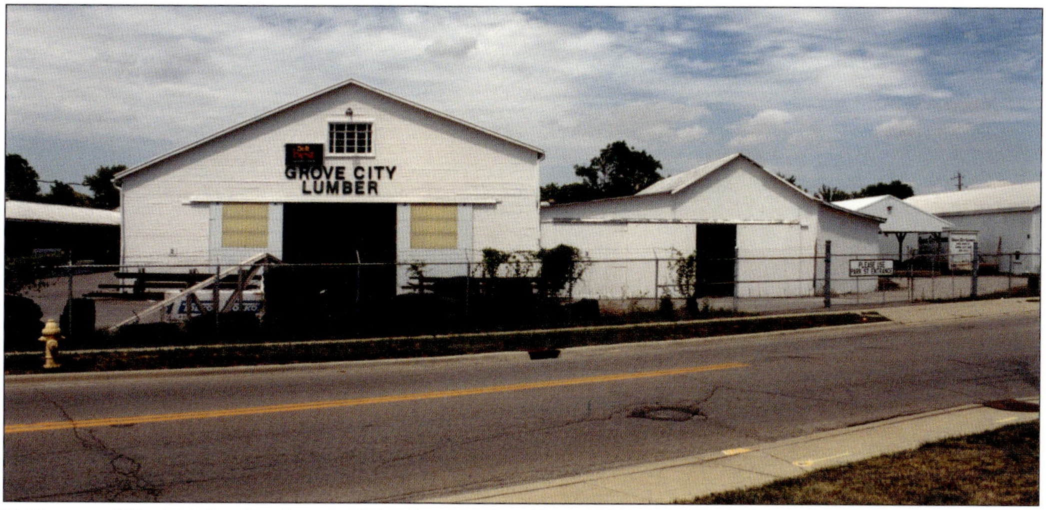

Following World War II, the need for lumber was great, as new homes and businesses were being built all over Grove City. For over 60 years, the Grove City Lumberyard, next to the railroad tracks, was a familiar sight to everyone in town. The lumberyard closed in 2001 and housed displays for the city's 2002 sesquicentennial celebration until it was torn down the following year.

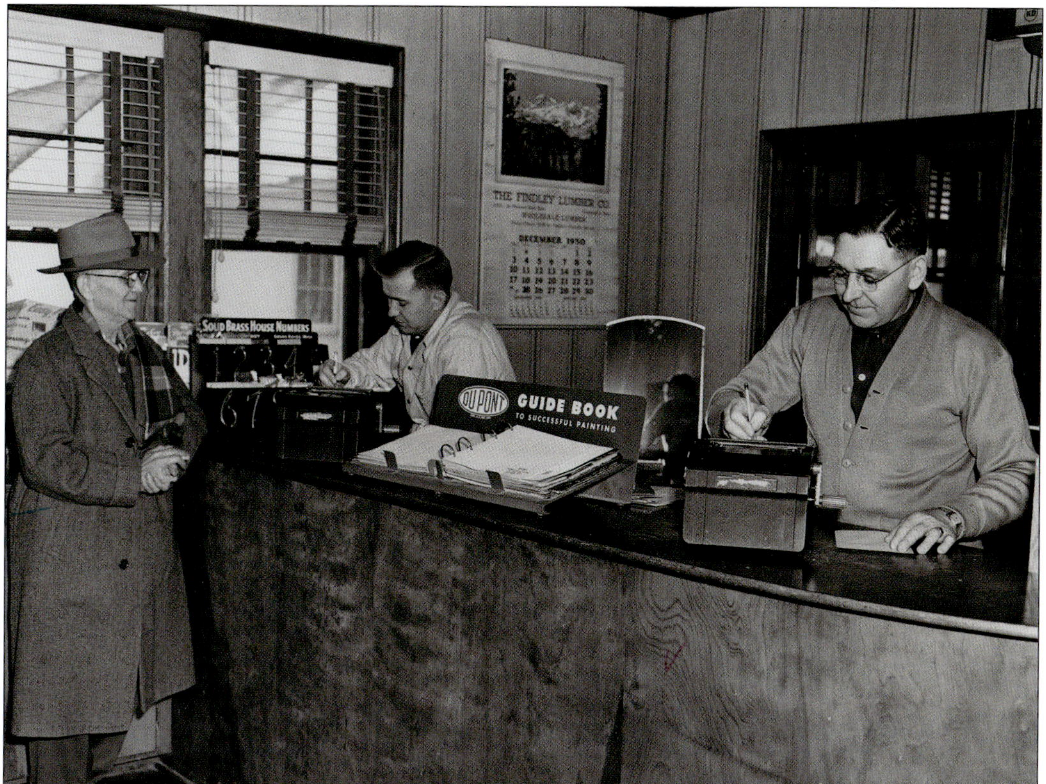

The Grove City Lumberyard formed in the mid-1930s in the aftermath of the closing of the Johnston and Grant lumber mill. Pictured is the lumberyard office as it looked in the 1950s. George Iftner (right) was the first person hired to work at the lumberyard. Also seen here are Don Baumgartner (center) and Phil Rond.

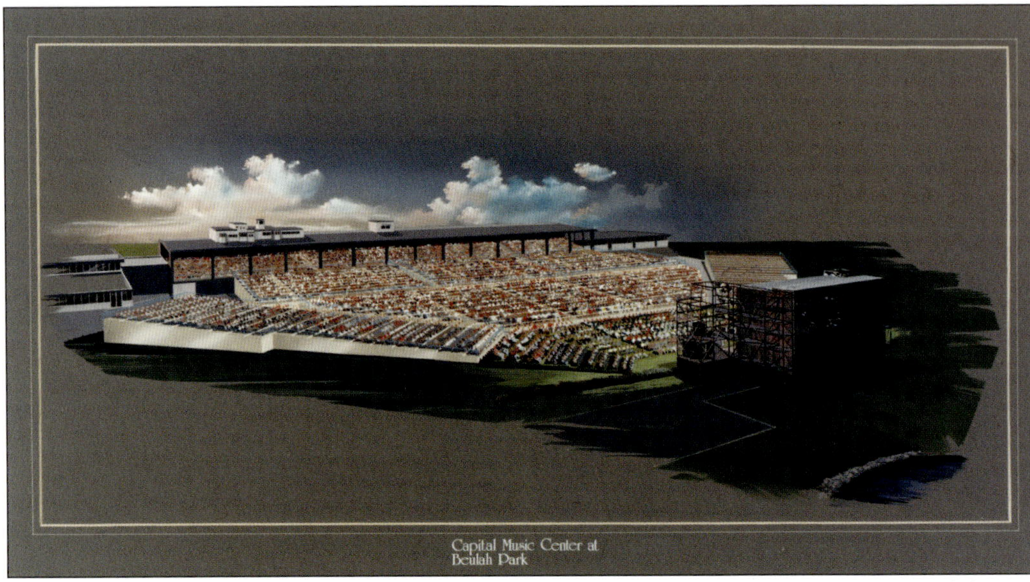

The summer-concert venue at Beulah Park got its start as Musicpark in 1973. Musicpark hosted well-known performers such as Ella Fitzgerald, Isaac Hayes, and Blood, Sweat & Tears. The concert series only lasted two years, but it was followed in the 1990s by Capital City Music Center, which opened with Frank Sinatra. Other legendary recording acts such as the Beach Boys, Jimmy Buffet, and Lynyrd Skynyrd also played the venue. Jimmy Buffett was the only sold-out performance, with approximately 15,000 fans in attendance.

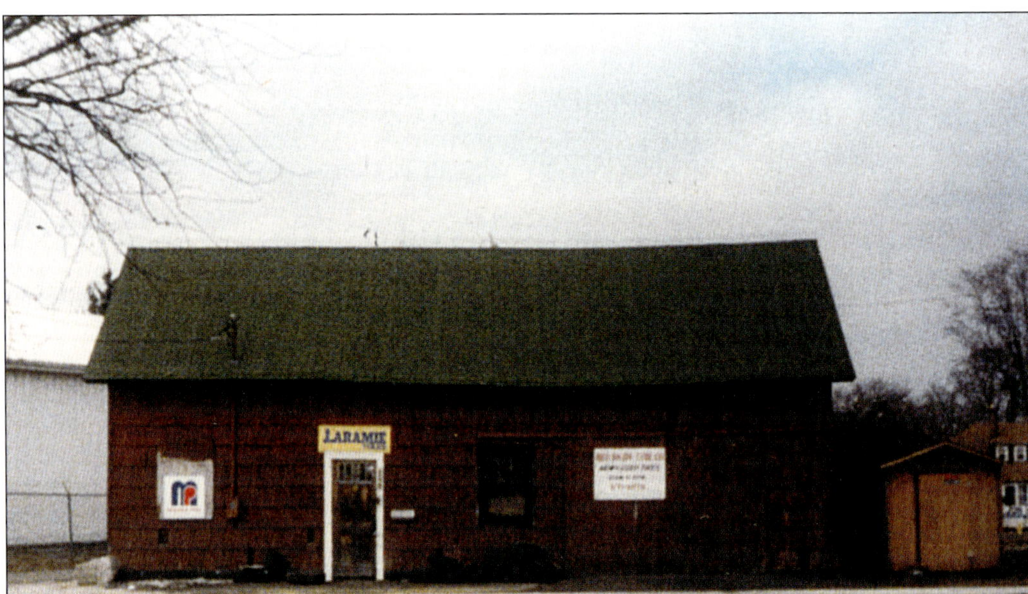

The Hensel & Son Blacksmith Shop, near the northwest corner of Grove City Road and Broadway, began operating in 1878 under businessman Joseph Buckholtz at the corner of Park Street and Broadway before moving to its second location in 1894. In later years, it sold tires and other automotive products. The building was torn down in the late 1980s to make way for the new Grove City City Hall.

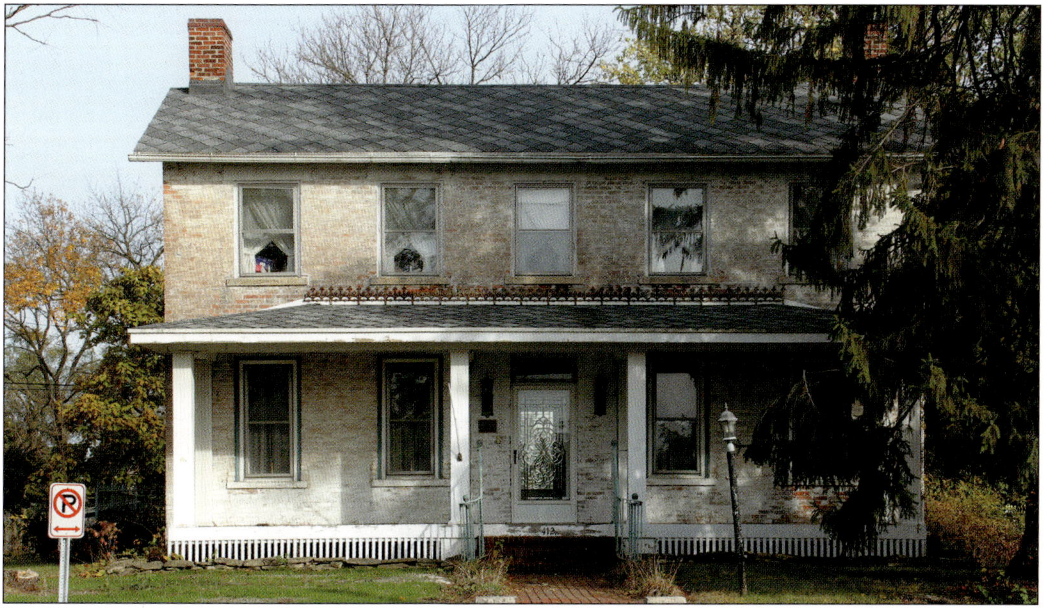

Grove City's first settlers were Hugh and Catherine Grant, who relocated to Grove City from Pittsburgh, Pennsylvania, in 1803. Having settled on the wrong property, the family built this home on their rightfully owned site in the 1840s after Hugh's accidental death. Shortly before her death in 2014, Ruth Sawyer Jividen, a direct Grant descendant, sold the property to the city for use as a public historical site.

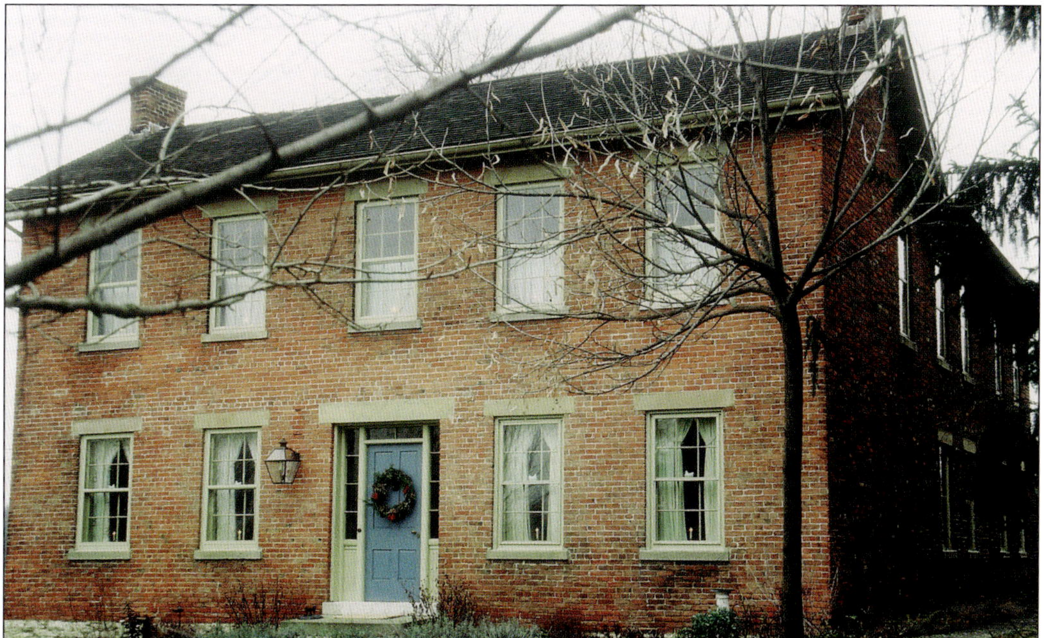

Originally known as the Landes House, the Maxwell House on Hibbs Road was erected by Samuel Landes in 1848 on part of a 1,200-acre land grant given to Revolutionary War surgeon Cornelius Baldwin for his service during the war. The home was turned into a popular local bed-and-breakfast in the 1980s and today is a private home.

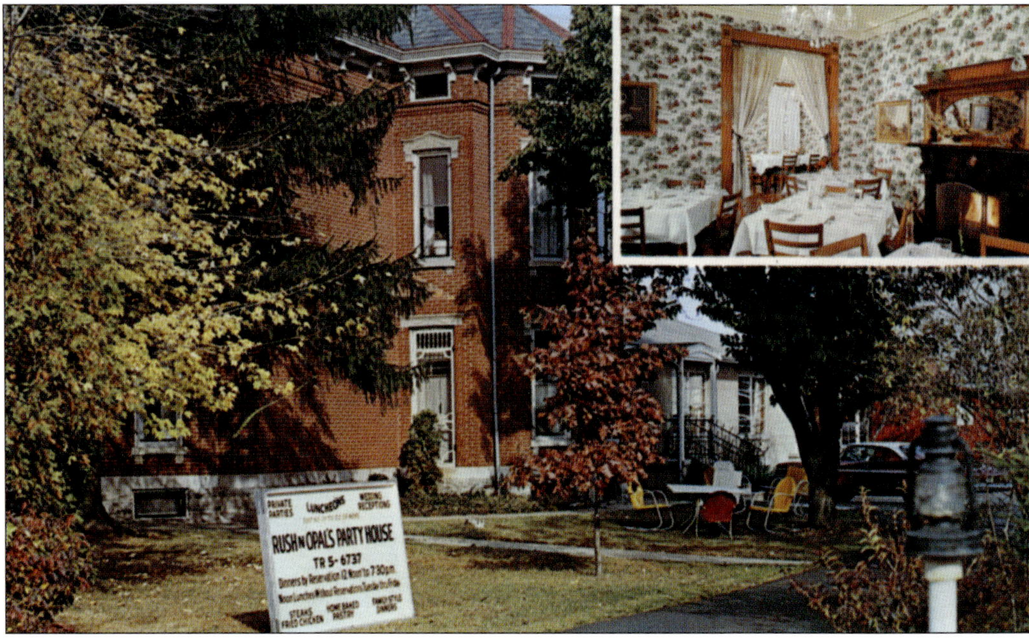

Opened in 1957 by Rush and Opal Thomas near the corner of Stringtown and Hoover Roads on the former Leithart property, Rush and Opal's offered a place to celebrate birthdays and weddings, in addition to dinner. Closed in the early 1970s, the building became a doctor's office, hair salon, and real estate office. Today, it is part of the Grove City United Methodist Church.

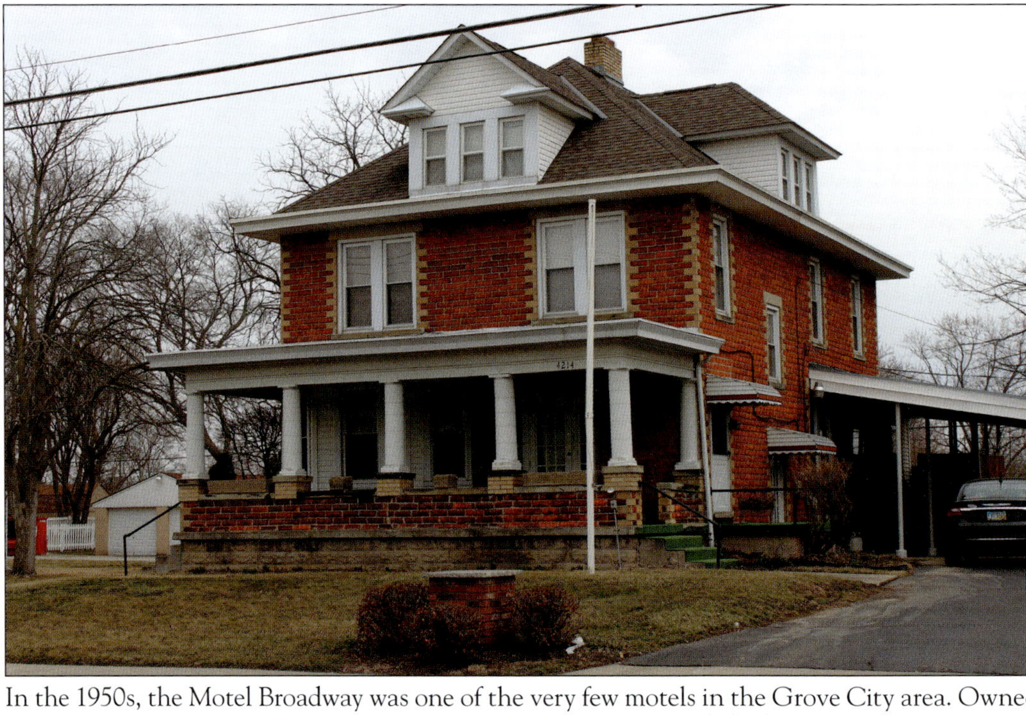

In the 1950s, the Motel Broadway was one of the very few motels in the Grove City area. Owned by Charles and Lona Wolfe, the motel had several cabins behind the house. Today Grove City has 15 motels and hotels, most located along Stringtown Road.

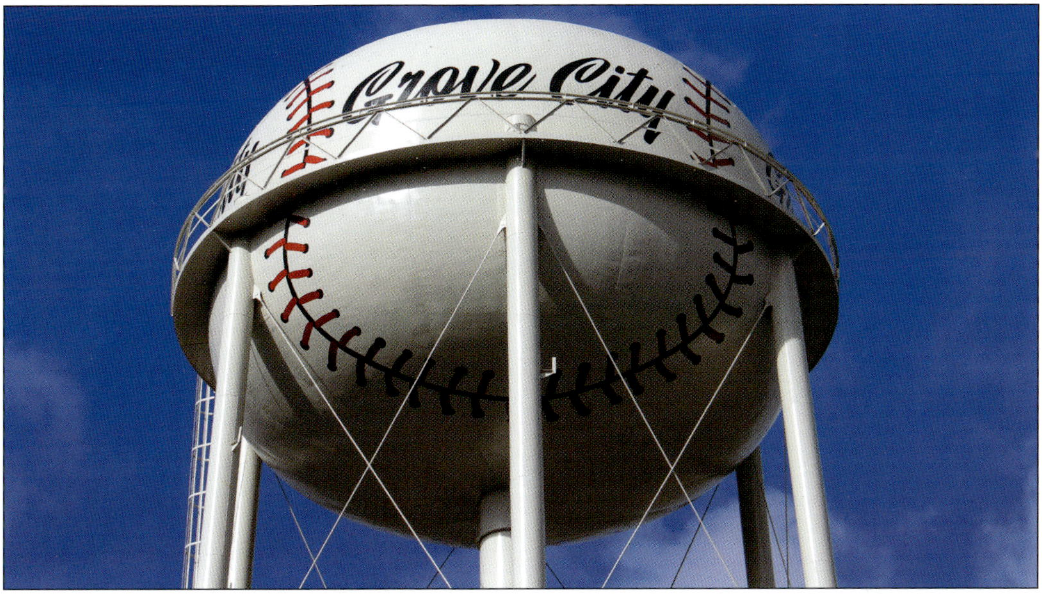

This baseball-inspired water tower was repainted in 2013 to reflect the city's long-standing passion with all things baseball. Having one of the earliest Little League programs in Ohio, Grove City reintroduced Little League in 2013. More than 700 kids play on 11 fields at Windsor Park, and the city is currently working on a "Dream Field" so that children of all abilities can enjoy the sport.

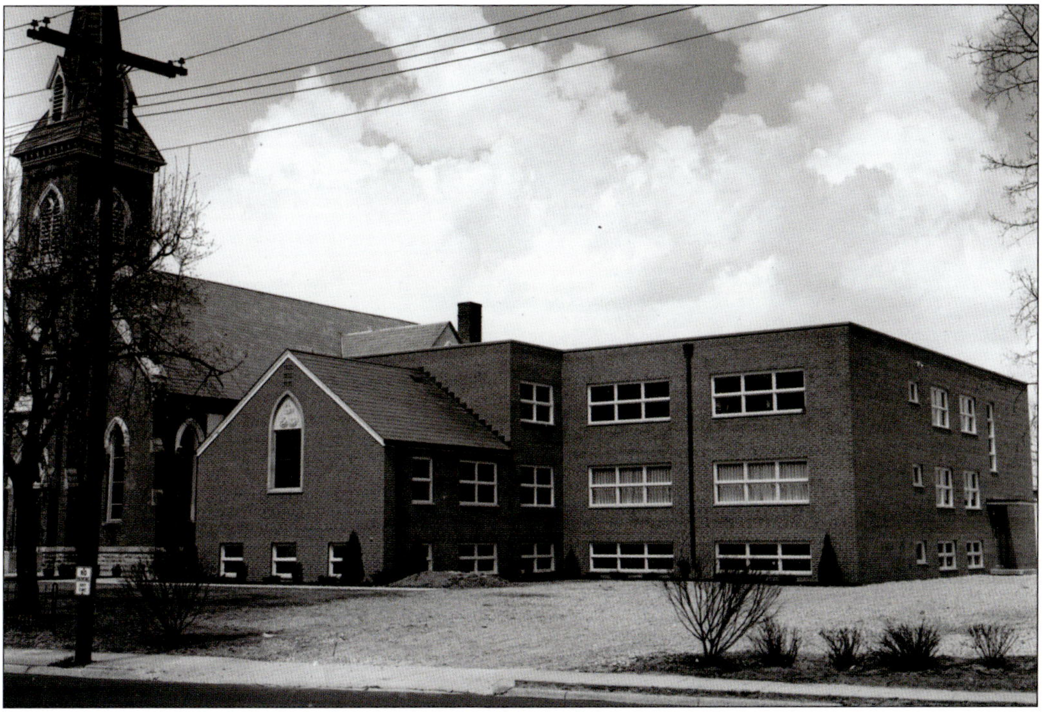

An education wing was added to the landmark St. John's Evangelical Lutheran Church, at 3220 Columbus Street, in 1957. The congregation formed in 1849 and built a small church in 1854 on the northwest corner of Columbus Street and Arbutus Avenue before constructing the present structure in 1889.

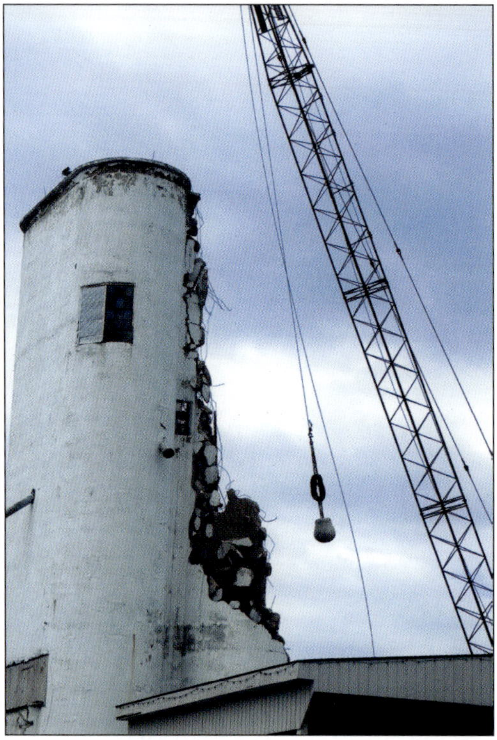

The grain elevators were constructed on the site of town founder William Breck's sawmill. The silo pictured here replaced the Gregg and Shafer flour mill that was destroyed in a fire in the 1920s. The demolition of the silos in 2007 was hard on the agriculturally nostalgic community. The farmers' exchange building still stands and today houses a number of local small businesses.

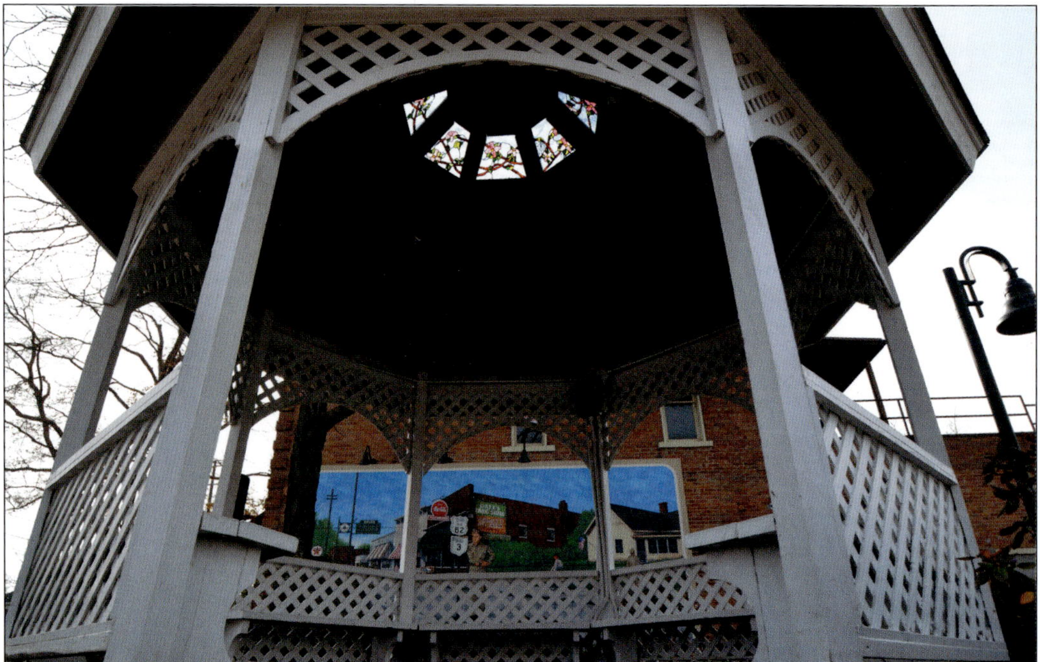

The town center gazebo was dedicated in honor of Betty Ford Evans on July 5, 2011, for her efforts on the Grove City Beautification Committee to improve downtown Grove City. Behind the gazebo is an historical mural depicting GI Clyde DeLong standing along US Route 62 and Ohio Route 3 while home on leave during World War II.

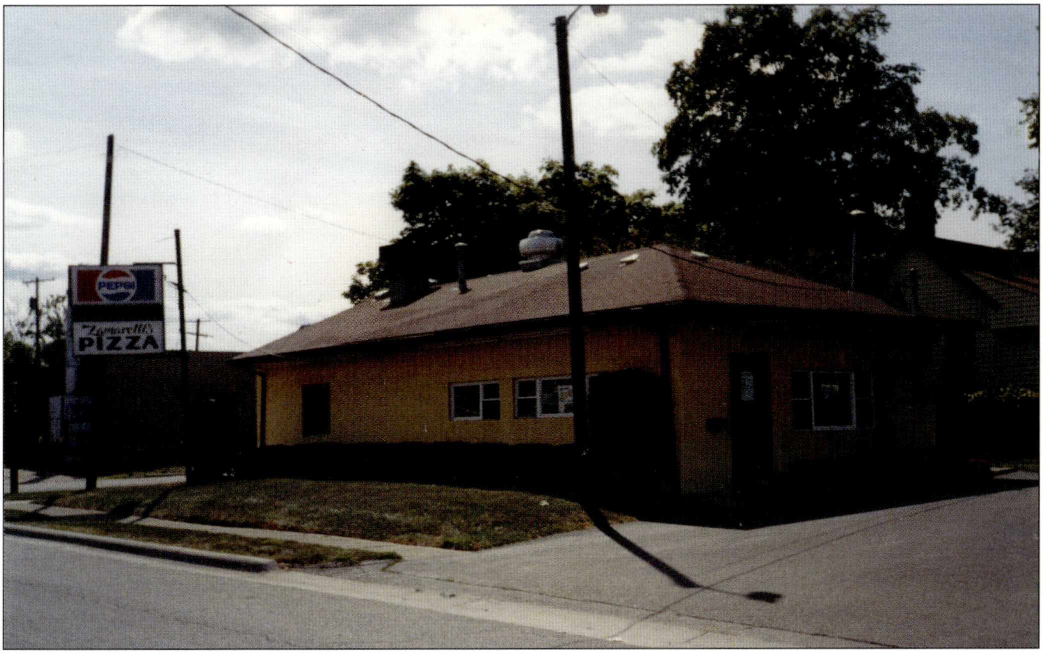

One staple of Grove City life for more than 50 years has been Zamarelli's Pizza Palace, at 4011 Front Street. The single location carry-out-only family business began with Andy and Kate Zamarelli in 1963, and the tradition of food, fun, and family continues today through Andy's daughter Tina and son-in-law Jack Middendorf, who are now in charge of this beloved Grove City institution.

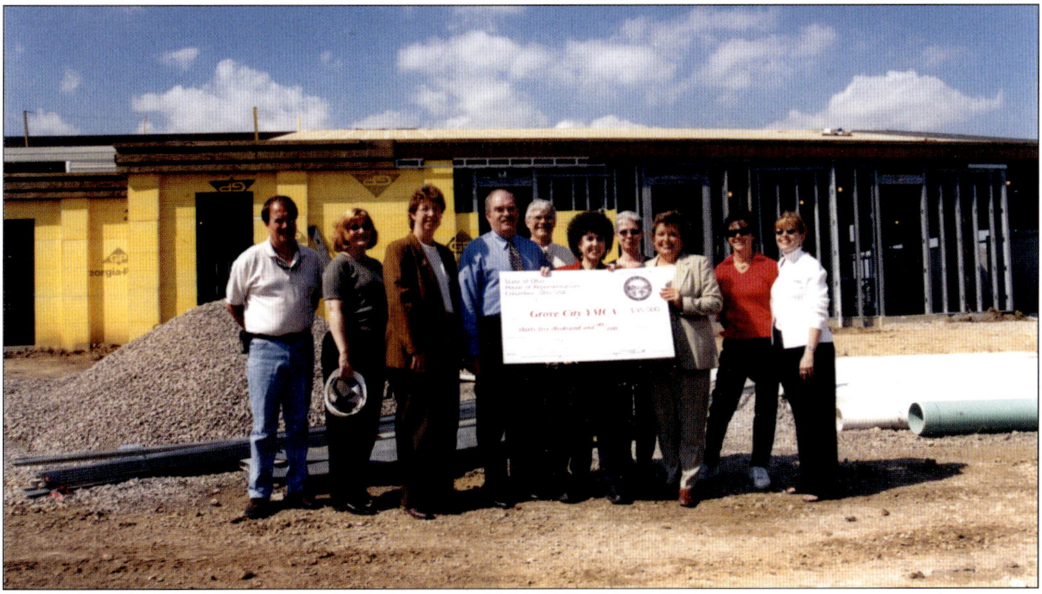

From left to right are Jackson Township trustee Dave Burris, Cheryl Brunton, Karen Crabbe, Central Ohio YMCA CEO John Bickley, Rick Brunton, state representative Amy Salerno, Sue Corbin, Mayor Cheryl Grossman, Jody Burris, and Tina Badurina. The Grove City branch of the YMCA opened in 2003 and serves 14,000 members, more than any central Ohio branch. In addition to free programs for cancer survivors and diabetes patients, Grove City's YMCA provides nearly 3,000 seniors with free memberships and almost $300,000 in membership aid.

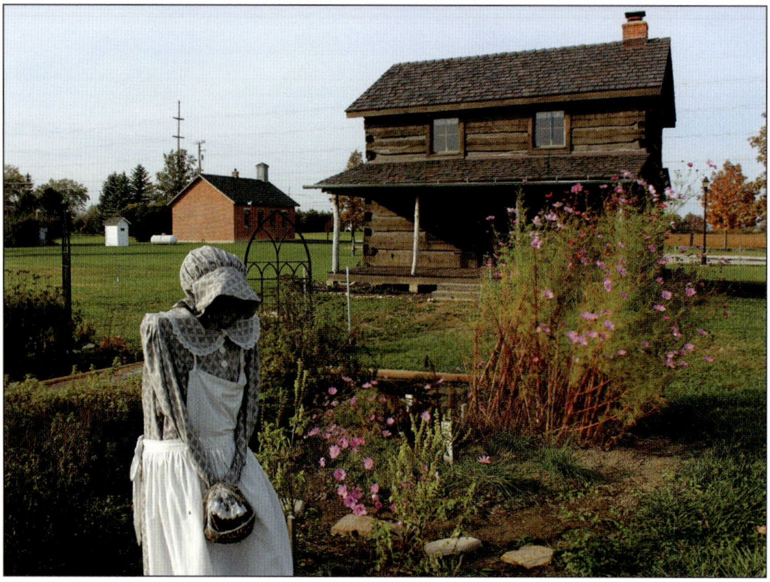

This scarecrow dressed as a woman of the 1860s stands guard in the garden at Century Village at Fryer Park. The garden has herbs and flowers that were prevalent during the mid-1800s. The park is maintained by the city in conjunction with volunteers from the Southwest Franklin County Historical Society.

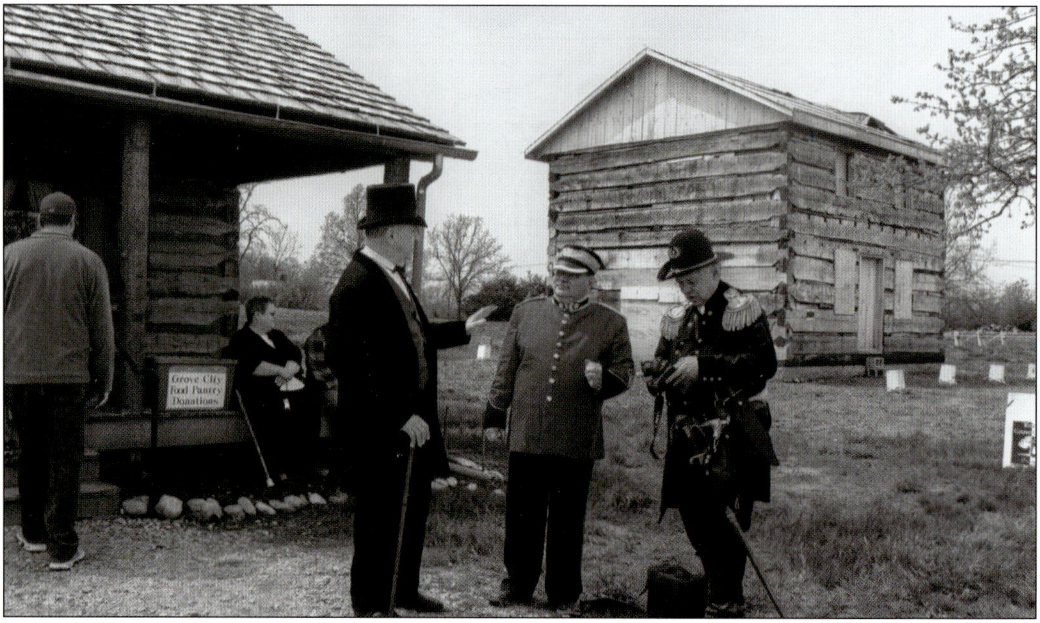

The encampment at Grove City is held every year at Century Village in Fryer Park. The event invites Civil War reenactors and craftsmen from that era to roam through the village's eight mid-19th-century buildings for an education-filled day. Pictured here is Bob Davis (left) posing as Gov. William Dennison, who served as Ohio's governor from 1860 to 1862. The event is sponsored by the Southwest Franklin County Historical Society.

Three

Churches' Stained Glass

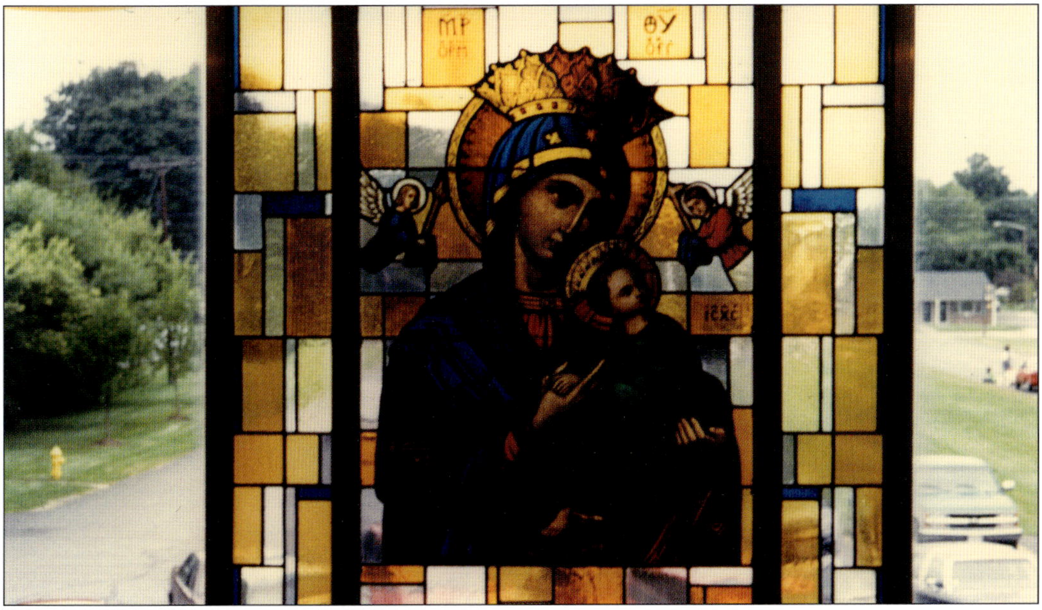

This stained-glass icon was the first image Our Lady of Perpetual Help parishioners saw when they entered the church in 1959. When the new church was built in 1999, the stained glass was relocated to the interior of the new building, where Mary's image greets parishioners as they enter the church. According to tradition, St. Luke created this icon, which depicts Mary comforting her son Jesus as archangels Michael and Gabriel look on.

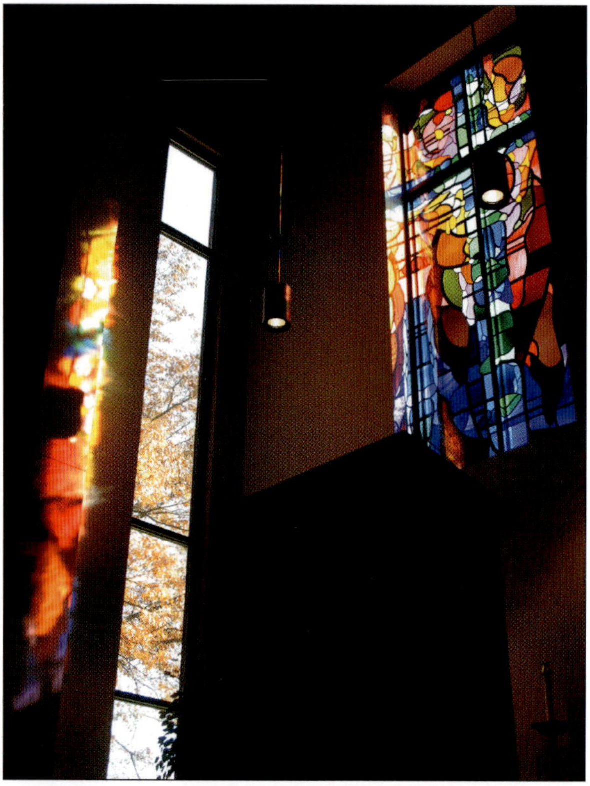

Bethel Lutheran Church opened its doors in 1968 on farmland owned by George and Martha Milligan. The tiny church grew rapidly. In 1997, it added an educational wing, and in 2005 a new sanctuary was dedicated. This stained-glass abstract was designed by Curtis R. Doll of Hanover, Pennsylvania. Doll stated that he wanted to make the dominant color blue due to its depth and because it is the most spiritual of all colors.

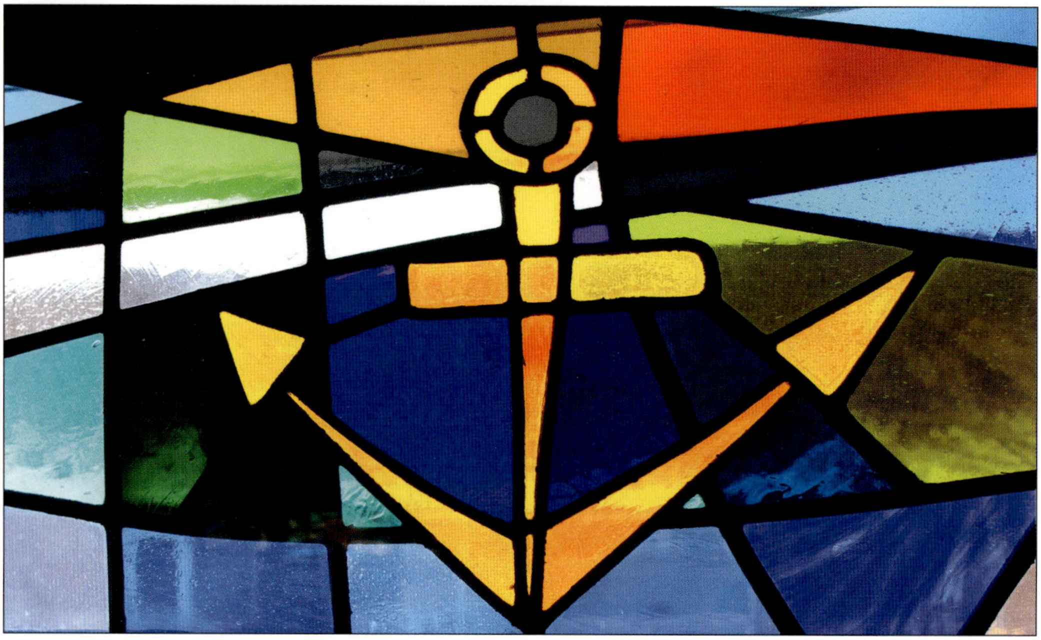

The First Presbyterian Church of Grove City took root in 1858 when the congregation at that time broke away from St. John's Evangelical Lutheran Church and formed their own. The 16 stained-glass panels in the sanctuary were installed in 1961 when the congregation built a new building on south Broadway on former farmland donated by Dr. A.B. and Mrs. Minnie White.

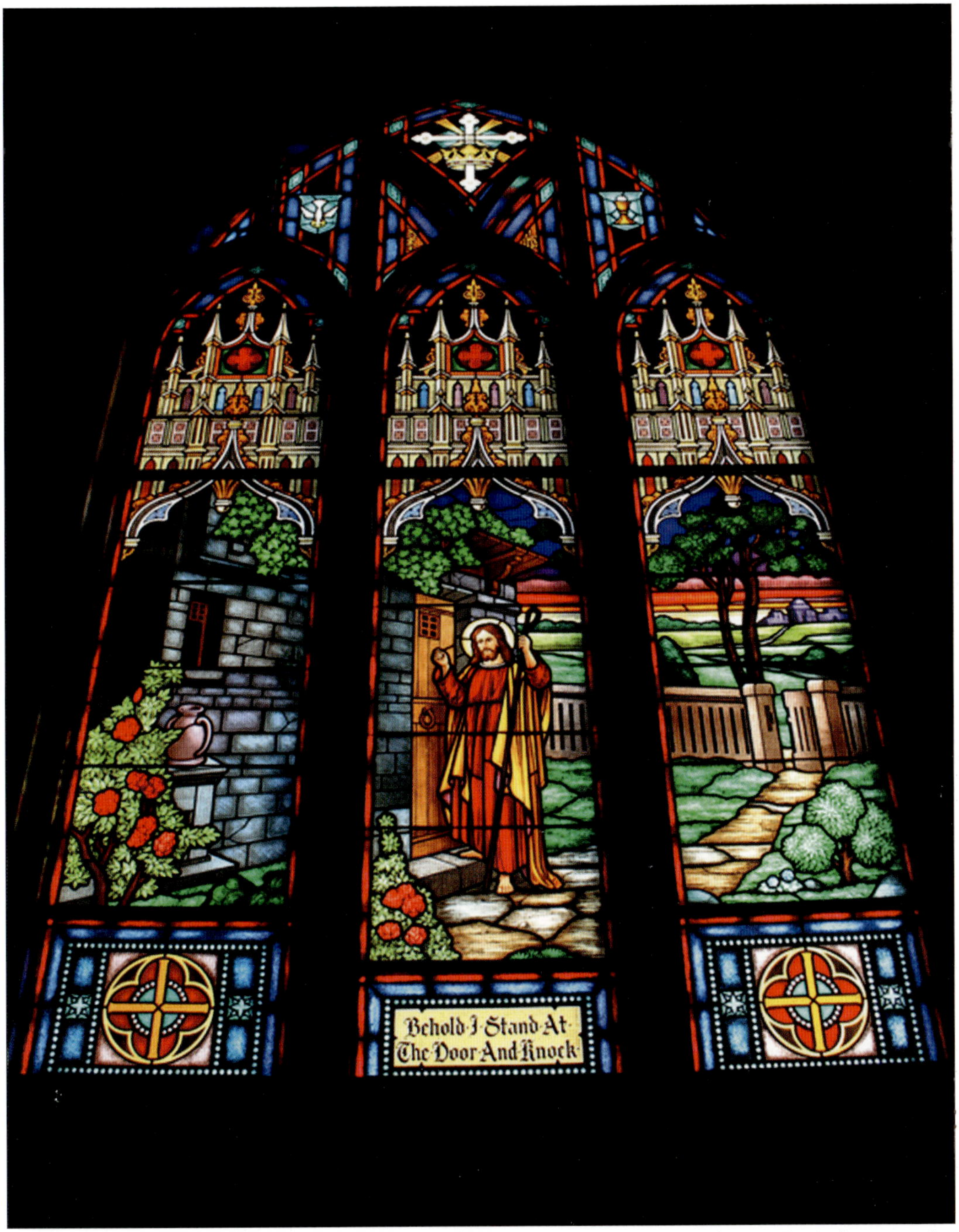

The congregation of Jackson Chapel United Methodist Church formed in 1850 and met in the home of William Breckenridge until they transferred to the Hopewell Church. In 1859, they built their first church, at the corner of White Road and State Route 104 (Jackson Pike). It is the second-oldest congregation in Jackson Township. In 1995, the church celebrated the Festival of Windows at the conclusion of a major renovation. The Gothic stained glass has been described as a jewel box for its magnificent windows designed by Michael Whapham. This window depicts Jesus saying, "Behold I stand at the Door and Knock."

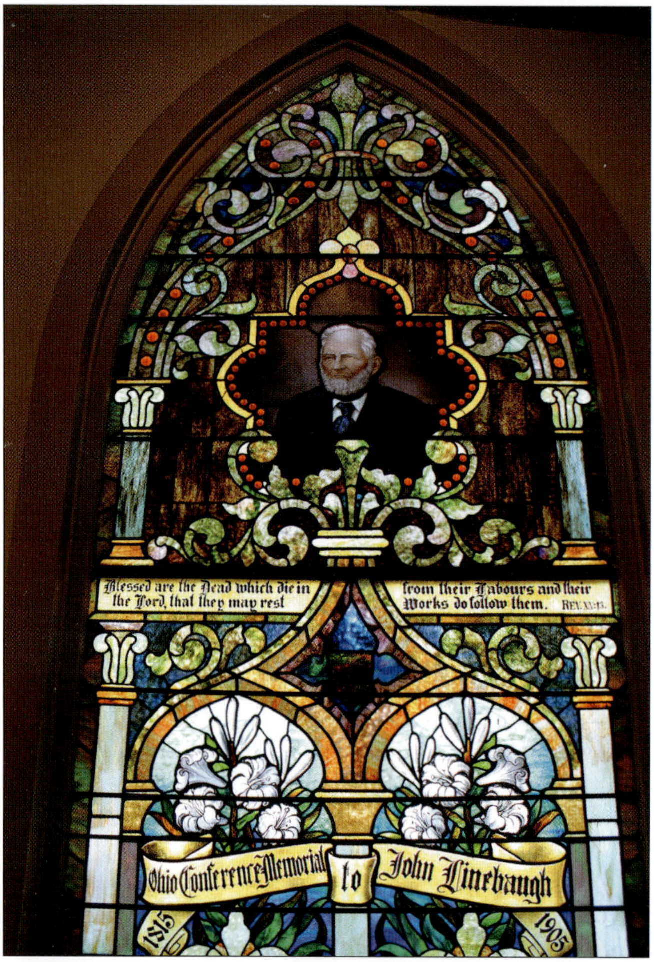

The congregation of Concord Chapel (later the Concord United Methodist Church) formed in 1847 and is considered the oldest congregation in Jackson Township. The church, built along Cottage Mill Pike (now State Route 665), was constructed in 1859 at the cost of $1,800. In 1905, the church underwent remodeling and dedicated this window to member John Linebaugh, who donated 700 acres of land to the Methodist diocese.

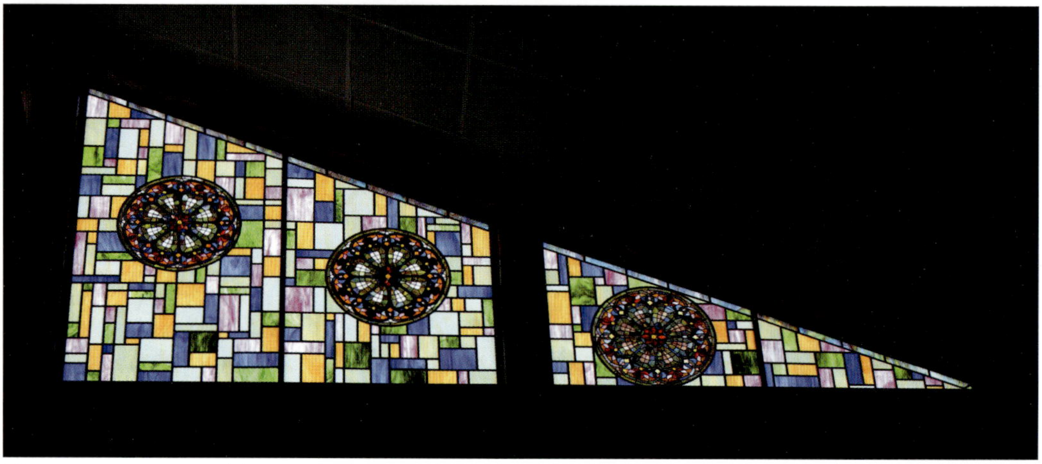

The congregation of Amazing Grace Christian Church developed from the former Church of Christ on Columbus Street and is now a nondenominational house of worship. The stained-glass panels at the crest on the east and west sides of the building were created by Franklin Art Glass. The church opened on Quail Creek Boulevard in 2006 and has 350 members.

This stained-glass window sketch of the annunciation of Mary was created for Our Lady of Perpetual Help Church by Maureen McGuire Design Association, Inc., located in Phoenix, Arizona. It tells the story of the angel's visit to the Virgin Mary when she is told she will bear the Christ child. This window was unveiled, along with five others, when OLPH's new church opened in 1999.

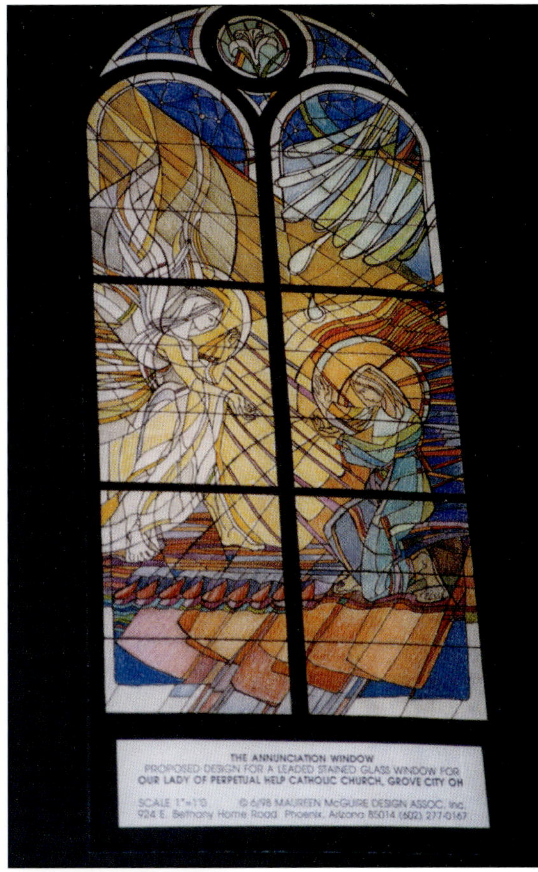

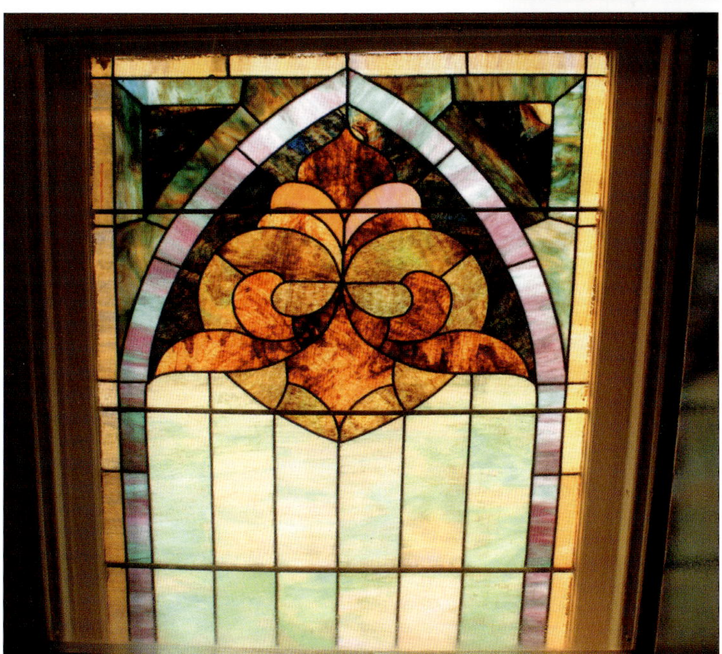

The congregation of Concord Methodist Episcopal Church, established in 1847, was the oldest church in Jackson Township until the building was sold in 2007. Today, it is Concord Chapel Animal Hospital. Several of its original stained-glass windows are still intact, including this window.

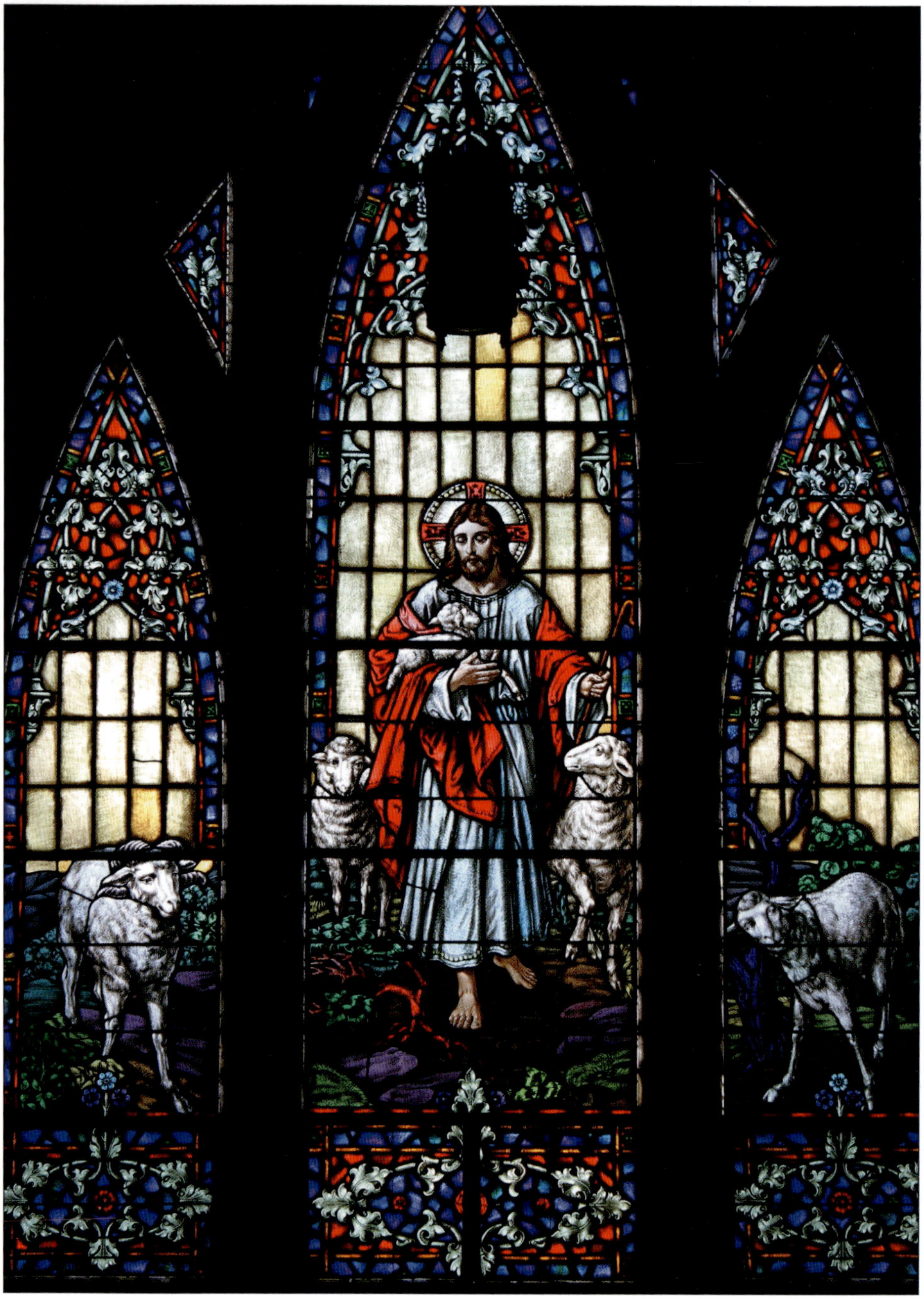

The Good Shepherd Window at St. John's Evangelical Lutheran Church was dedicated as part of a renovation of its sanctuary and extension of the chancel in 1937. The window was designed by Max Frank of Associated Art Glass. St. John's was formed in 1849 by German Lutherans and is the oldest congregation in Grove City. The present building was constructed at a cost of $11,000 and dedicated on May 12, 1889. Some of original stained glass from that era can be seen in the sanctuary and bell tower today. In 1920, a new parish house was added to the east in keeping with the same style of architecture. In the mid-1950s, the parish house was torn down and replaced with a new educational wing.

The congregation of Highland Baptist Church began meeting in an area school in 1964 until construction could begin on their building at 3460 Hoover Road in 1965. The congregation has 600 members. Highland Baptist is a gospel-centered community with an eclectic mix of music and dramatic and artistic expression.

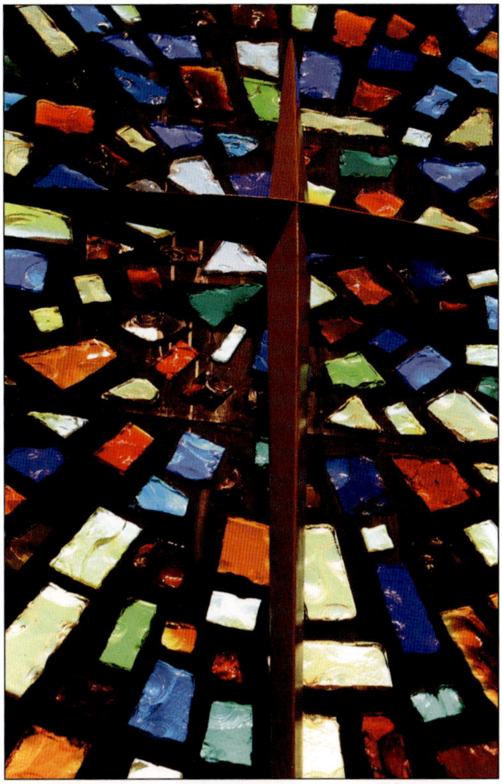

The Evans Gazebo, also known as the town center gazebo, at the corner of Grove City Road and Broadway, is dedicated to the late Betty Evans, who owned a floral business on Broadway for over 50 years. The eight panels at the top of the gazebo reflect a floral pattern on a sky-blue background.

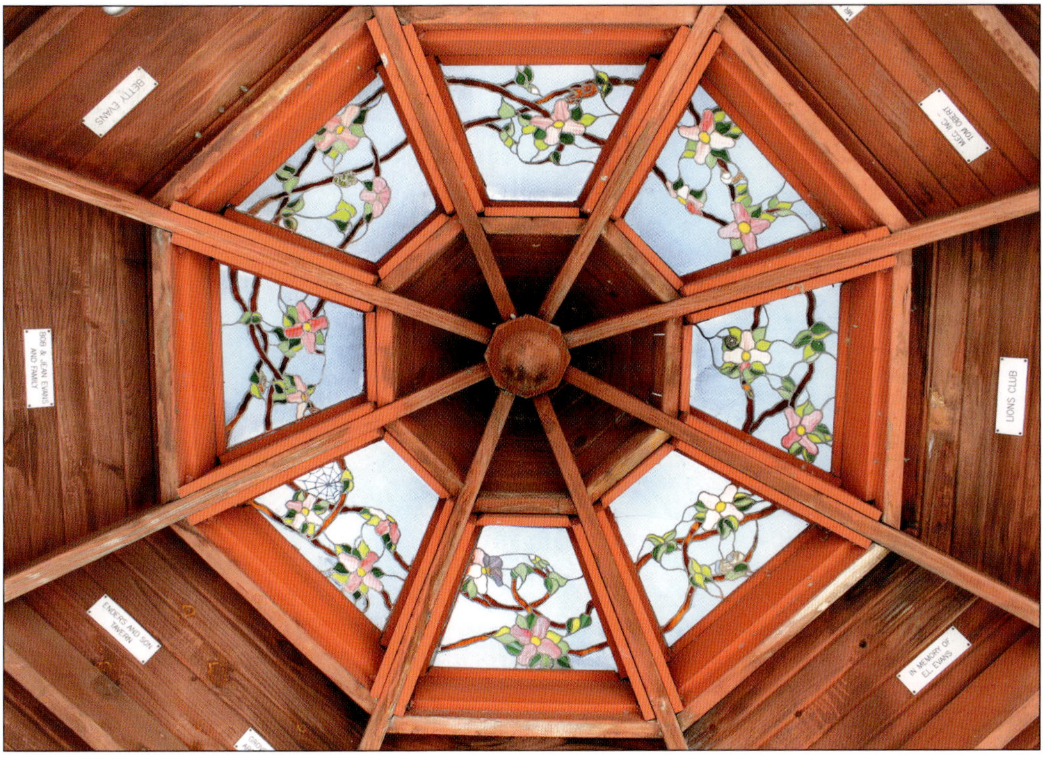

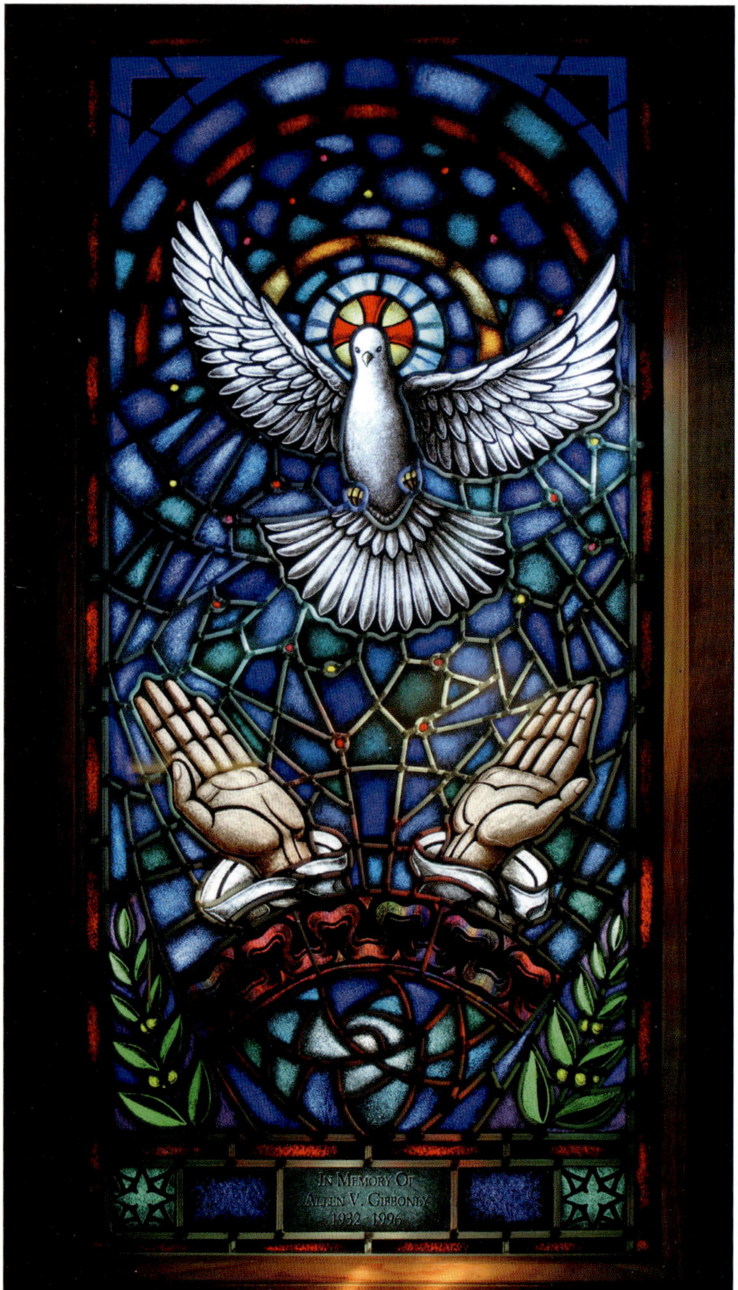

The present Jackson Chapel United Methodist Church, at 4473 Jackson Pike, was constructed in 1901 on a tract of land granted for the new edifice by Margaret Breckenridge and her son Frank. The chapel was renovated in 1995 and some new windows added. This window in the north door of the church was designed by Michael Whapham of the Franklin Art Glass Company. The window is called *The Spirit of the Dove in God's Hands* and depicts God's hands reaching out to receive people into heaven. It is dedicated to the late Allen Gibboney, a lifelong member of the church. The door is used by pallbearers after funerals to carry out caskets as doves accompany souls to God.

Four

Community Cornerstones

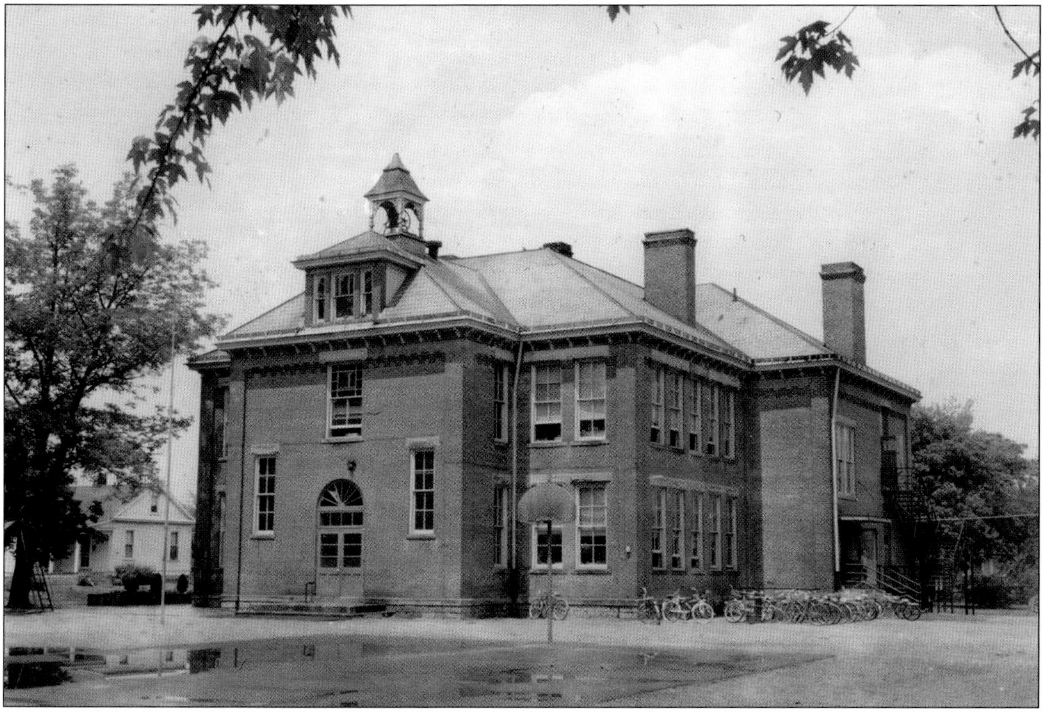

A wooden school stood on the lot between Arbutus Avenue to the west and Third Street to the east from 1853 to 1888, when this brick schoolhouse, known as the old Park Street School, was constructed. In 1894, the first classes for Grove City High School opened for students on the upper floor. A public school stood on this block for 111 years before the building was demolished in 1964.

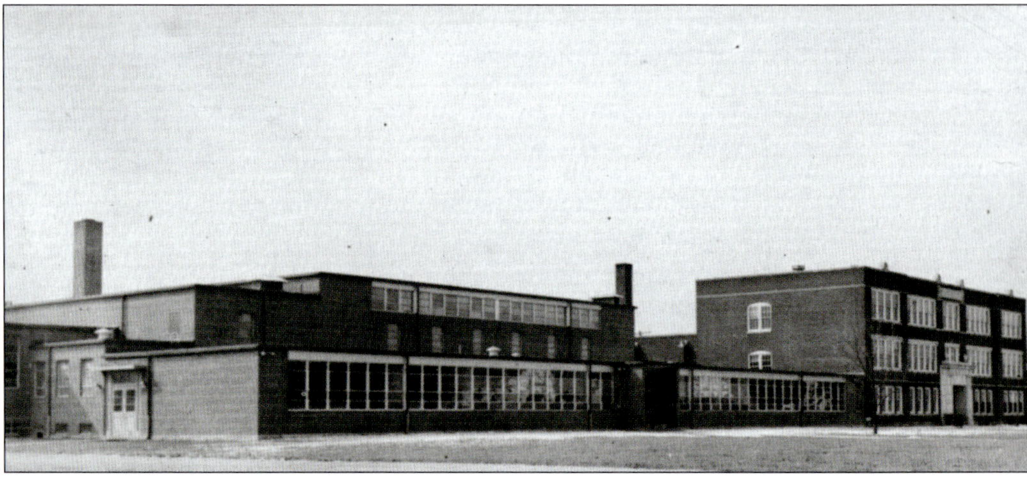

Pictured here are the old Jackson Township-Grove City High School, built in 1928 (far right), and the addition, built in 1956 (left). Until this time, it was the only high school in the South-Western City School District. In 1970, it was converted to Park Street Middle School. The old building was demolished in 2000, and the site now is home to Park Street Intermediate School, which has students in grades five and six.

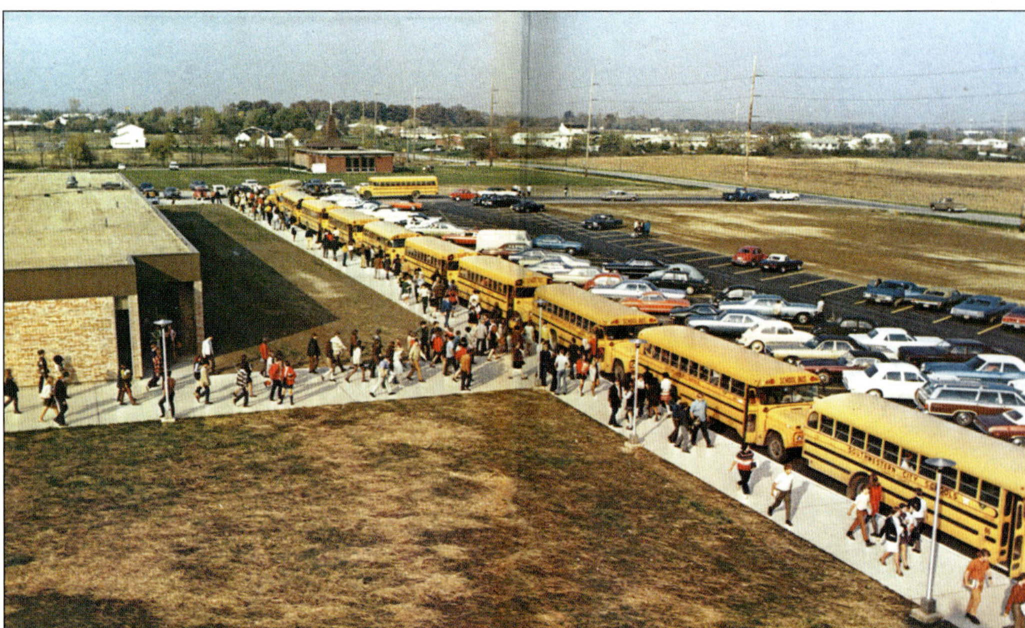

The new Grove City High School opened at 4665 Hoover Road, on property formerly owned by the Milligan family, for the 1970–1971 school year. Standing nearly alone on the west side of Hoover Road, the school had yet to be annexed into the city when it first opened.

Grove City High School's football program has a long and storied history, beginning with its first victory against Ashville in 1929. The Greyhounds had undefeated regular championship seasons in 1939 under coach John E. "Pete" Trego, 1972 under coach Chuck Brockmeyer, and 1990, 1991, and 1996 under coach Brian Cross. The Greyhounds experienced their 300th win on October 1, 1991, by defeating Canton McKinley. Pictured are Cross (left) and assistant athletic director Jim Lester.

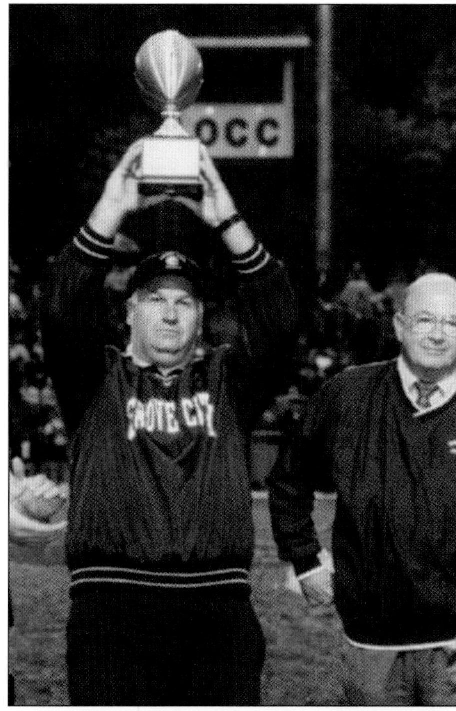

During the late 1920s, when the state shut down greyhound racing, a group of businessmen donated money to the high school in a public-relations move to save the local racetrack. Afterward, the school designated the greyhound as the team mascot. Throughout the school's history, several greyhounds have been a part of the team. Pictured here is Faultless, the adopted mascot during the 1970s. The National Honor Society held fundraisers to raise the $12 monthly feeding of Faultless. Today's school mascot, Ruby, is owned by athletic director Tom Willison.

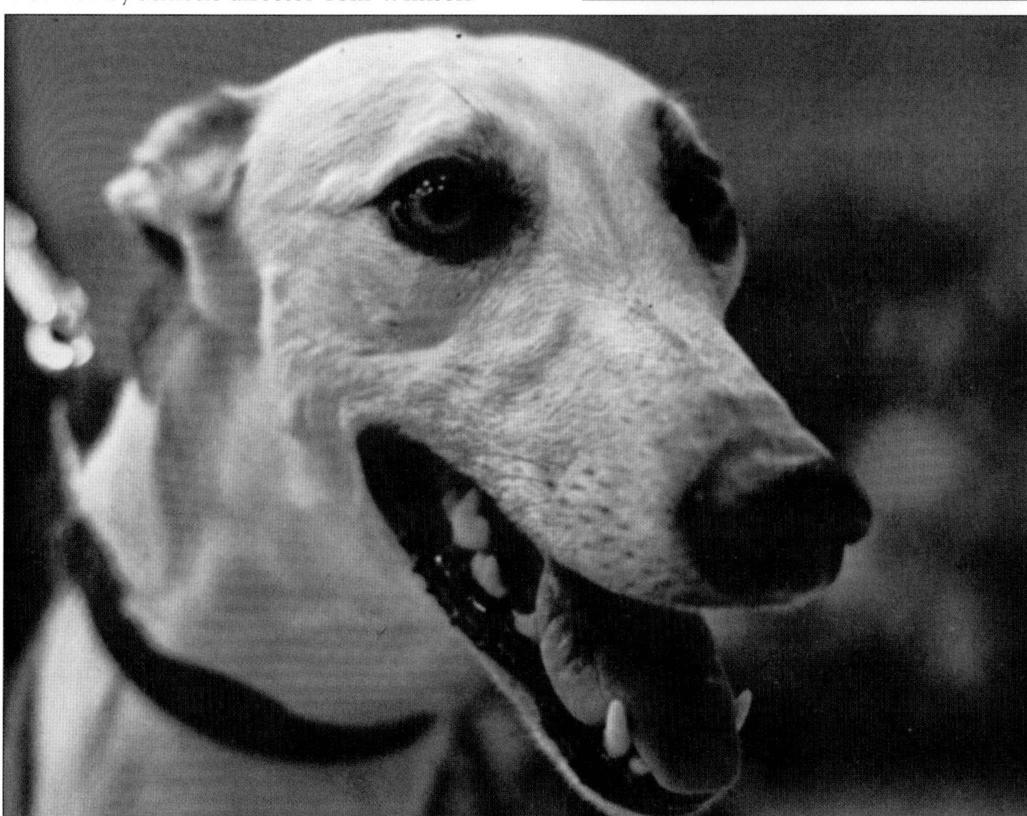

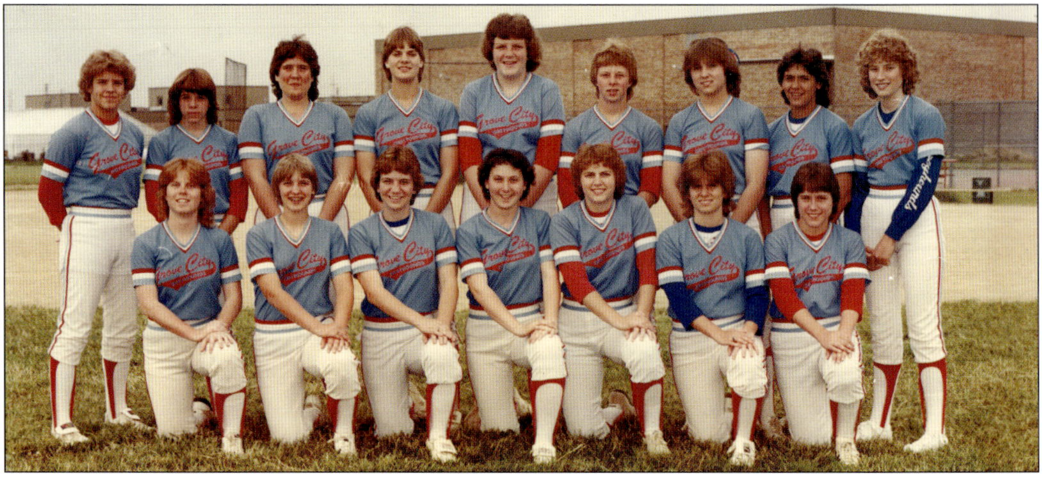

Coached by Ron Hutcheson, the Grove City High School girls' softball team won the school's first AAA state title in 1983 by defeating Tallmadge High School. Pictured here are, from left to right, (first row) Denise Walters, Tracy Smith, Lisa Norris, Kim McKeon, Teresa Eisel, Kathy Merriman, and Crystal Lilly; (second row) Lori Patzer, Karen Holmes, Sherry Zeller, Audie Hayes, Dortha Ford, Kerry Gleich, Jenny Ruoff, Tracy French, and Audry Rollins.

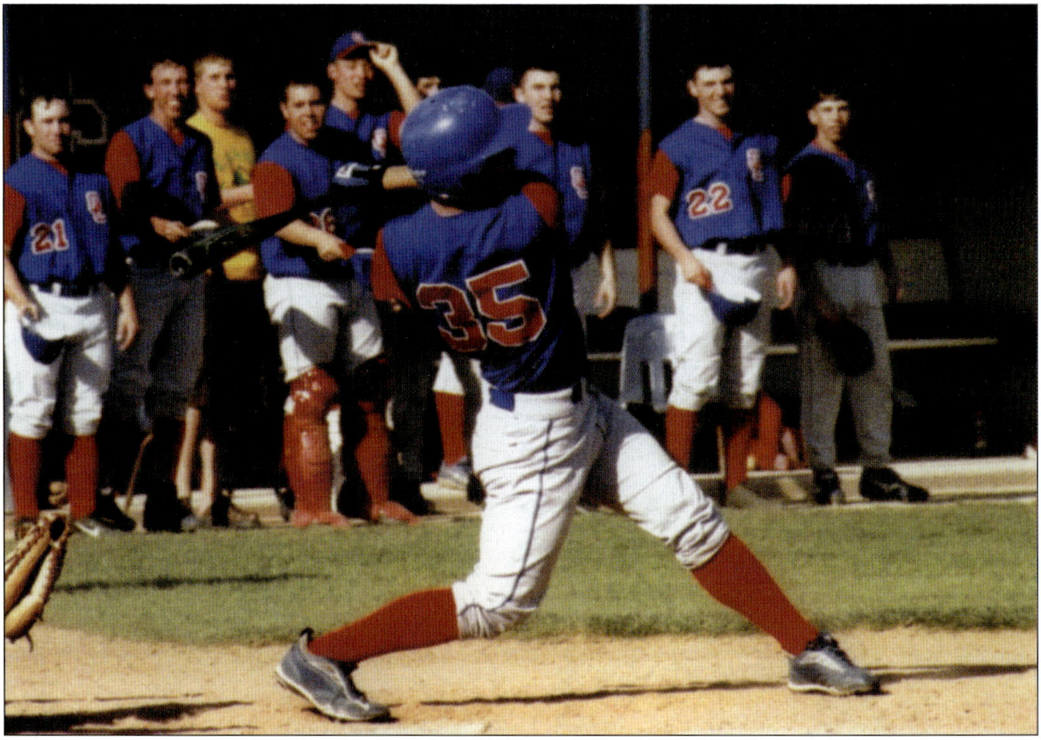

Grove City has a history of great baseball teams and coaches. Coach Elmer Houdashelt's team won the Mid-Eight League and a district championship his first year as head coach in 1958, followed by nine more league championships. Coach Mark Wylie coached from 1977 to 1986 and earned seven sectional championships, three district championships, and one regional championship. Coach Jim Habermehl was at the helm from 1987 to 2008 and is the longest-serving coach for any major Grove City High School sport.

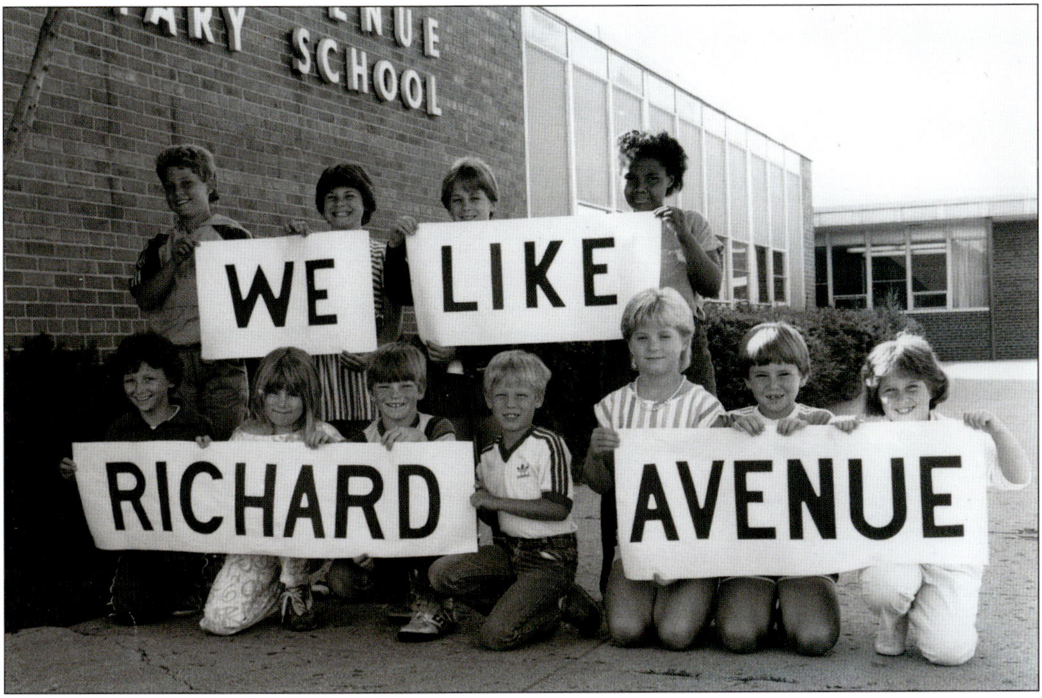

Richard Avenue Elementary School was built in 1957 to serve a rapidly growing population. From 1957 to 1960, enrollment in the South-Western City School District soared, with 1,000 new students entering the system each year. Richard Avenue was the fourth elementary school to be built within the corporation limits of Grove City. It was demolished in 2015 and will be replaced with a new building.

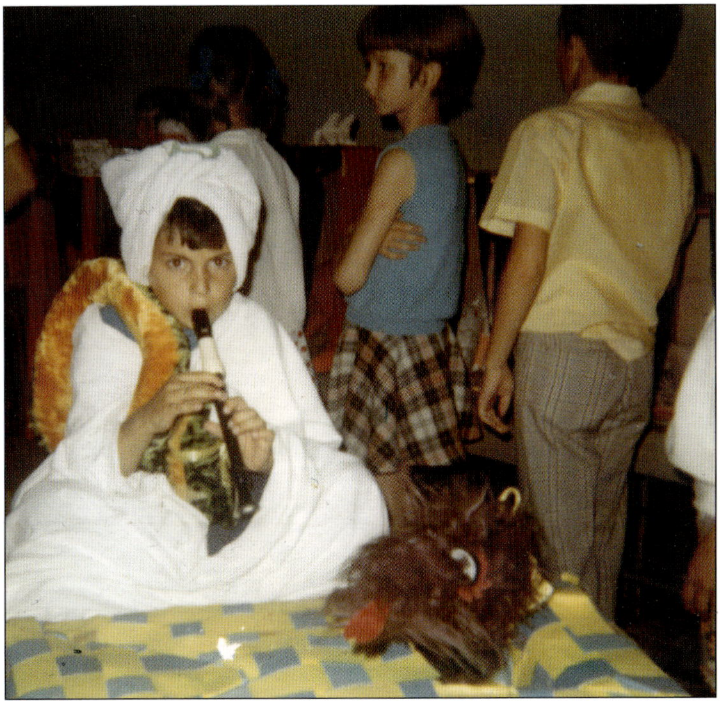

Gary Buckingham is shown playing snake charmer at a Richard Avenue School circus in 1970. Gary is the son of Roy Buckingham, who helped start one of the city's early organized teenage program, Teens Unlimited. Gary currently serves on the city's historical commission.

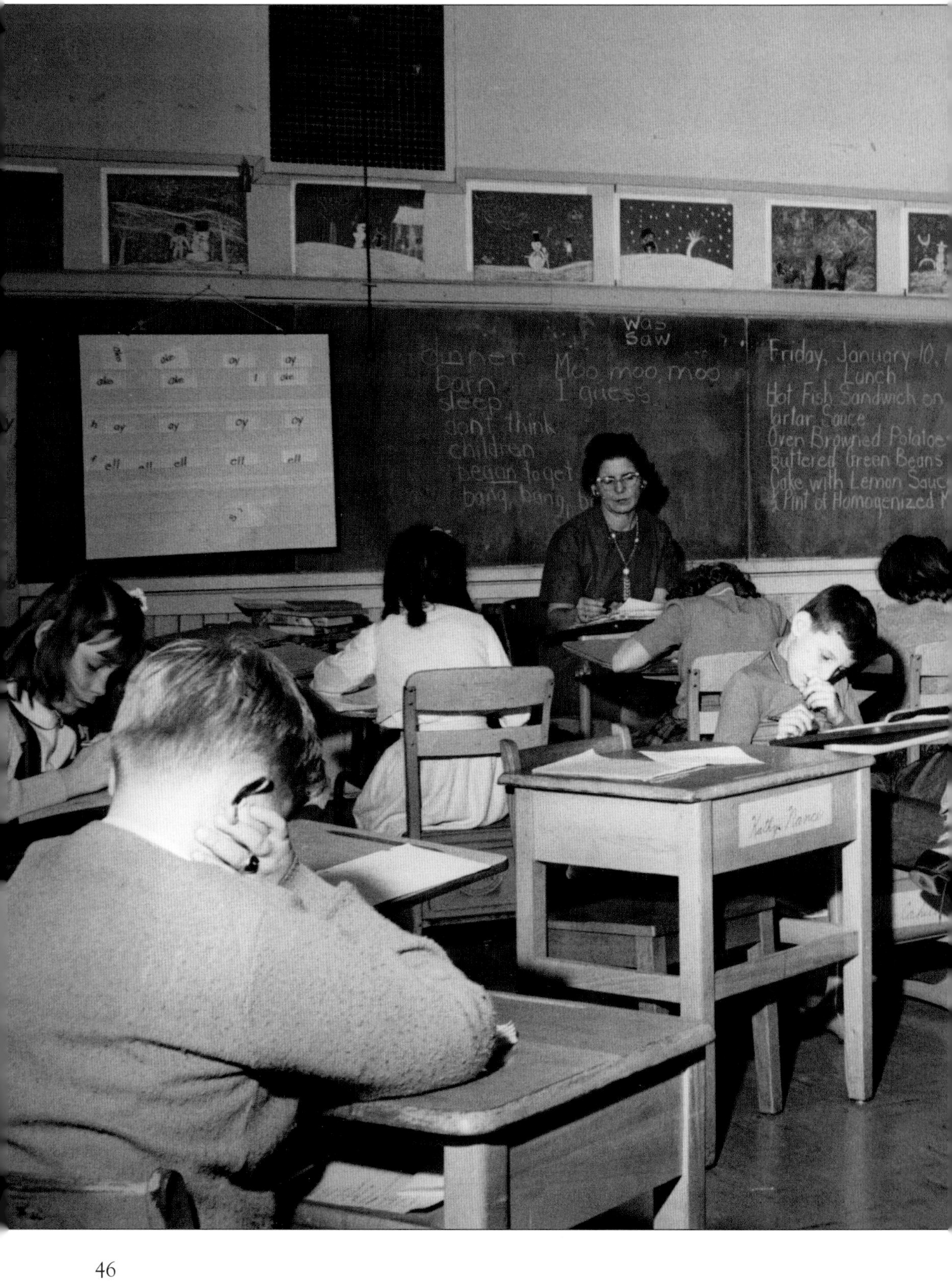
was
saw
dinner
barn
sleep
dont think
children
began to get
Moo, moo, moo
I guess
Friday, January 10,
Lunch
Hot Fish Sandwich on
Tartar Sauce
Oven Browned Potatoe
Buttered Green Beans
Cake with Lemon Sauc
Pint of Homogenized

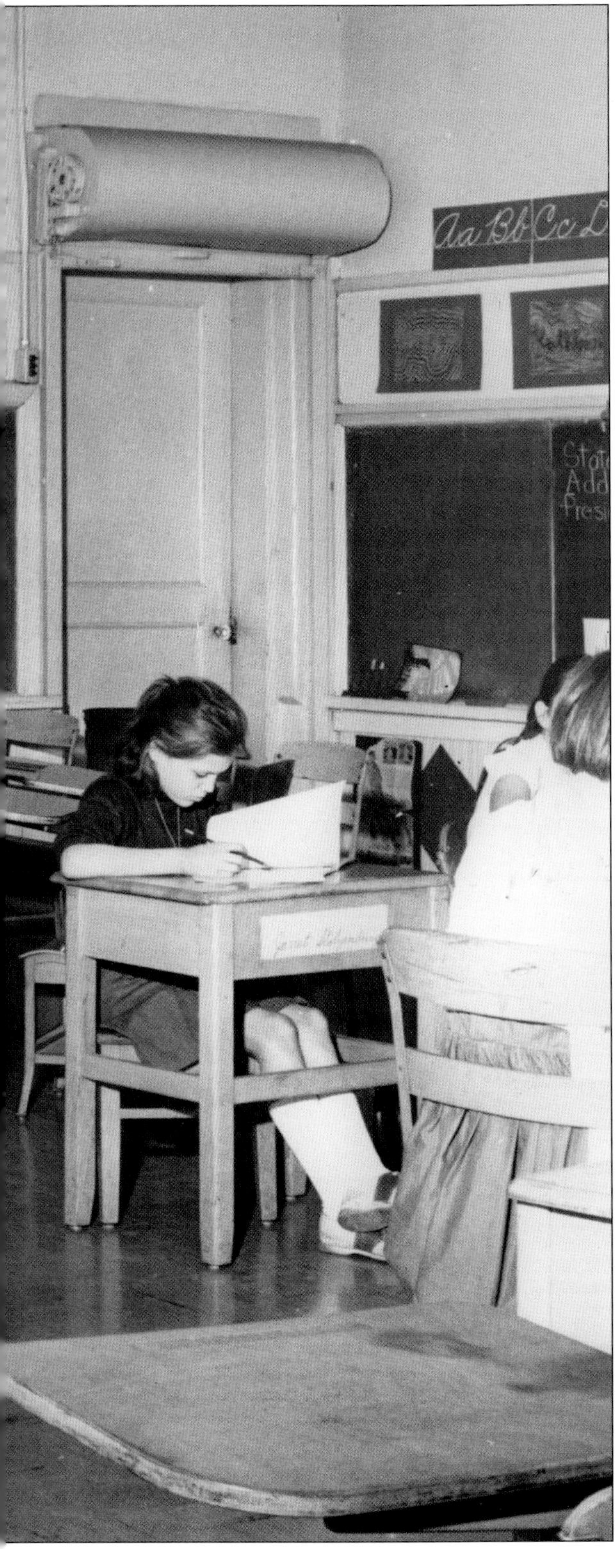

The old Park Street Elementary School was an educational beacon for Grove City's children until it was closed in 1964. The two-story brick structure was preceded by a two-room wooden building on the same site, built in 1853. Until its demolition, the school was one of the oldest in Ohio, having been constructed in 1888. In 1895, a high school was started in the upper story and was a three-year course of study. This photograph was taken on January 10, 1964, during the school's last year. Note that the lunch menu is written on the blackboard and is still a standard lunch today. Faculty for the school's final year included principal James Harmon, Carol Grossman, Florence Smith, Frances Neff, Nelle Bowman, Robert St. John, Nedra Carlson, Mollie Owen, Faye Alban, Florene Williams, and John Scalise.

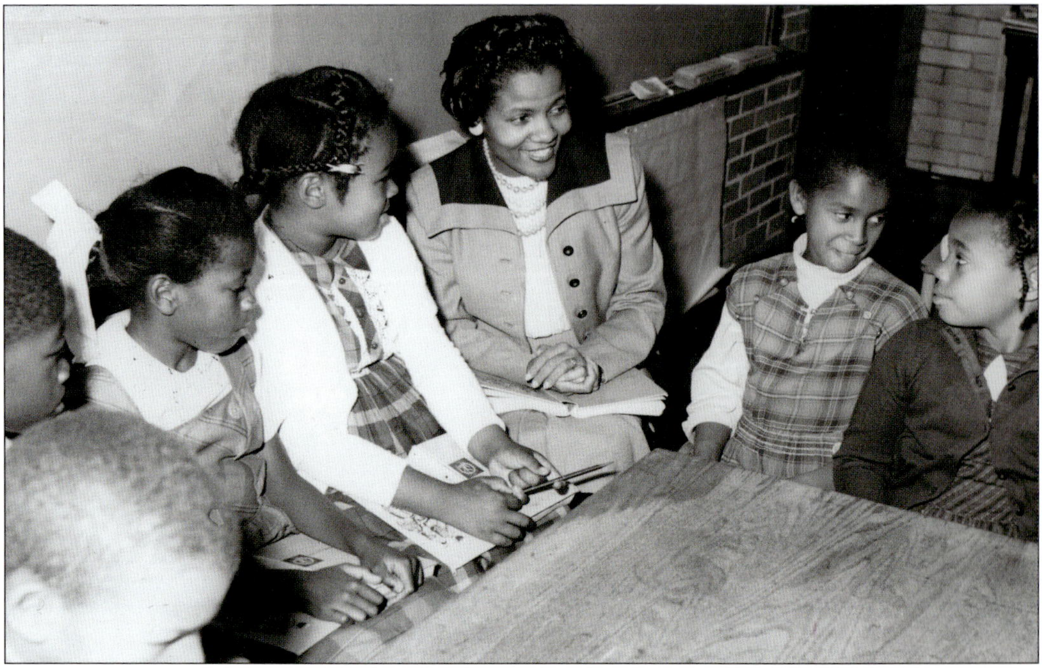

Urbancrest Elementary School consolidated into the newly formed South-Western Local School District in 1956. Others consolidated into the new district that year were Franklin Township Local District, Prairie Township Local District, Pleasant Township Local District, and Georgesville Local District. Urbancrest School closed in 1981, and the children were transferred to other schools in the Grove City area.

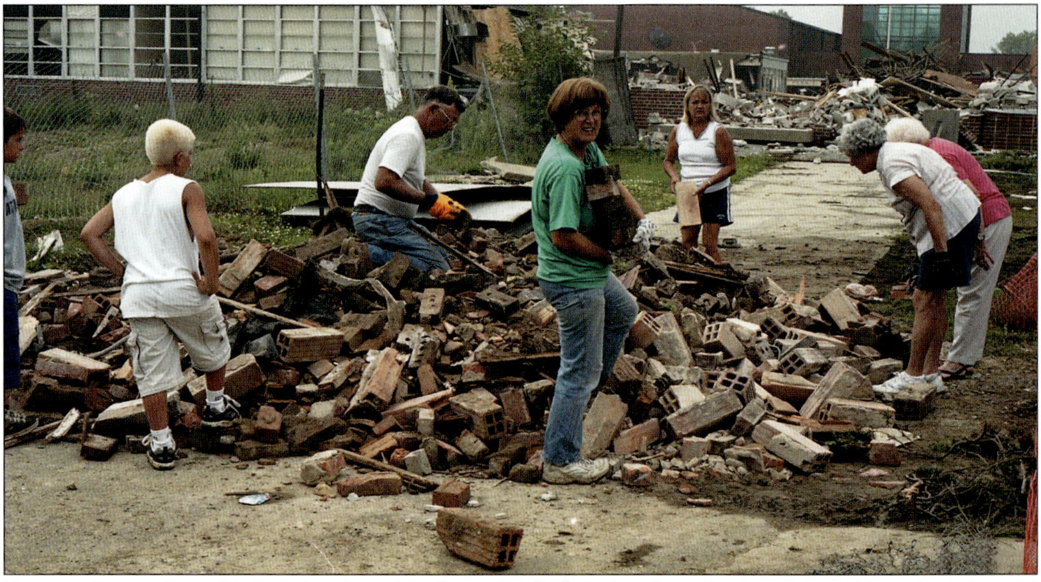

Former Grove City High School and Jackson Middle School students were saddened as the old brick building at 3191 Park Street, partly built in 1928 and in 1956, was torn down in 2000. The former building housed Jackson Township's only public high school (part of South-Western City Schools since 1956) until the new Grove City High School opened in the fall of 1970. Today, the site is the home of the recently built Park Street Intermediate School.

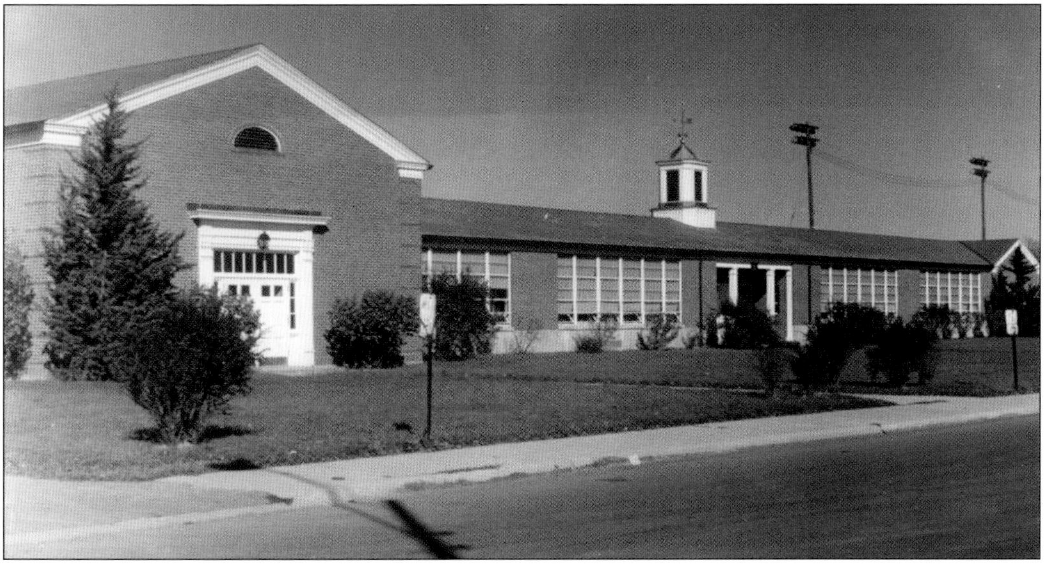

Kingston Avenue Elementary School, at 3226 Kingston Avenue, was built in 1949 as the village's second elementary school after the Park Street Elementary School. On January 1, 1956, Grove City's schools merged with five local systems and one exempted village district to form South-Western City Schools. Today Kingston is the oldest remaining school building in Grove City but is being leased by Grove City Parks & Recreation.

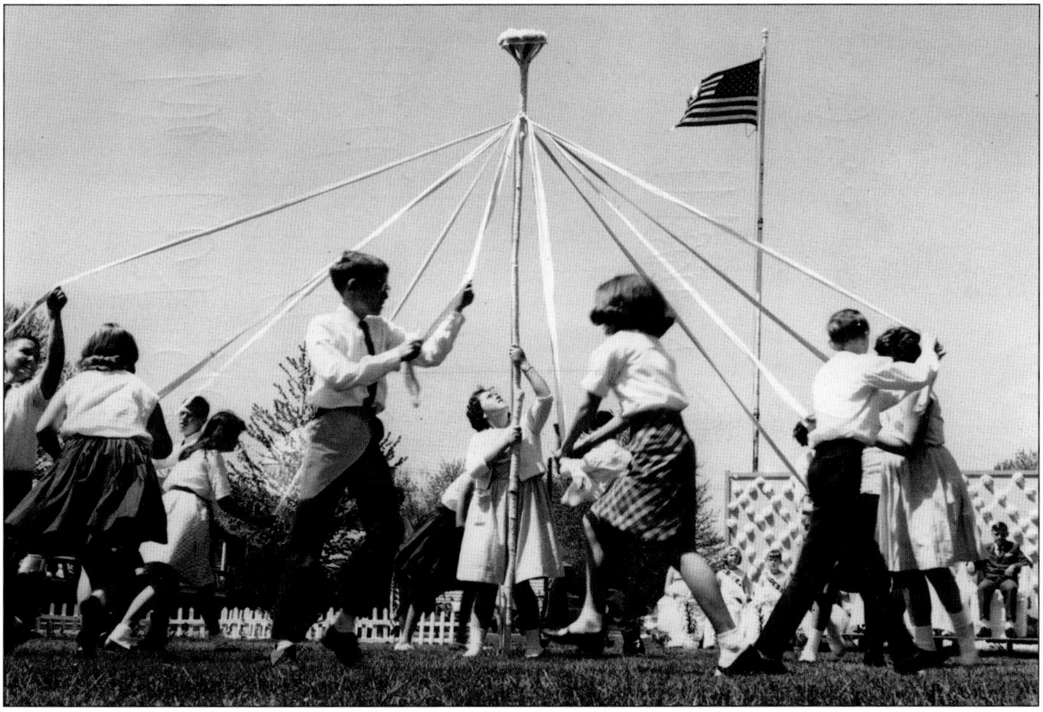

Despite May Day celebrations becoming less frequent in schools during the 1960s, the students at Kingston Elementary School carried on the tradition with a celebration in 1966 complete with a May Queen and a maypole. Twirling around the pole is Barb Moore, and off to the far right is Sue Ruoff Zeszotek in a skirt made by her mother, Dorothy Ruoff.

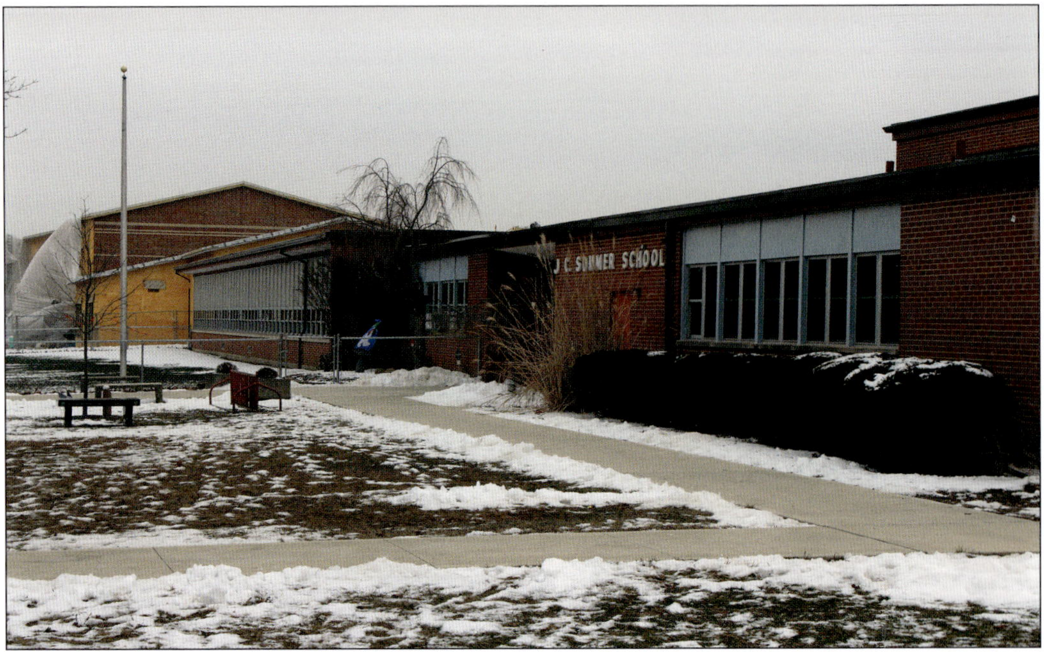

J.C. Sommer Elementary School, at 3055 Kingston Avenue, is seen with its replacement building under construction. The original building was completed in 1956 for students in first through eighth grade. Today, the school educates students in first through fourth grade. In March 2012, the district passed an Ohio Facilities Construction Commission bond issue to pay for new construction.

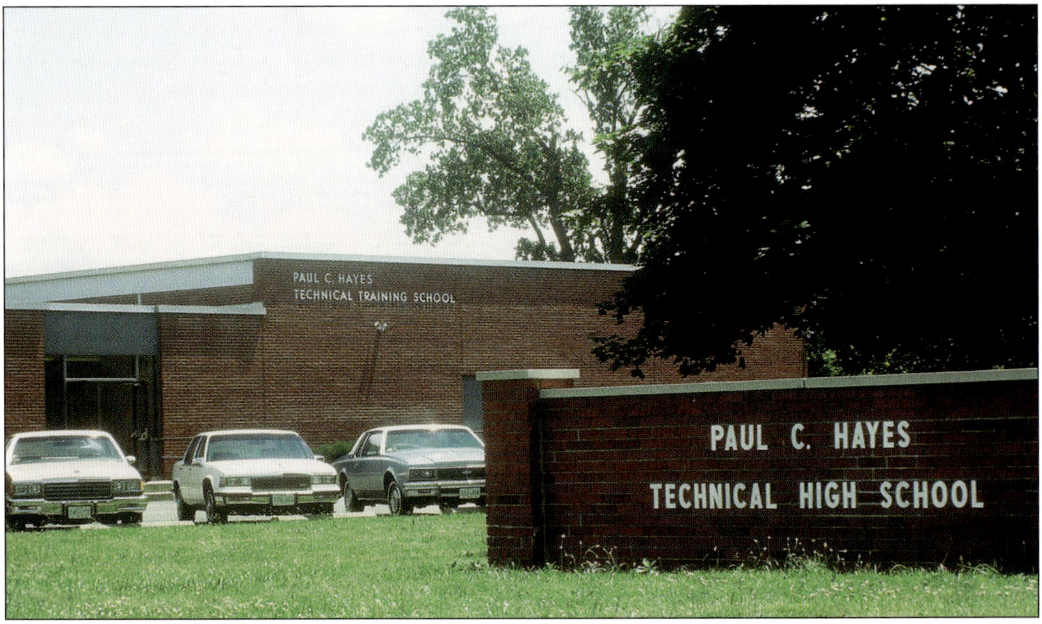

Paul C. Hayes Technical High School opened in 1966 and served students in South-Western City Schools for more than 40 years before being transformed into Hayes Intermediate School following the opening of the South-Western City Schools Career Academy in 2002. Juniors and seniors from all over the district attended Hayes in large part to gain skilled training in order to establish post–high school careers.

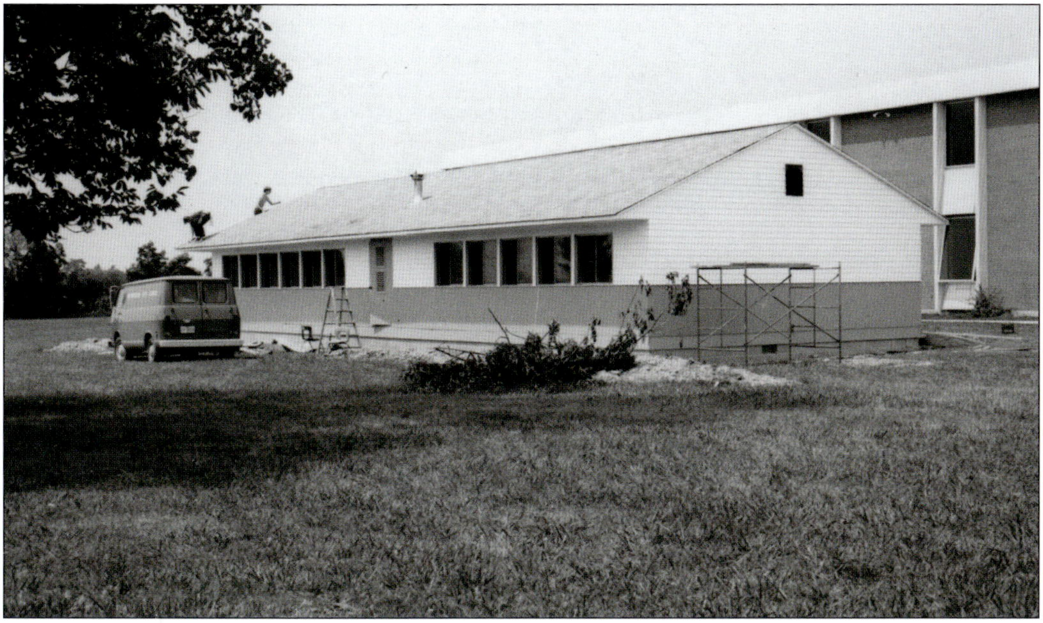

Brookpark Middle School, at 2803 Southwest Boulevard, opened as Brookpark Junior High in 1964 to educate students from seventh through the ninth grades. Now called Brookpark Middle School, the student population consists of students in seventh and eighth grade. It was the second junior high in Grove City, following Jackson Junior High, and the first one built specifically for that grade range.

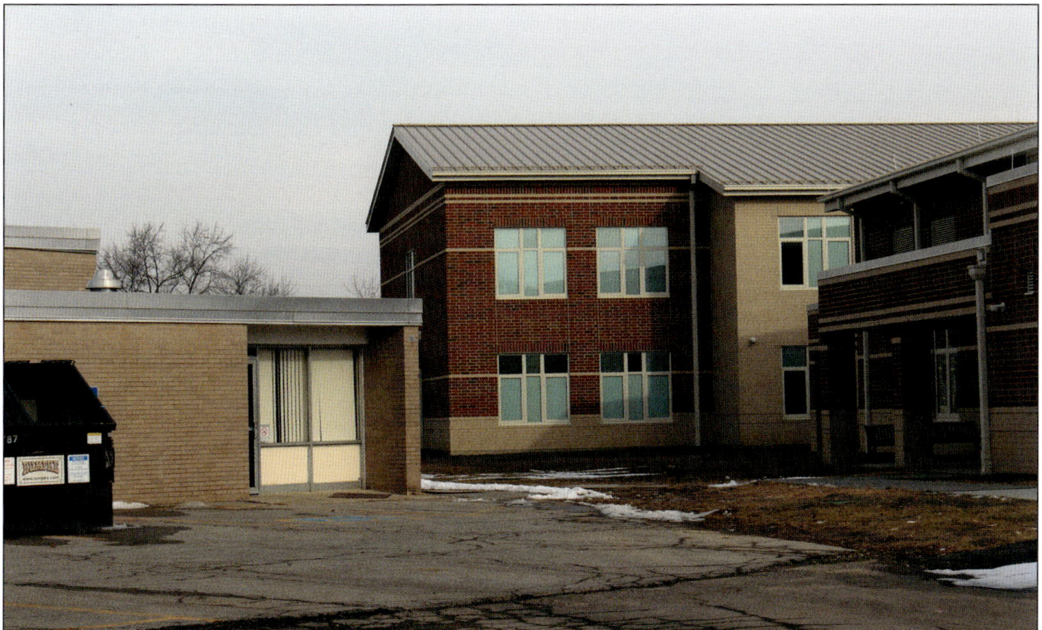

Monterey Elementary School was originally built in 1963, and its first principal was LeMoyne Brokaw. It has been replaced by a new building of the same name that opened in September 2014. Seen here is the old building standing back to back with its replacement. The old building is scheduled for demolition.

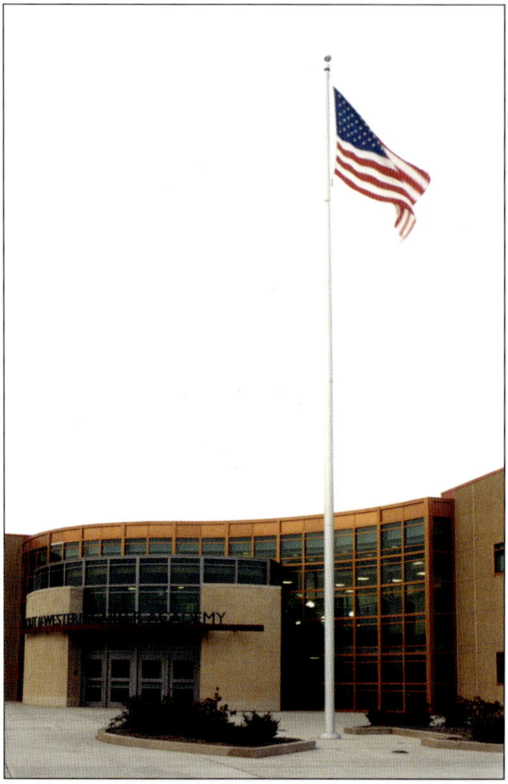

A successful bond issue in 1998 resulted in new schools in the South-Western City School District, including the South-Western Career Academy. The building opened in the fall of 2002 and serves juniors and seniors, offering training in a variety of career fields. It replaced Hayes Tech (now Hayes Intermediate) and joined Central Crossing High School and Holt Crossing Intermediate School on the new campus at Holt and Big Run South Roads.

Players on the Central Crossing High School Comets football team made school history as they stormed the field for their first-ever playoff appearance in 2014, under the direction of head coach Chris Harr. The Comets lost the Division I postseason football game to Cincinnati's St. Xavier High School, but the season's top accomplishment was an important milestone for the local high school.

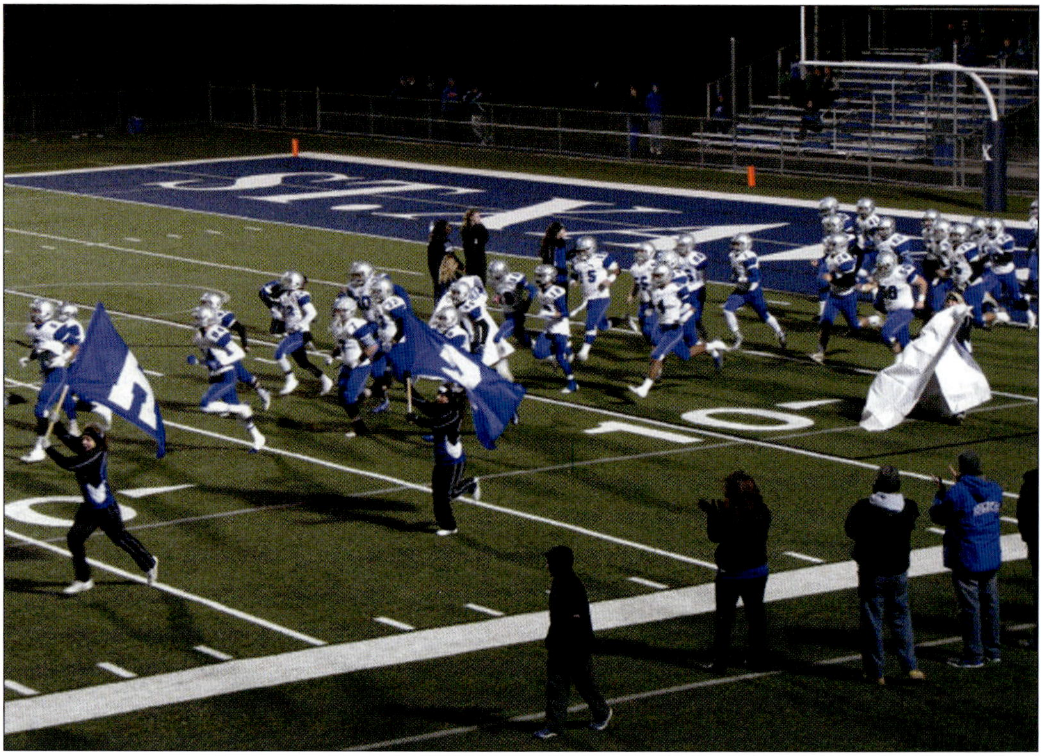

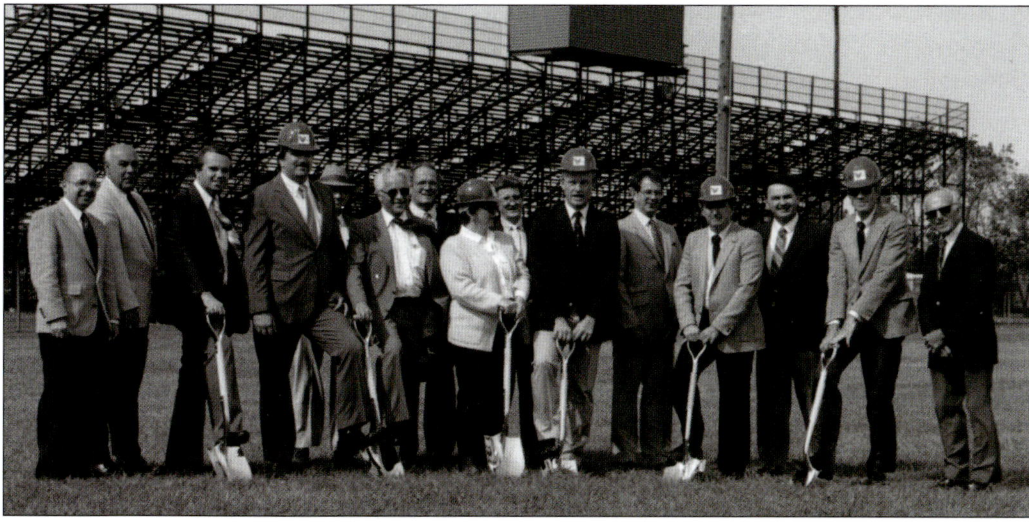

One of the projects voters approved by passing a $14.5-million bond issue for South-Western City Schools in 1984 was the construction of three identical recreation centers located at the three high schools in the district. Here, community and school leaders participate in the ground-breaking ceremony for the center at Grove City High School in October 1985. The shared community/school-recreation centers opened in September 1986.

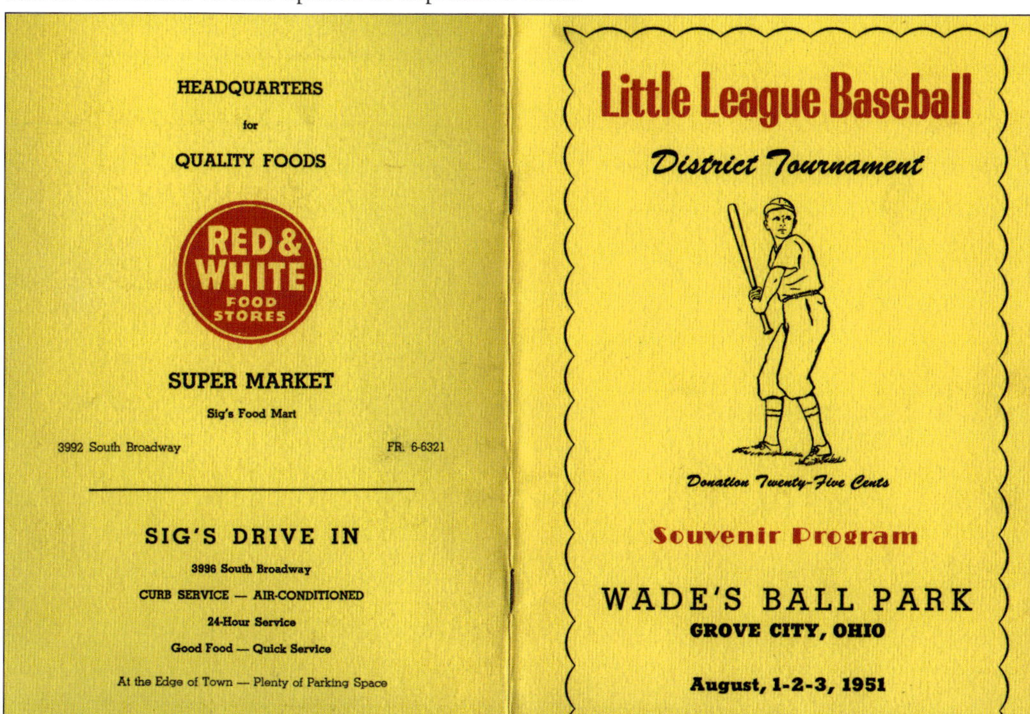

From 1950 to 1978, Little League Baseball was a fixture in town, as thousands participated in the sport. Tournaments held in the community drew teams from around the region to Wade's Field, and then Windsor Park, as the city's reputation as a baseball town continued to grow. After a 35-year hiatus, official Little League Baseball returned in 2013. Even during the absence of Little League, recreation and travel baseball continuously thrived.

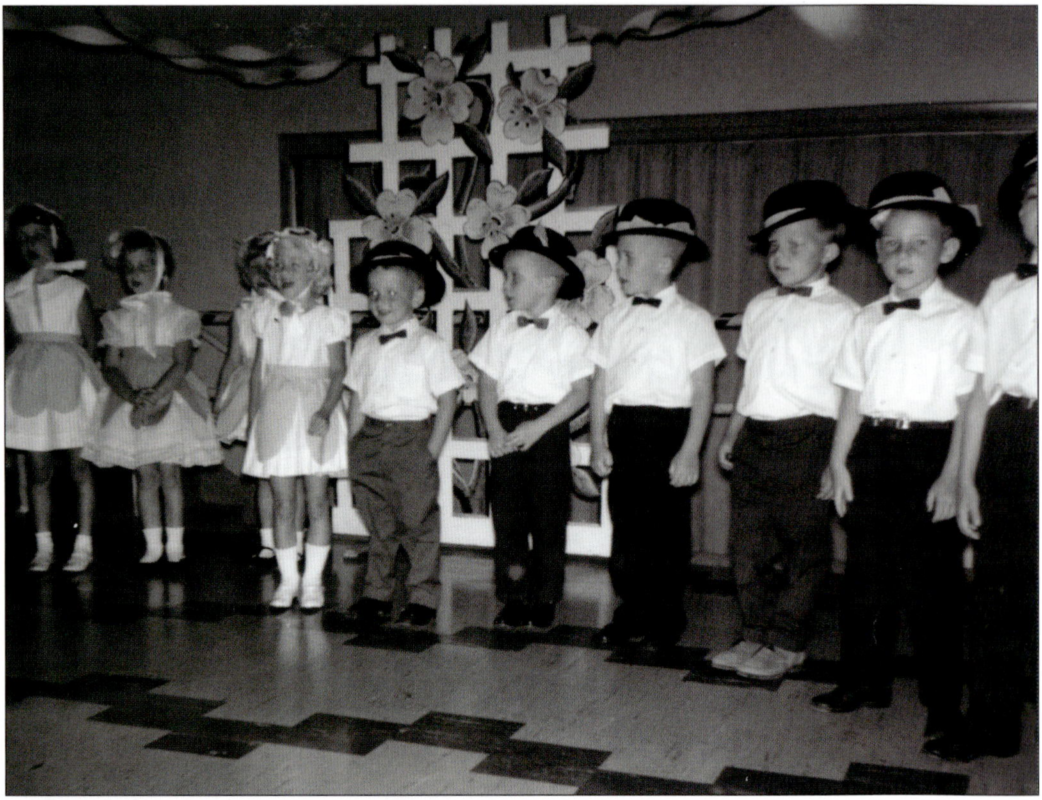

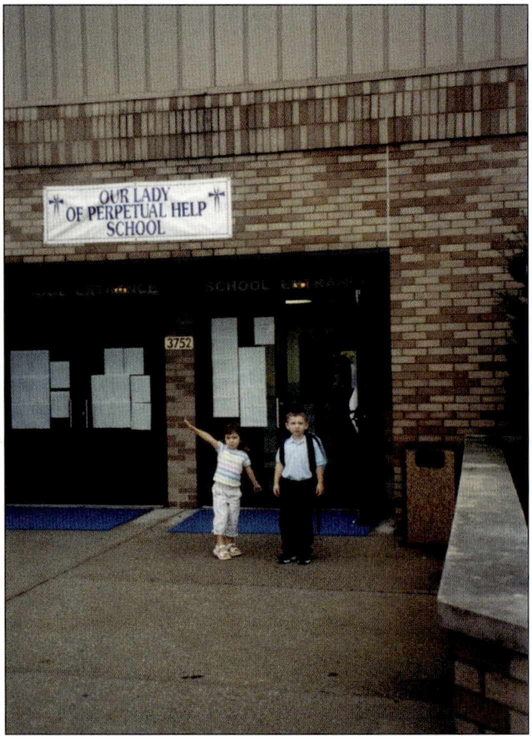

St. John's Lutheran Church opened a nondenominational nonprofit preschool and kindergarten in March 1957. The first kindergarten teacher was Grace Thomas, who was assisted by Mary Lawrence, a registered nurse. St. John's was the first kindergarten program in the area, predating the public school system.

Pictured here are Camille and Michael Lanese on the first day of kindergarten in 2003 at Our Lady of Perpetual Help School, which was founded in 1960. In 2009, the campus added a preschool to the kindergarten through eighth grade school in a building previously occupied by Murph's Gym. Today, the school has an enrollment of about 350 students and is committed to service projects both locally and internationally.

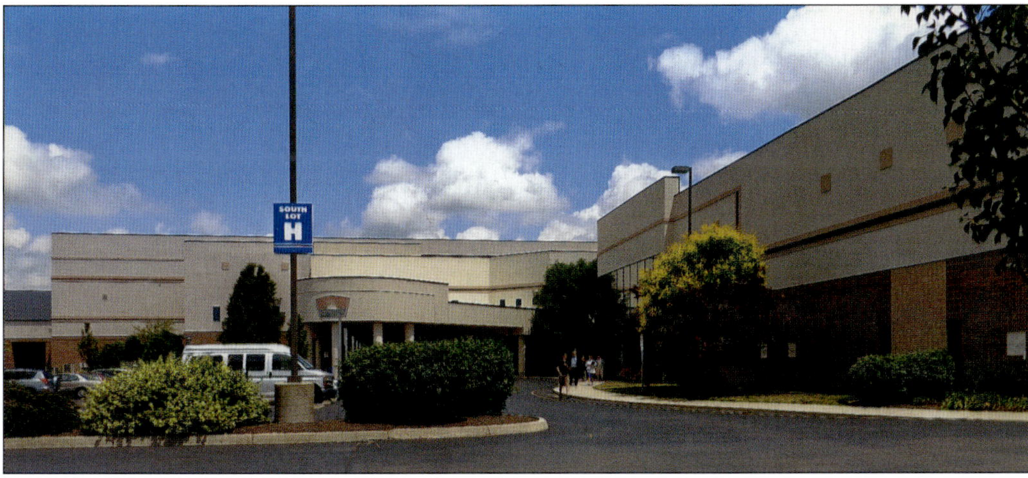

Pictured is the Grove City Church of the Nazarene, which opened its worship center in November 1998 and has one of the largest congregations in the city. Grove City Christian School, serving students from kindergarten through the 12th grade, and Huffaker Community Sports Complex sit behind and just south of the church. The sports complex is the permanent outdoor home of Grove City Christian High School's athletic programs. It is also home of the Columbus Comets professional women's football team.

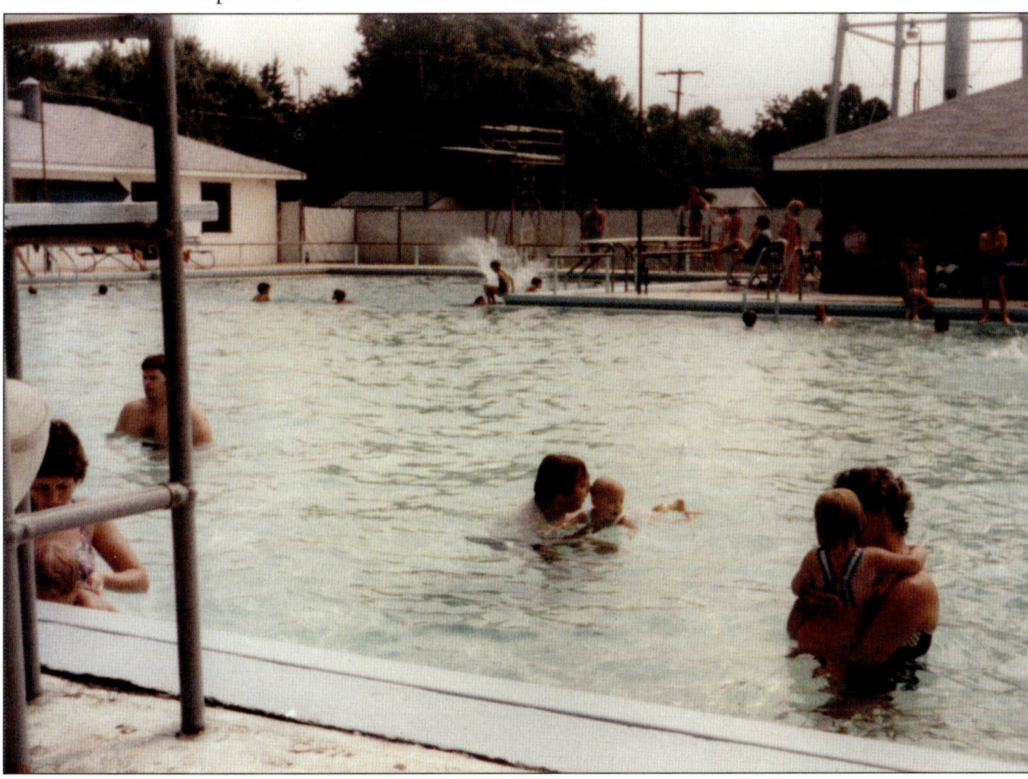

The Twin Towers Swim Club was the center for summer fun, beginning with its opening in 1957 until it closed in the late 1990s. Note the high dive, low dive, and one of the water towers in the background. Twin Towers also had a concession stand, a baby pool, and a second adult pool. Pictured in the center are Barry Babbert and his daughter.

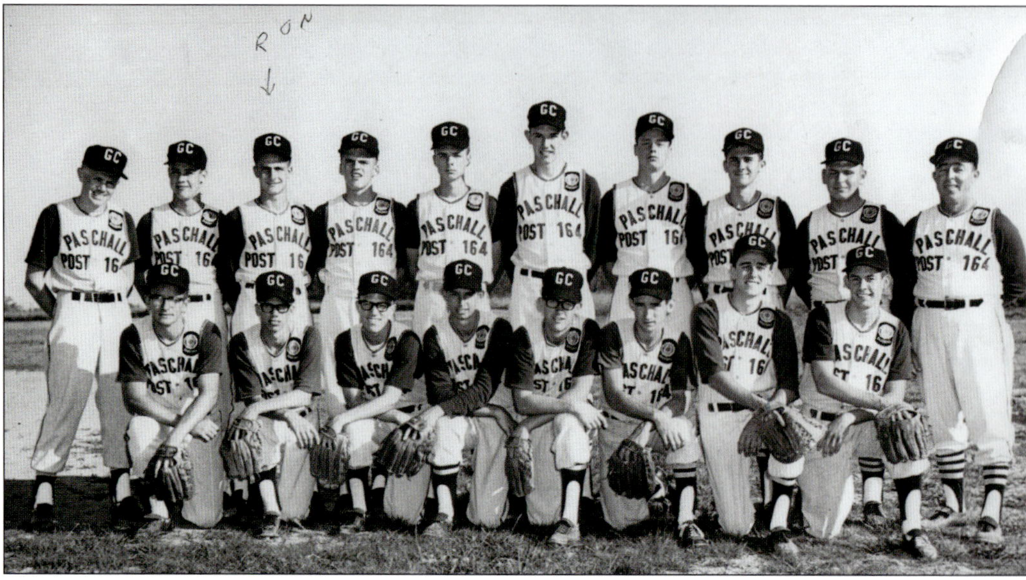

Grove City's Paschall Post 164 baseball team won the state American Legion Baseball Tournament two years in a row: 1965 and 1966. Pictured here is the 1965 team. From left to right are (first row) Rondale Chinn, Bob Grooms, Mike Waples, Ron Hennes, Mike Workman, Roy Steinhoff, Eddie Harris, and Tom Murphy; (second row) Jim Cowgill, Ralph Reeves, Ron Burket, Dave Beets, Brock Schmidt, George Fannin, Tom Boos, John Geddes, Dick Gutheil, and Paul Harris.

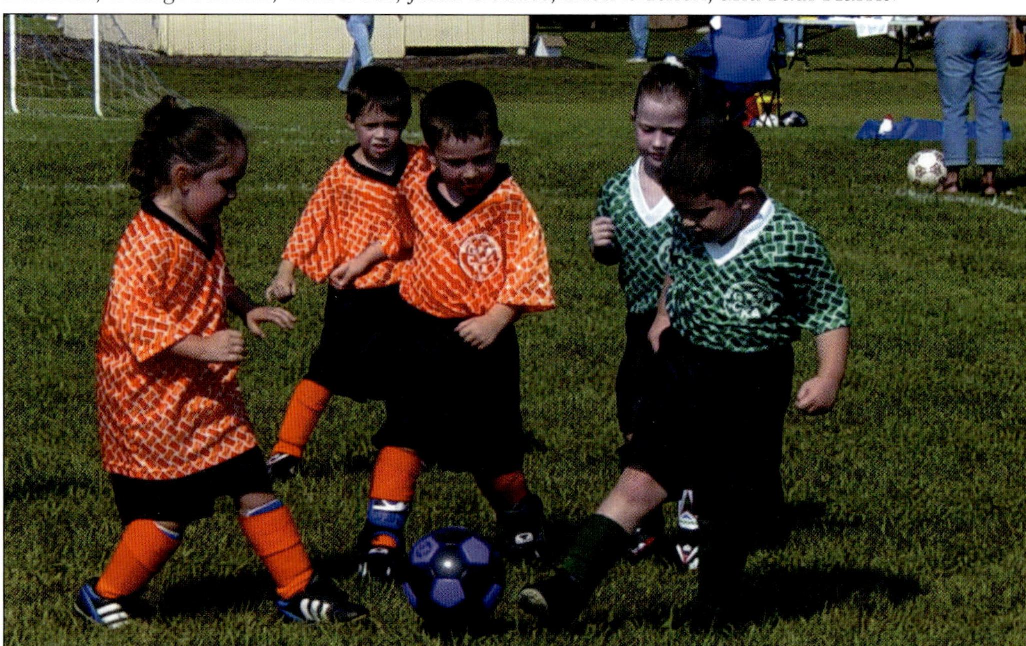

These kids are participating in the Grove City Kids Association (GCKA) soccer program at Murfin Fields. GCKA started in 1967, but did not have a permanent home until Murfin Field was dedicated in 1979 after the death of the entire Thomas Murfin family in a plane crash. To honor the family's devotion to soccer and GCKA, Murfin's father donated $100,000 to support the field and the program. Today, more than 2,000 athletes compete on the site's 51 acres.

Gary Shyu (pictured) and his wife, Cathy, first opened China Bell Restaurant in April 1988. Through good service, tasty cuisine, and community involvement, the eatery has become a favorite among residents and visitors alike. It is known for its free dessert sundae machine and the Shyu's ability to adapt to changing times and tastes of their customers. Recent additions include the Hole-in-One Lounge and drive-through service.

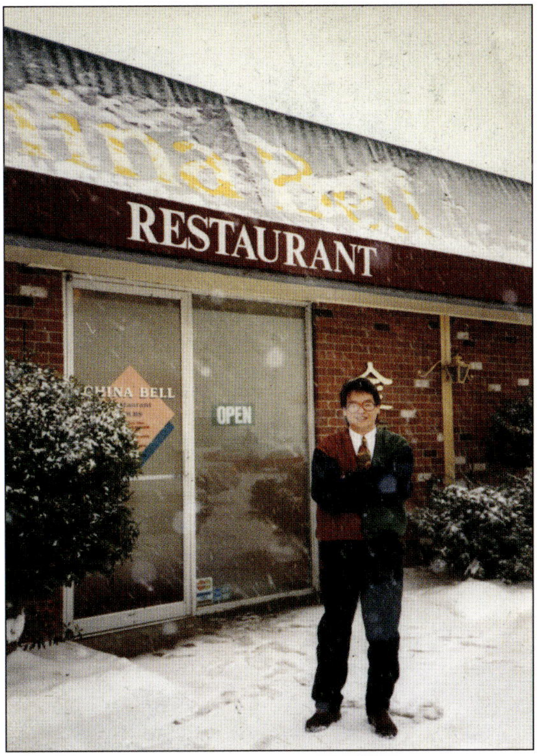

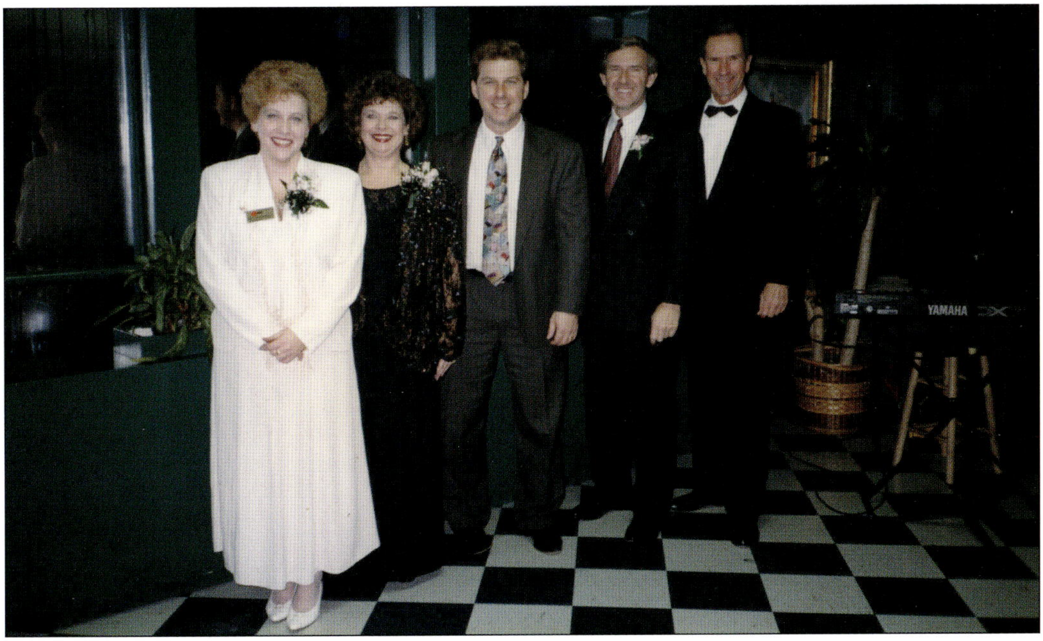

Shown here from left to right at Beulah Park's Jockey Club are outgoing chamber of commerce president Mary Lou Giovanelli, incoming president Sherol Saxton, NBC4 news anchor Cabot Rea, Mayor Ike Stage, and Buckeye Boys Ranch founder Les Bostic. The chamber began in 1978 with 89 members and now serves more than 500, with 18 original members. Signature events include the Arts in the Alley Festival, Taste of Grove City, and the summer-long farmers' market.

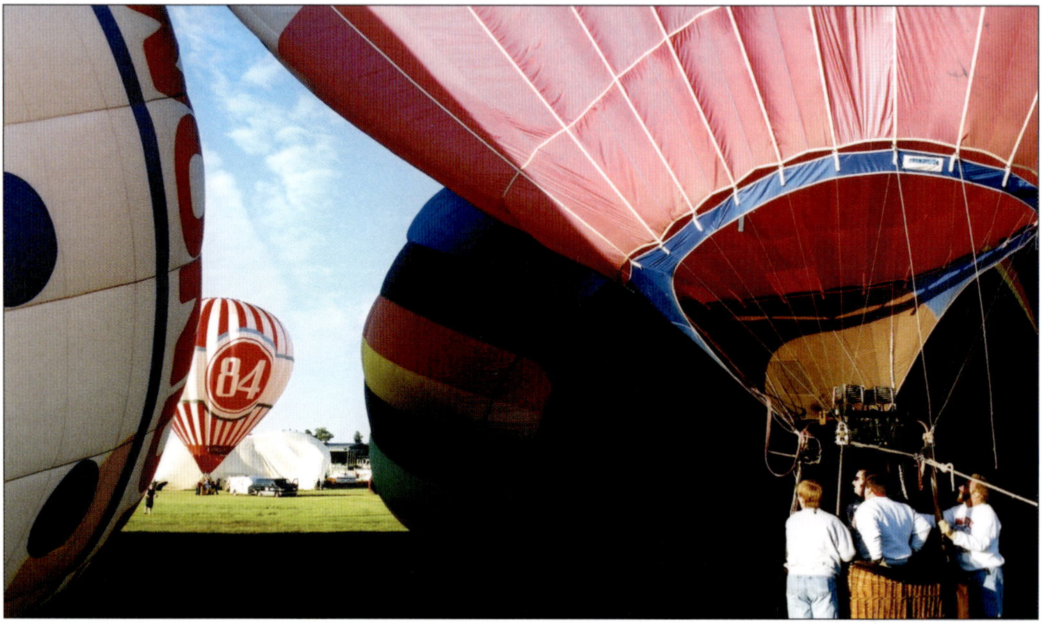

Hot-air balloons became a hallmark of Grove City summers when Big Bear Balloon Festival launched at Beulah Park. It ran for several years before the Big Bear grocery chain went out of business. The city reestablished the balloon event in the mid-2000s. Balloons Off Broadway was moved back to Beulah Park in 2008 and renamed Balloon & Tunes. The event continued every summer through 2013.

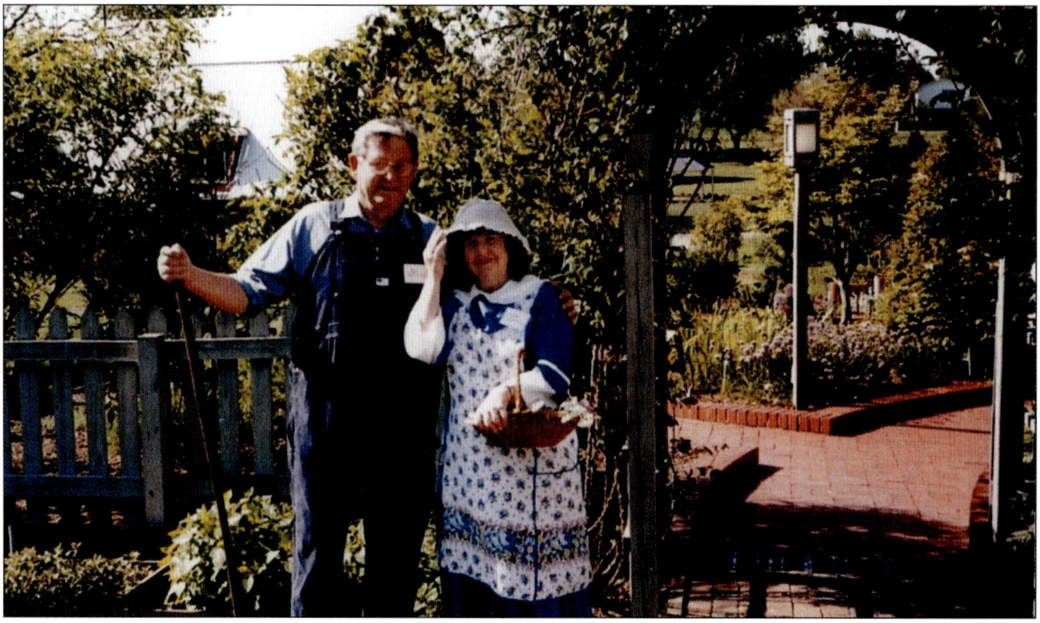

Volunteers Keith Monteque and Jan Noltemeyer are dressed up as farmers Adam and Catherine Gantz at the herb garden sale at the Gardens at Gantz in May 1995. The grounds include the Gardens of Yesterday, Today, and Tomorrow. The popular annual herb plant sale includes demonstrations and workshops. In 2011, the city added a labyrinth modeled after a medieval garden maze at Chartres Cathedral in France.

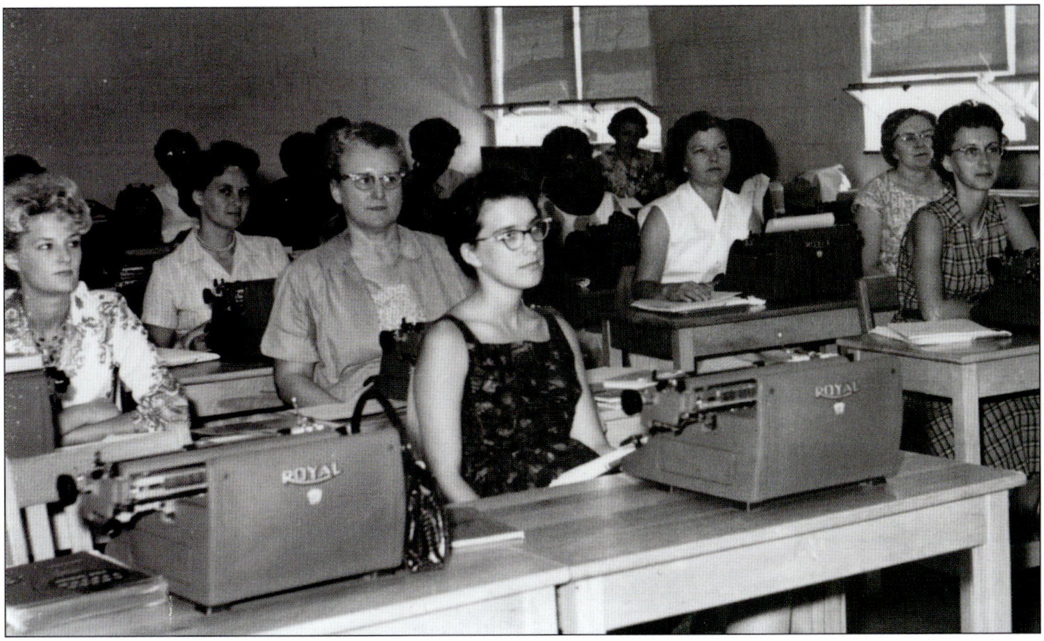

This photograph of adults in the 1960s participating in South-Western City Schools adult education program shows the district's emphasis on assisting people who want to upgrade their skills. Business offerings included shorthand, typing, keypunch, and investments. Adult education started with one class of 10 and expanded rapidly. Classes met at various schools within the district. Note the manual typewriters.

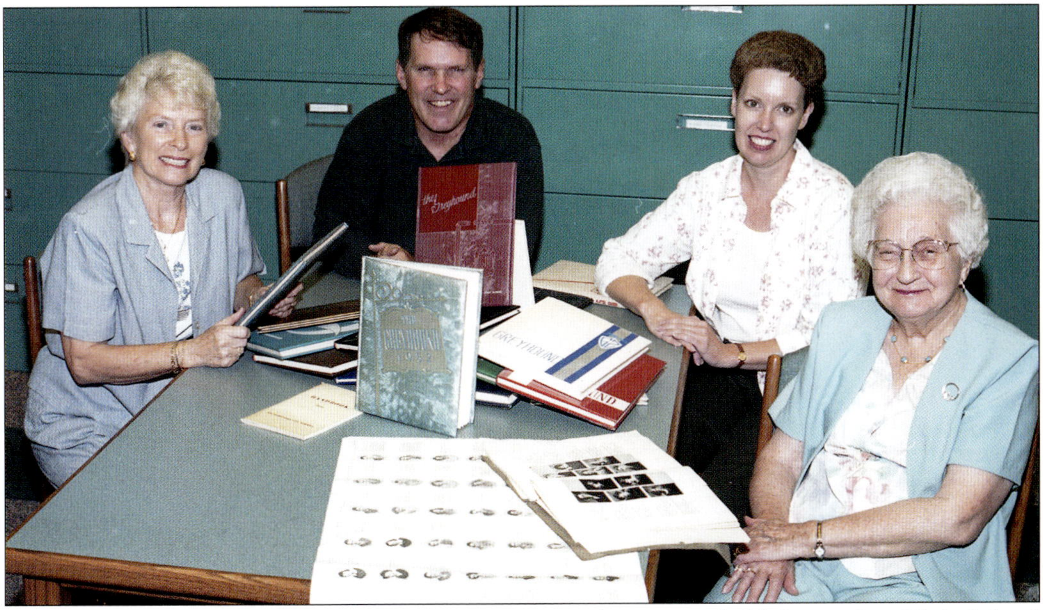

The Grove City Library is a repository for Grove City history and old Grove City High School yearbooks. Shown here in the 1990s are, from left to right, Dottie Keene Mounts, Bill Ferguson Jr., Bethanne Gibboney Johnson, and Martha White Mounts working to collect yearbooks. The library also has a collection of Franklin Heights High School and Central Crossing High School yearbooks.

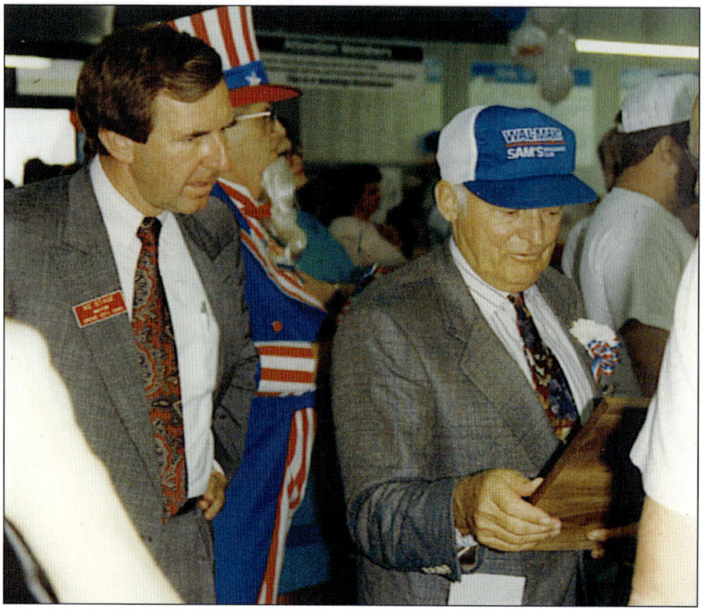

Pictured here are Mayor Ike Stage and Wal-Mart founder and CEO Sam Walton (right) during Walton's 1991 visit to central Ohio shortly after the development of the Wal-Mart Distribution center located off of Southwest Boulevard. Walton, founder of the world's largest retailer, is shown in his trademark baseball cap. Wal-Mart Distribution, which had a rocky public-relations start, is currently the city's largest private employer, with over 1,300 employees.

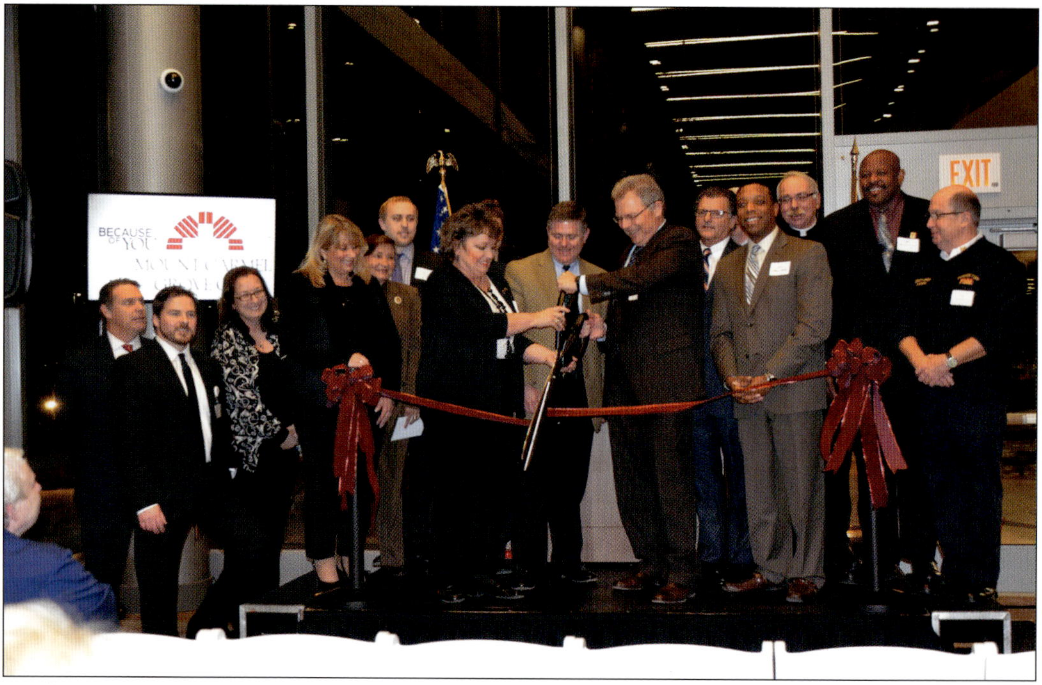

At the ribbon-cutting for the new Mount Carmel Grove City Emergency facility in January 2014, the Reverend Frederick Campbell (back row, second from right), bishop of the Catholic Diocese of Columbus, offered a blessing to the room full of local dignitaries. An adjacent 54,000-square-foot medical building was completed that spring. In early 2015, Mount Carmel announced a $355-million investment in the community, as plans for a seven-story 210-bed facility were unveiled in March 2015. The hospital plans on adding 1,500 new jobs, which will make it the largest private employer in Grove City.

First Baptist Church of Grove City started in 1955, when 17 people gathered in the Grove City High School music room. In 1956, the church broke ground for a new building on Kingston Avenue with the Reverend Richard Bowser as pastor. In 1992, King's Kids Daycare opened its doors. The congregation relocated to Orders Road in 2010, and the Reverend Jerry Neal serves as the current pastor.

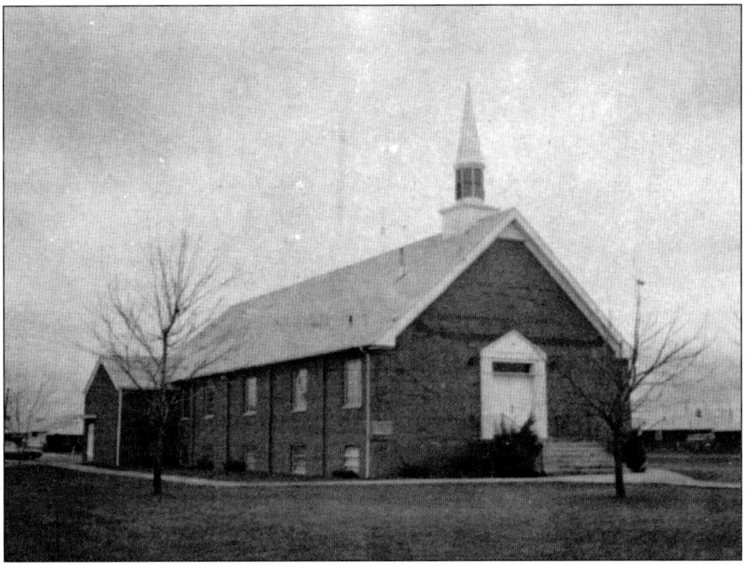

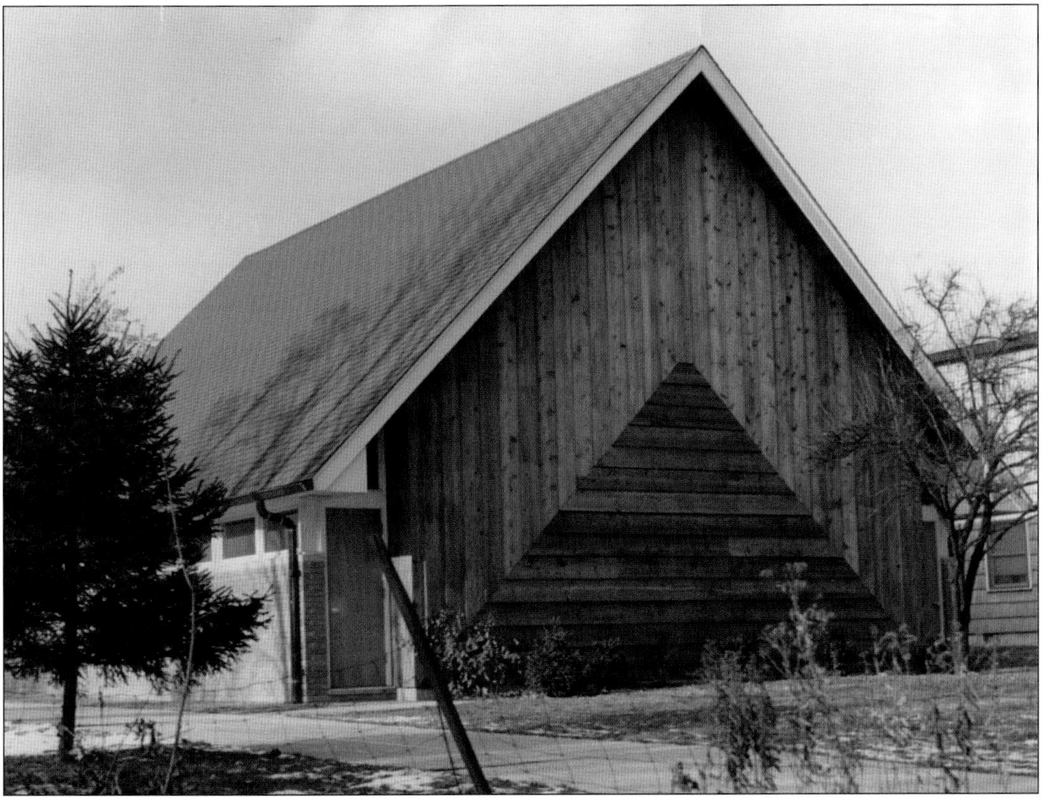

The congregation of First Presbyterian Church of Grove City was formed by 16 members of St. John's Evangelical Lutheran Church, who organized in 1856 with village founder William Breck among the first trustees. A wooden church was built near the railroad tracks in 1858 and later moved west on Park Street. In 1884, a new church was built at the corner of Broadway and Kingston Avenue and razed in 1955. The present church, shown here, was constructed in 1957.

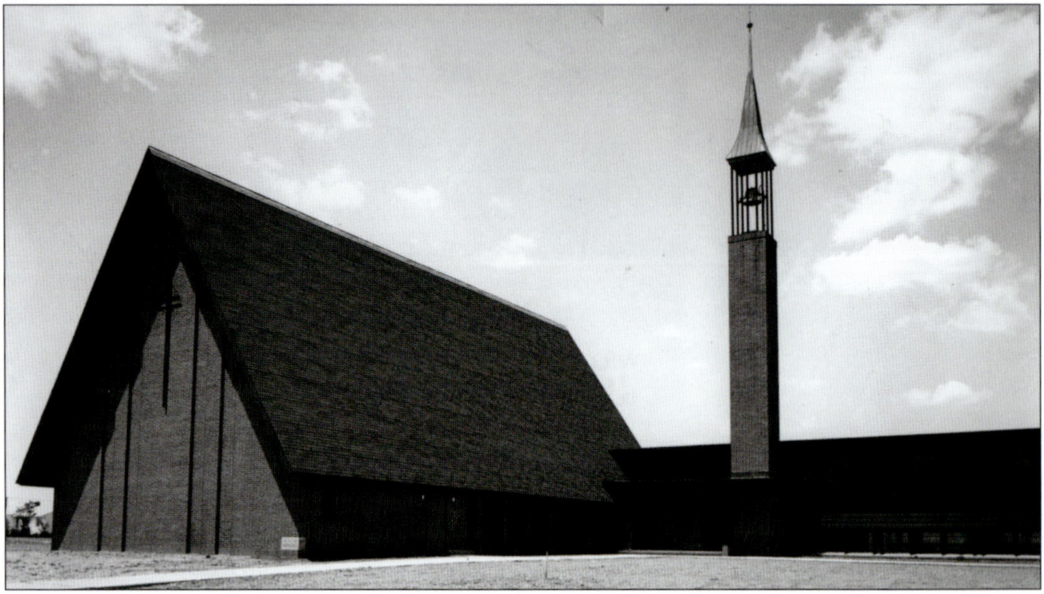

The congregation of Grove City United Methodist Church began in 1859, meeting in a wooden structure on the corner of West Park and Front Streets. The frame church was moved west to Lincoln Street in the 1880s, and then a brick structure was erected on the site in 1905. That structure had elegant pews and a massive brass chancel until destroyed by fire. On Palm Sunday 1957, ground was broken for a new building at the present church site at 2684 Columbus Street. The bell from the old church was moved to the present building and is still there.

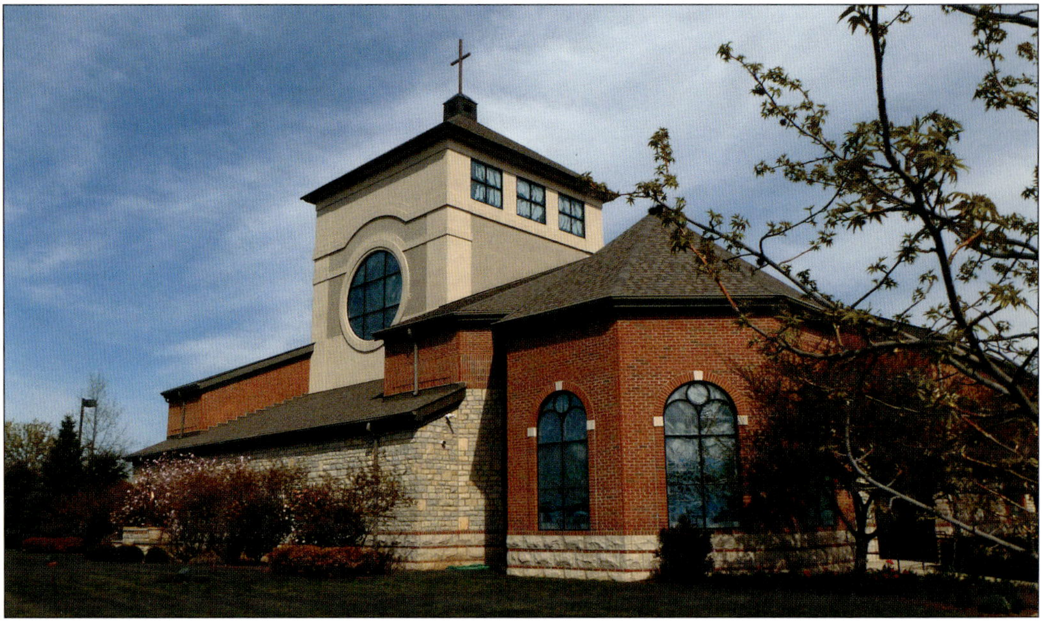

Our Lady of Perpetual Help Catholic Church first opened in the Kingdom Theater in 1954, and 121 parishioners attended the first mass. By 1959, the church congregation had outgrown the theater and relocated to their current site, a former greyhound racetrack. In 1999, the congregation again outgrew their confines and built the current church on the same property. Today, Our Lady has about 7,000 registered parishioners. Fr. Dan Millisor is the pastor.

Five

SERVICE IN THE CITY

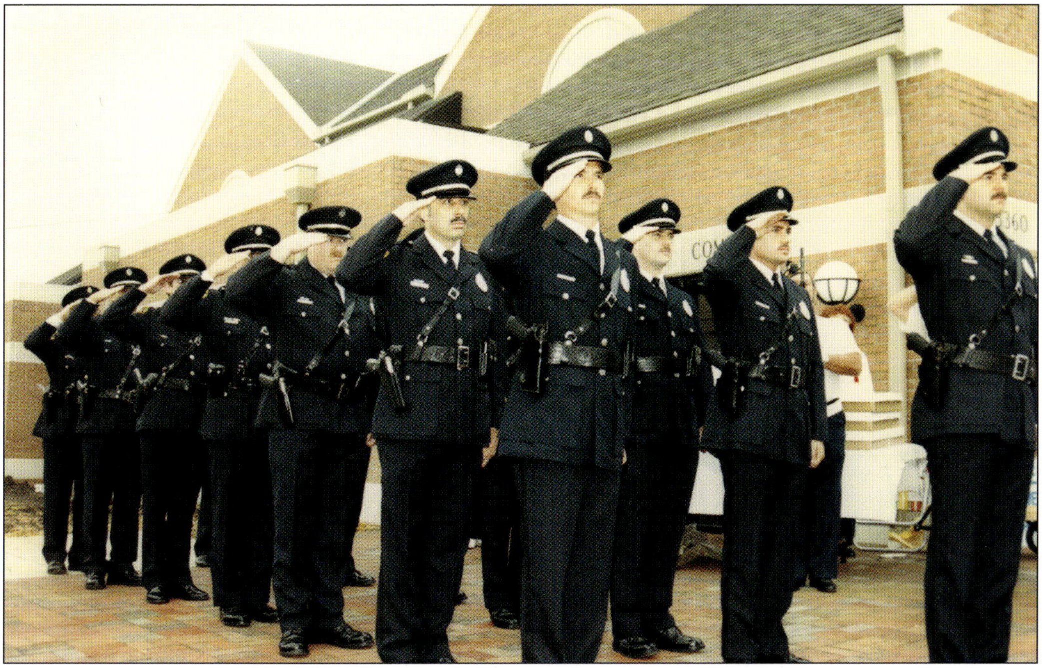

Standing at attention are members of the police department during the opening ceremony of the $1.7-million municipal safety complex in September 1989. The building houses the police force, holding cells, a mayor's court, and administrative offices. The department is CALEA certified (Commission on Accreditation for Law Enforcement Agencies), an award given to only about 10 percent of the nation's police organizations. Bricks and cornerstones from the old jail were built into the new entranceway.

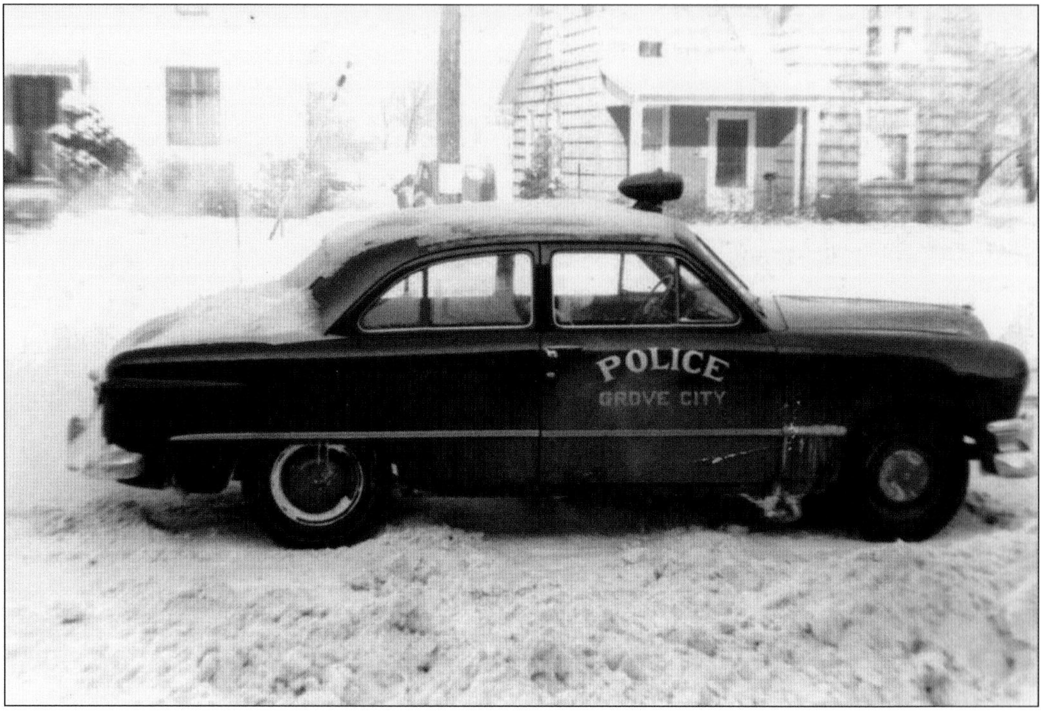

Robert Dienst Sr., owner of Beulah Park, donated the city's first patrol car, reportedly to help with traffic control in and out of Beulah Park. Dienst, known as "Mr. Beulah," also graded and repaired the streets due to the increased race traffic. This patrol car dates from the early 1950s. Notice the car only had front doors to prevent backseat passengers from leaving prematurely.

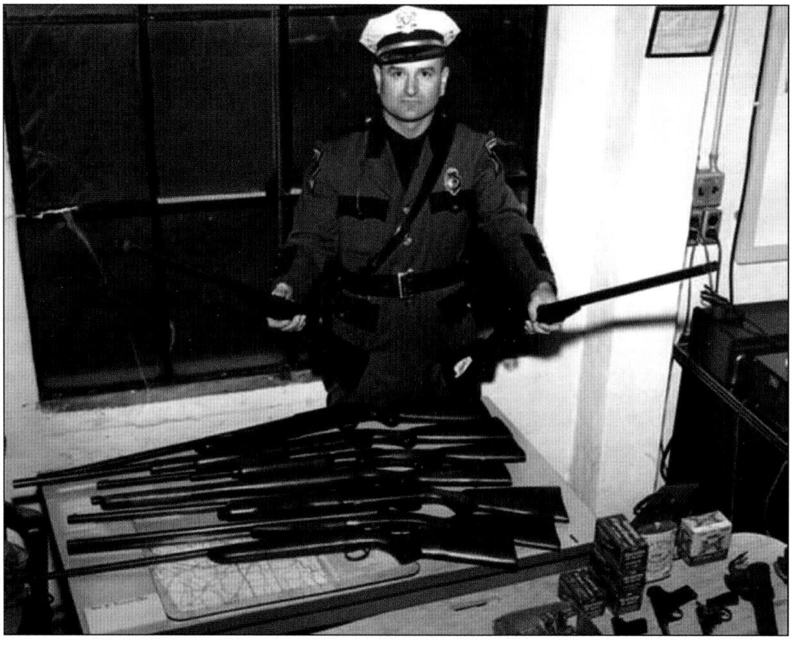

On January 7, 1956, Grove City patrolman (later captain) Ray Ruoff pulled over a suspicious car heading through town. As it turned out, the three men in the automobile had robbed a sporting-goods store in Steubenville. Ruoff is pictured here with the stash of rifles, handguns, knives, gunpowder, and ammunition he found in the trunk.

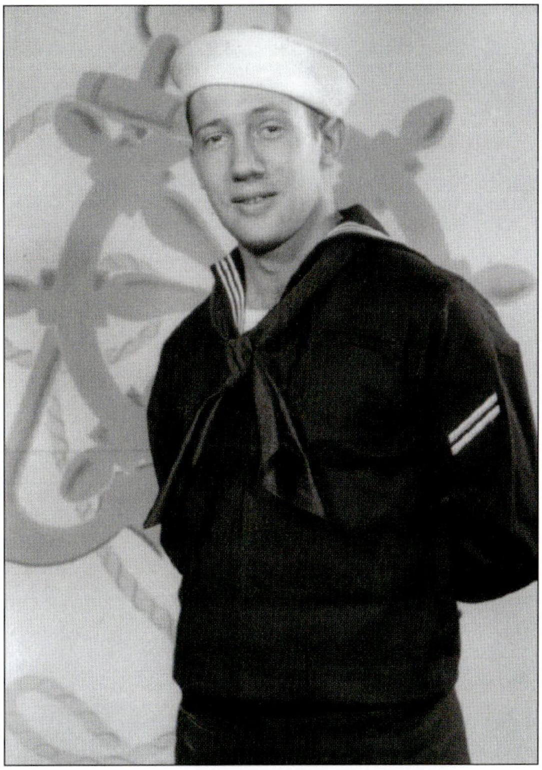

Pictured is Earl Nicholson, who served in the US Navy during the Korean War on the USS *Hornet*. Nicholson, a charter member of the Ohio Historical Society and local historian, served on city council from 1984 to 1992. He was also a commercial artist who worked at Battelle Memorial Institute and combined his passion and talent for both art and history by creating two historical murals in the town center, as well as various artwork for school and community events.

Jackson Township Fire Station 202 at 3756 Hoover Road was built in 1965 at a time when farm fields stretched through the area as far as the eye could see. Taxpayers complained that it was "too far out in the country" but changed their minds quickly as subdivisions began to spring up. Today, the structure is the Jackson Township Administration Building.

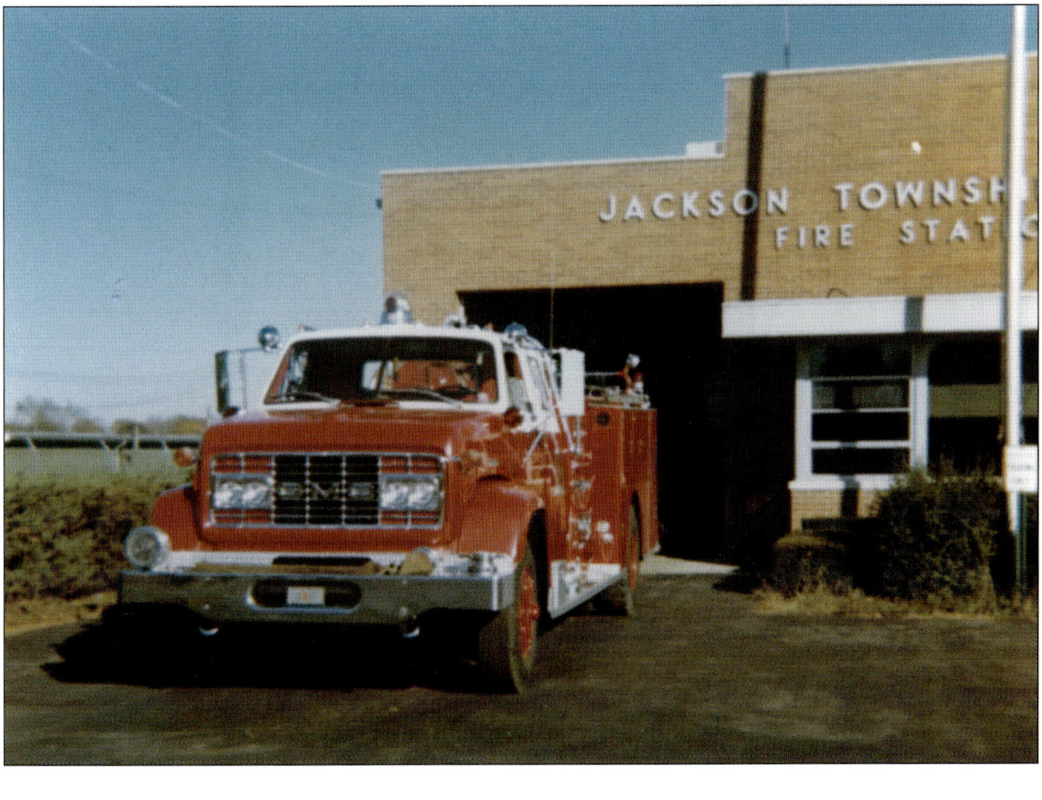

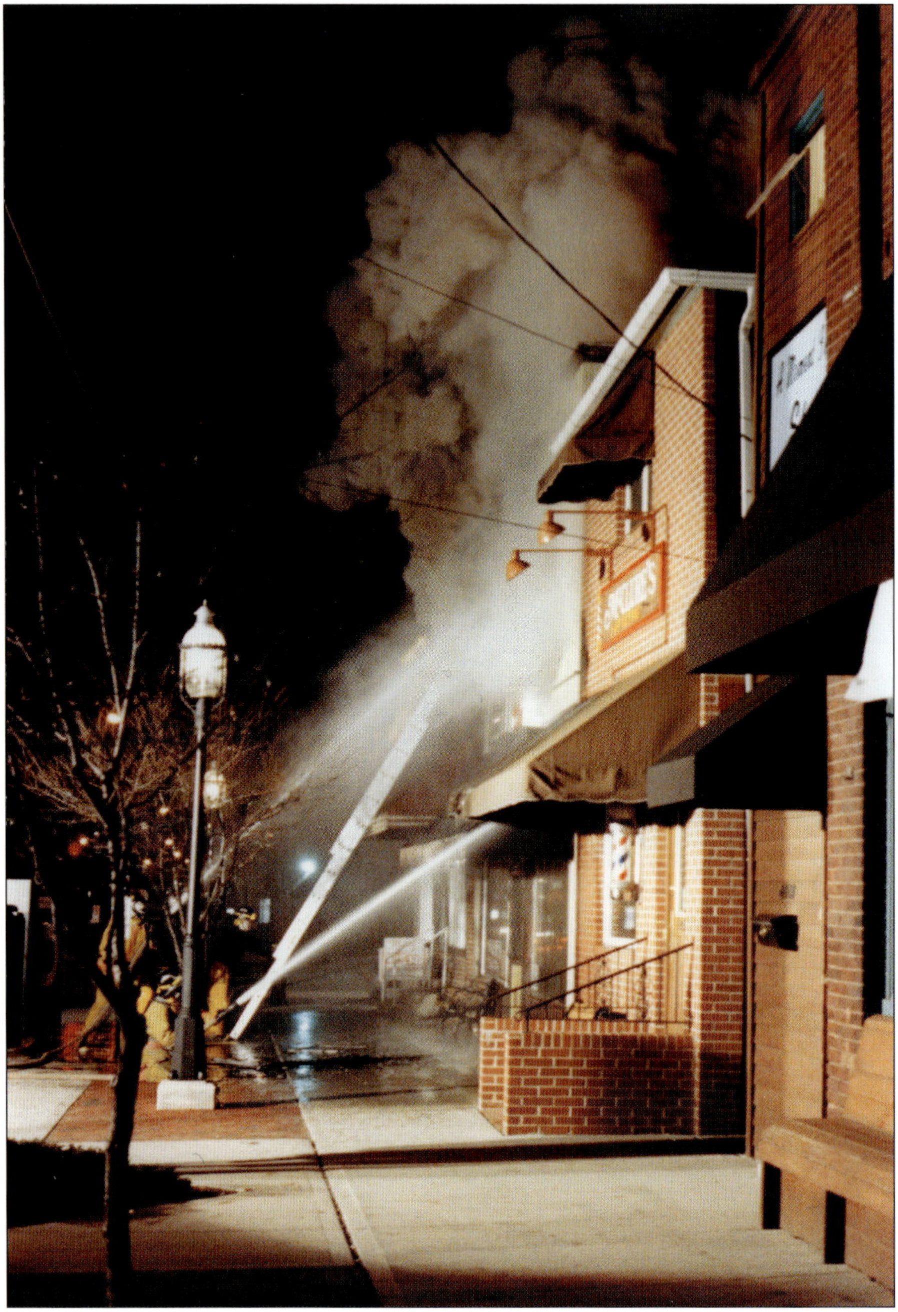

On November 26, 1991, a fire started in the Aaron Ashton Kung Fu Studio, in the heart of the town center, and spread rapidly to the Shedrow Tavern next door. Both buildings were destroyed, and a third business, McClure's Haircutting, was badly damaged. The Jackson Township Fire Department was joined by Franklin, Pleasant, Prairie, Hamilton, Norwich, and Scioto Townships plus units from Columbus and West Jefferson. A total of 106 firefighters fought all night in 15-degree weather until the blaze was extinguished. In the aftermath, the Shedrow was torn down and replaced by Parker's Tavern. The Ashton Studio building was torn down and is now green space. A historical mural of the town center in the 1920s is now on the north wall of Parker's Tavern.

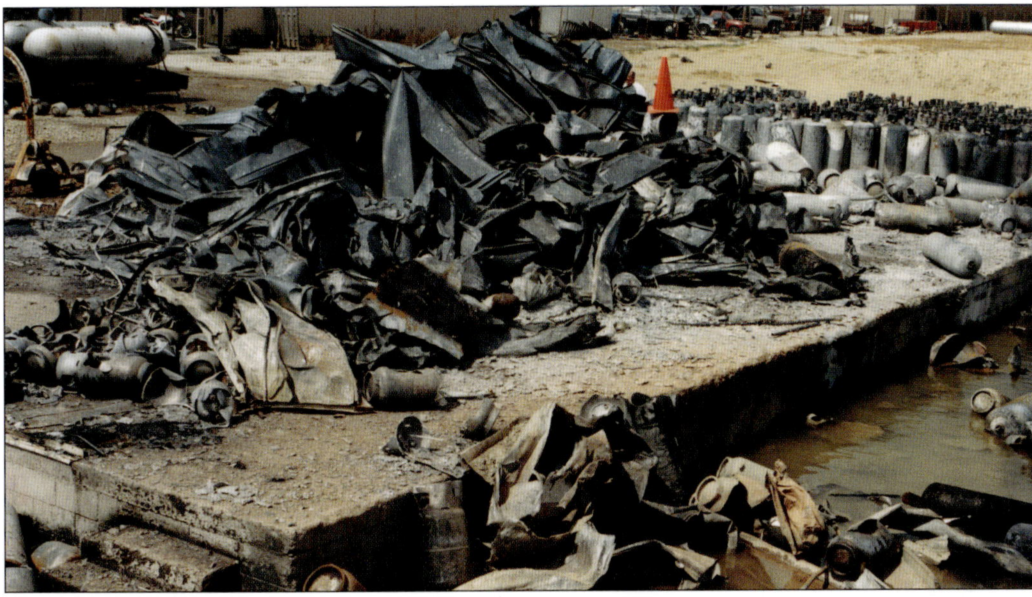

A major catastrophe was averted at 2:30 p.m. on July 8, 1996, as static electricity ignited a propane tank at the Ferrellgas Company, at 4401 Broadway, causing multiple explosions. As 30-gallon canisters rocketed in every direction, the Jackson Township Fire Department prevented flames from reaching five additional 30,000-gallon tanks that could have leveled most of the south side of Grove City. Two hours later, a second fire caused by static electricity ignited at the Bonded Oil Station at 3612 Broadway, where a car caught fire during fueling.

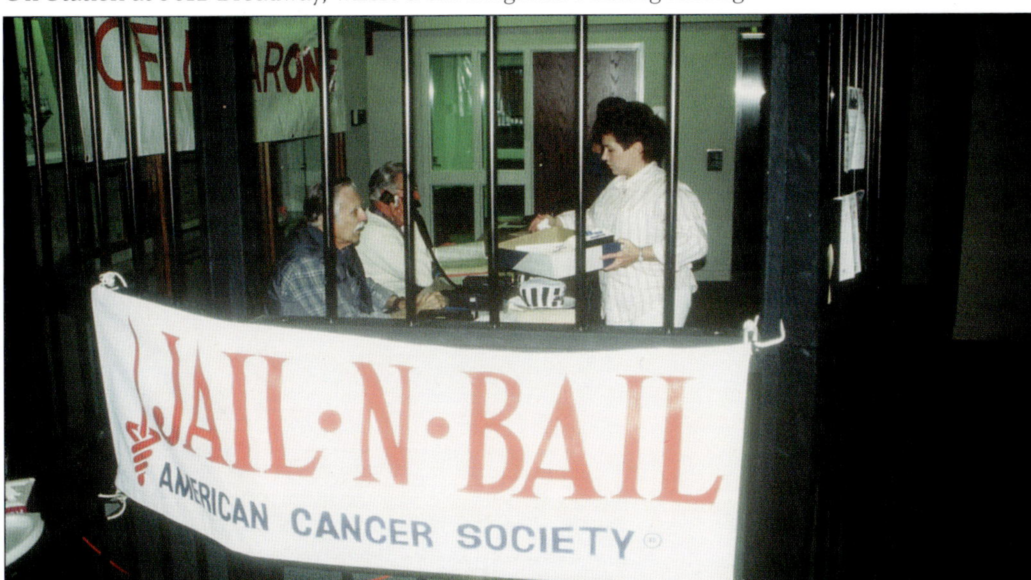

Several charities from the 1980s through the 1990s participated in Jail-N-Bail to raise money for research and education programs. Area residents filed phony warrants and had friends arrested and taken to a fake jail at city hall. The warrants required a $25 donation, and bogus charges were issued before the perpetrators headed to a kangaroo court. Three of the organizations that participated in Jail-N-Bail over the years were the American Cancer Society, March of Dimes, and the Muscular Dystrophy Association.

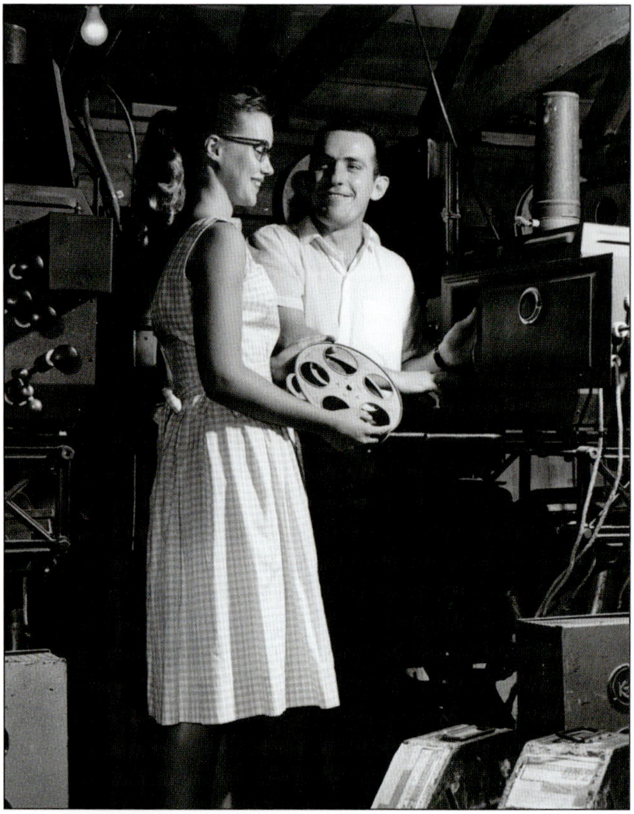

Kids of all ages were entertained on warm summer weekends in the early 1960s at Windsor Park, the town's oldest community-sized park. The Grove City Jaycees sponsored free movies for the community. This vintage movie projector was used by the Grove City Jaycees to show free movies at Windsor Park during the summer. The projectionist is Jaycee Bill Ferguson, seen with Patty Purdum.

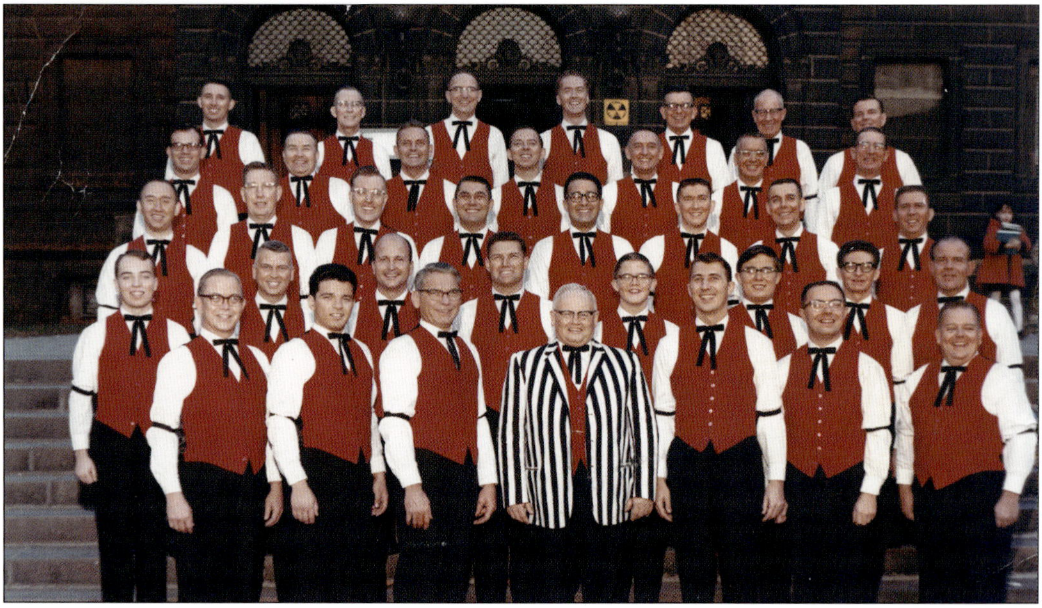

The Society for the Preservation and Encouragement of Barbershop Quartet Singing in America (SPEBSQSA) was extremely popular in Grove City during the 1960s. Frank Buffington (front, far right) was the music educator for the Johnny Appleseed District of the organization, which competed in singing competitions throughout the United States and Canada.

Presenting the Buckeye Tennis Classic trophy are, from left to right, Gov. John Gilligan, Jimmy Connors, Les Bostic, and Jack Nicklaus. During the 1970s and 1980s, Buckeye Boys Ranch founder and director Bostic organized the classic to raise funds for the ranch. An estimated 30,000 fans cheered on tennis greats such as Connors and Arthur Ashe. In 1981, the classic raised more than $150,000, making it one of the world's most profitable charities at the time.

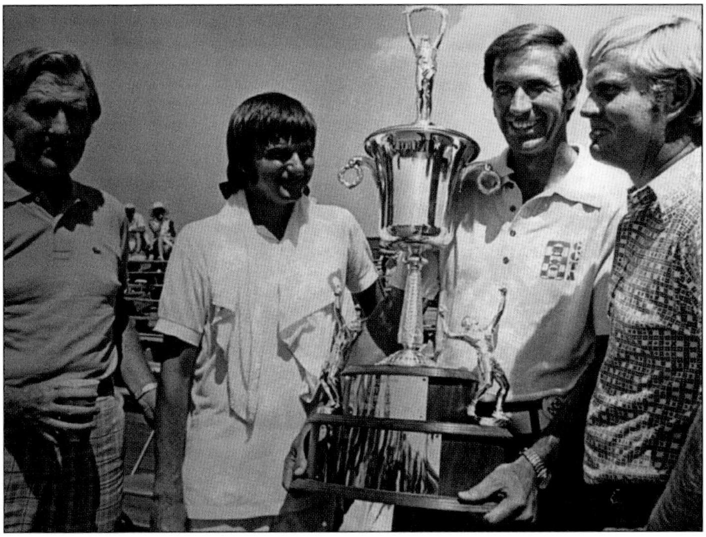

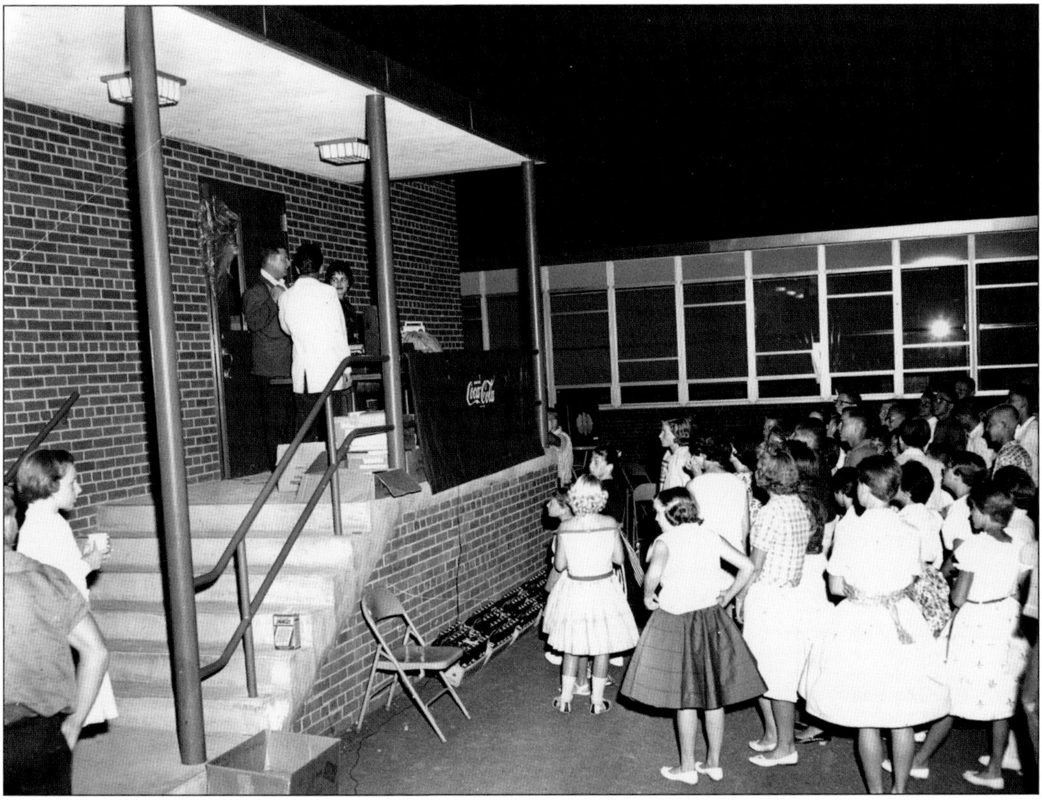

Sock hops were all the rage in the early 1960s, and this photograph shows a Teens Unlimited dance in the east parking lot of old Grove City High School. The disc jockey for the event was WTVN-AM's Gene Fullen. Note the array of poodle skirts worn by the girls.

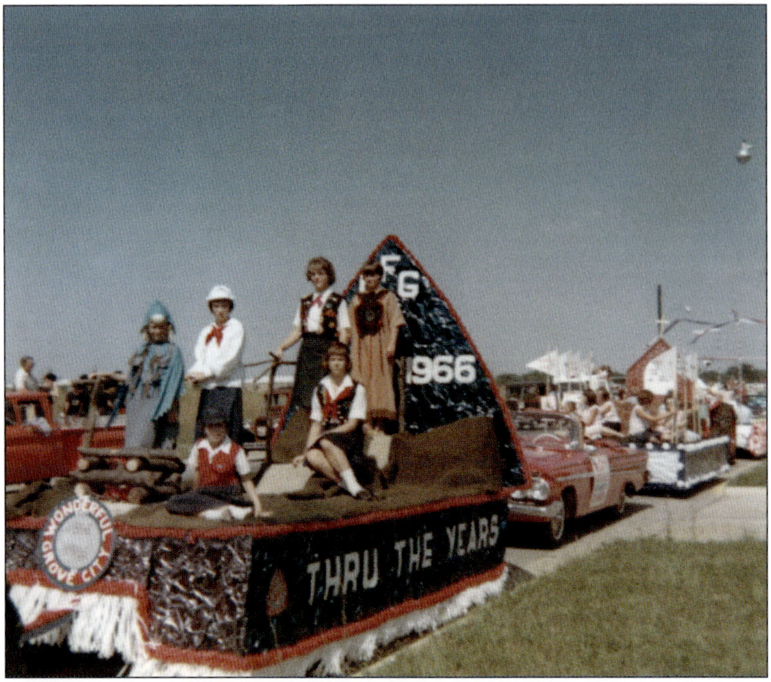

Taken in 1966, this photograph shows the Blue Birds in the street-fair parade. Organized in 1912, Blue Birds were the younger version of the Campfire Girls, the original sister organization of the Boy Scouts. Pictured here are Kristi Mixer (red tie), Beth Rawson (seated right), and Cindy Noltemeyer in a handmade Blue Bird costume sewn by her mother, Jan Noltemeyer.

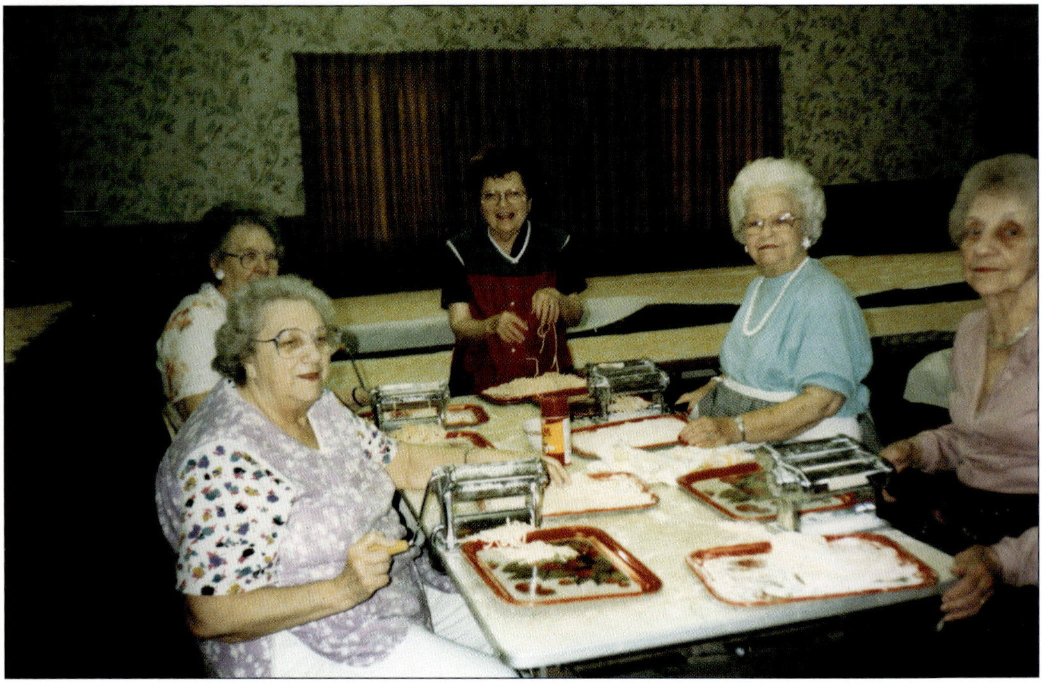

The Grove City Community Club is well known for its Noodle Ladies, who make hundreds of pounds of noodles for Election Day and Arts in the Alley. The group formed in 1917 as the Girls Community Club during World War I so members could assist the American Red Cross by knitting, sewing, and providing picnics for soldiers on leave. The club is still active today. From left to right are Helen Corkwell, Kathryn Darnell, Nadine Cordesco, Sidney Weygandt, and Mona Mulvany.

Paul Miller, in drag, belts out "Ain't She Sweet" at a performance of the E.L. Evans Senior Center's Humdinger Band. The band was formed in the early 1980s by Diane Mills and has a waiting list to become a member. The group performs concerts throughout the year.

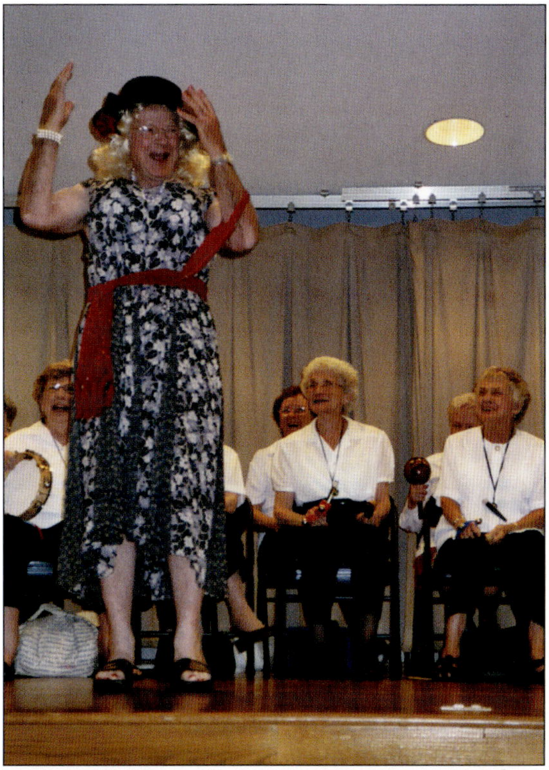

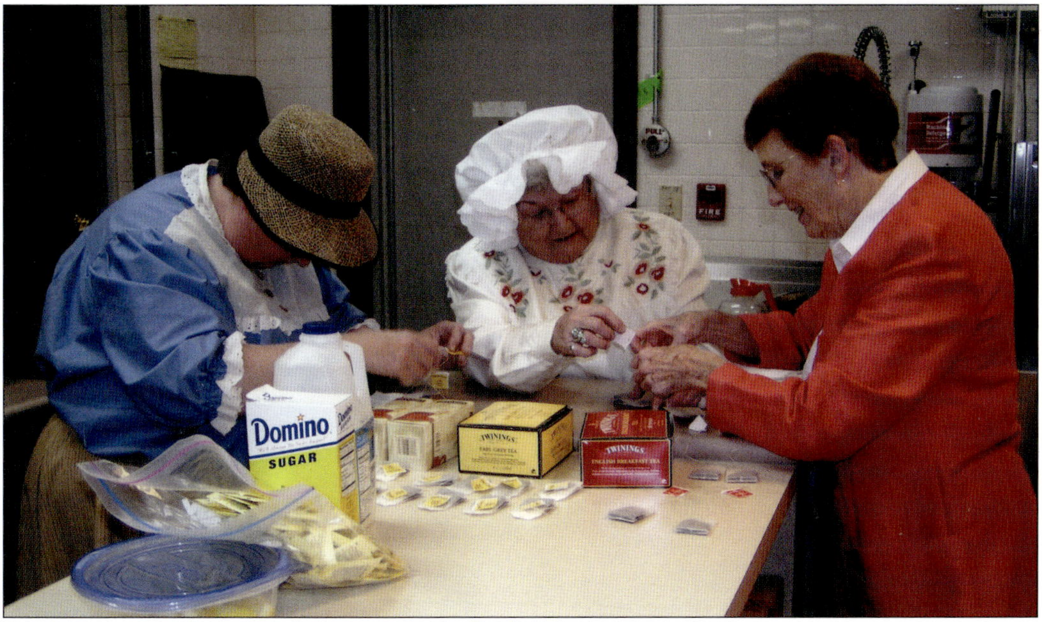

The Women's Civic Club of Grove City formed in 1917 as a social group to improve education and culture in the community. In the same year it was formed, the group founded the first public reading room in Grove City at the First National Bank. Pictured are, from left to right, Amy Hipple, Dorothy Hipple, and Anne Brown prepping tea for the group's English High Tea on April 23, 2005. Hipple has been a member of the club since the 1950s.

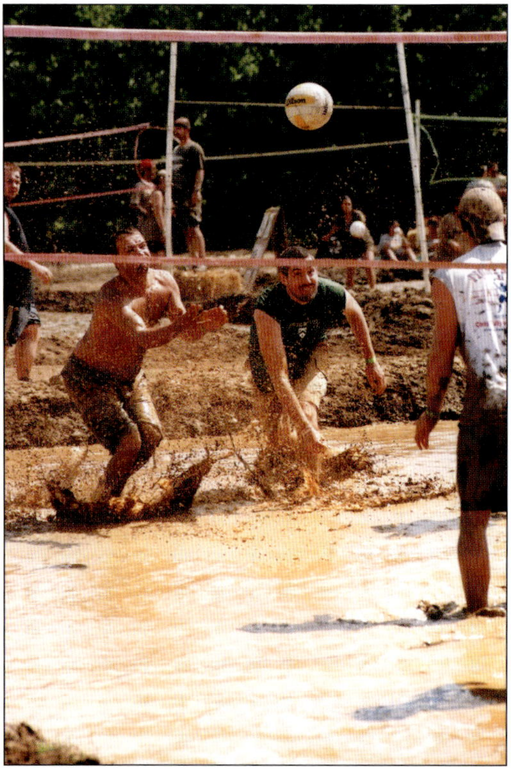

Beginning in 2001, the Central Ohio Epilepsy Foundation hosted its annual mud volleyball fundraiser at Beulah Park. A moneymaker for the organization since 1985, officials said they were pleased to have a permanent home for the tournament at Beulah, which drew upwards of 3,000 players. The tournament took place there each summer until 2013.

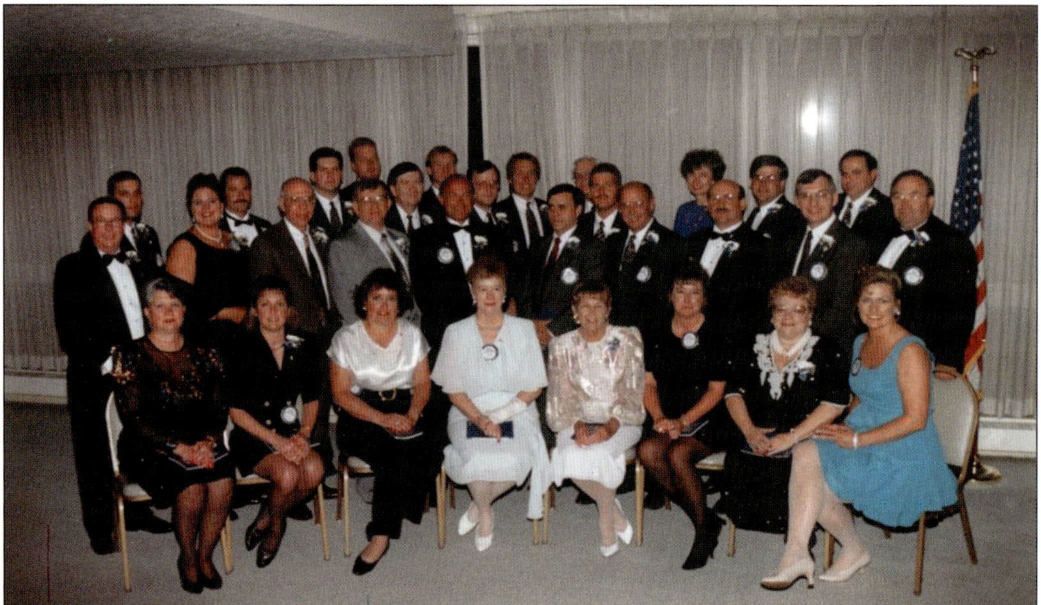

The Rotary Club of Grove City was first chartered in 1996. One of its largest projects to date has been donating $50,000 to the Eagles Pavilion at Rotary Lake in Fryer Park, a city project partially financed in partnership with the Fraternal Order of Eagles, whose international headquarters are located in Grove City.

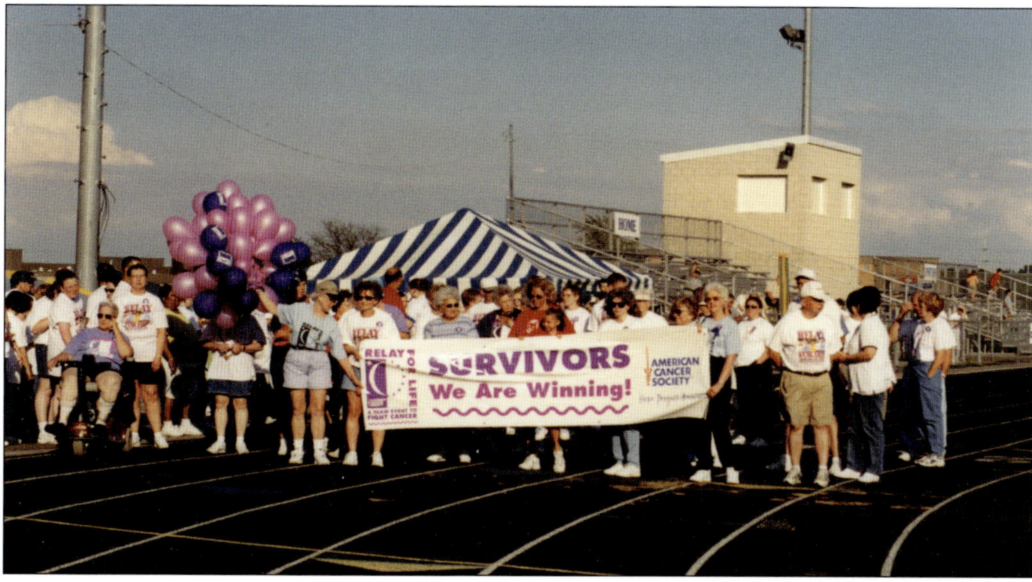

Relay for Life is a nationwide fundraiser benefiting the American Cancer Society. The Grove City relay began in 2002 and has become a staple one weekend every June. Teams are formed, cancer survivors are honored, family and friends who lost their battle are remembered, and money is raised to help fund cancer research and find a cure. Relay for Life is held at the track at Grove City High School.

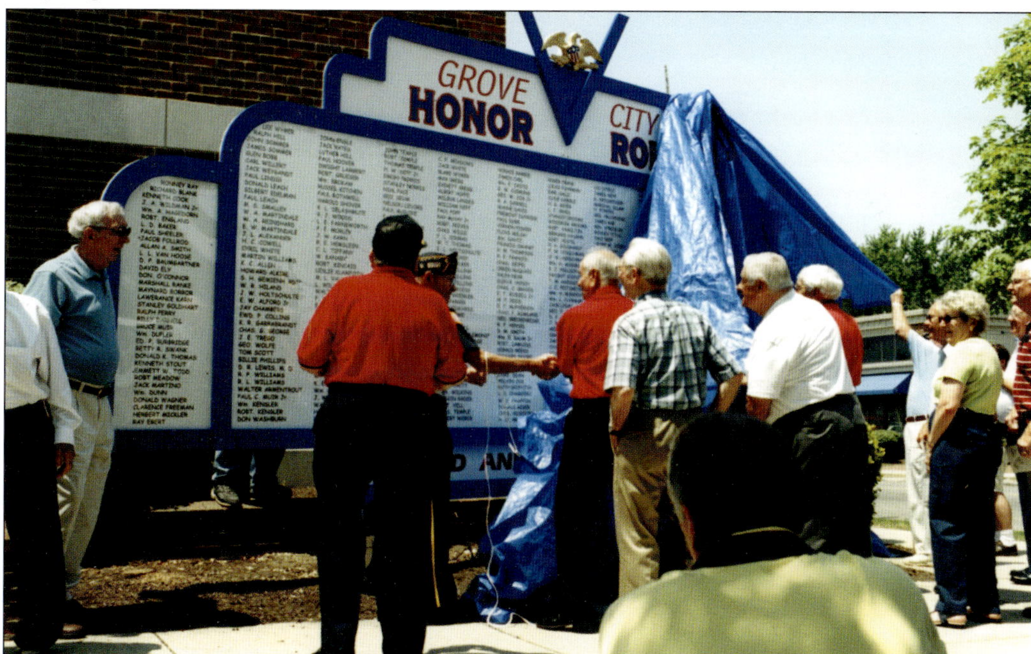

During World War II, the local VFW post dedicated an honor roll billboard on October 31, 1943, commemorating the more than 500 local service members who were on active duty at that time. A replica of the honor roll was moved to the American Legion Post on McDowell Road in 2000. In 2014, local artist David Maple's rendition of the original billboard was unveiled in the post's memorial garden.

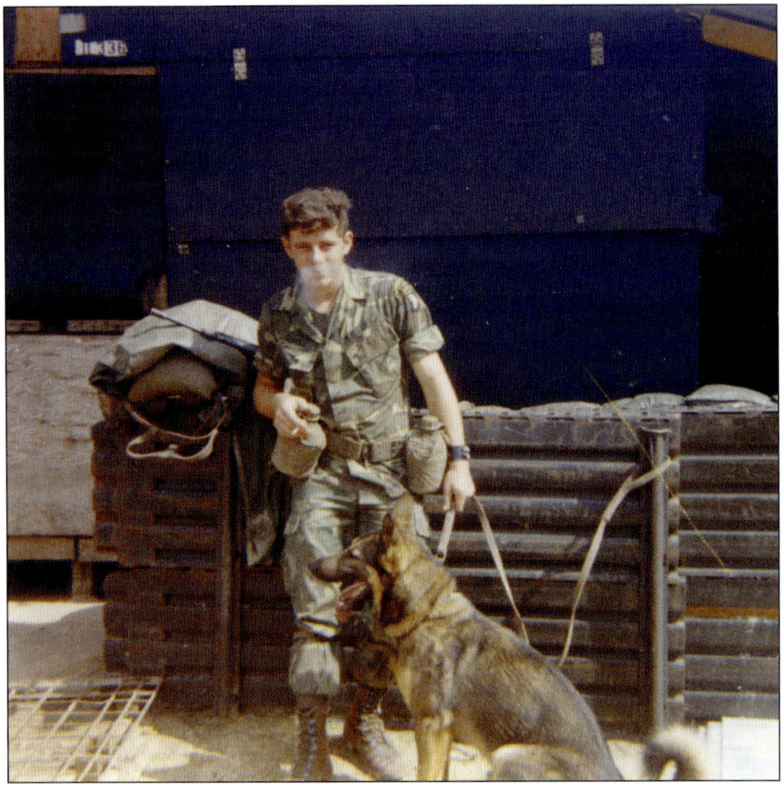

Ed Reeves poses with his scout dog Prince while attached to the 47th Scout Dog Platoon, 101st Infantry Division, in Phu Bai, Vietnam. Reeves served from October 1970 to July 1971 and was awarded the Bronze Star when Prince discovered eight enemy booby traps and alerted Reeves, thereby protecting the platoon. Grove City had four sons killed in action during the Vietnam War: 1LT Robert Lee Grooms, CWO Richard L. Holycross, PO3 Gregory Asbeck, and CPL Terry Webb.

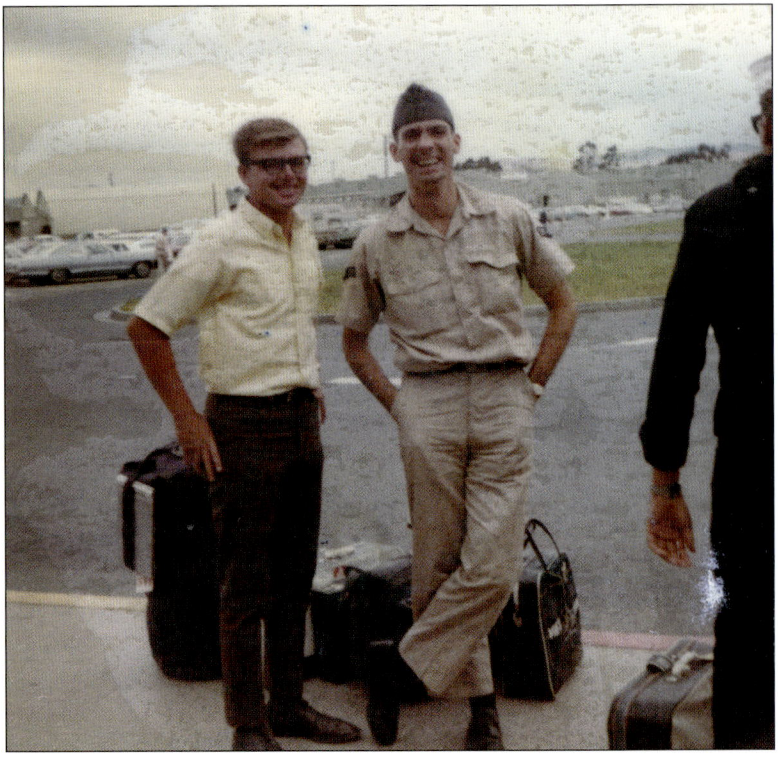

Air Force sergeant Steven Walters is pictured here in 1968 upon his return from Binh Thuy Airbase, South Vietnam, where he served in the 632nd Security Police Squadron. Walters has since retired from both the Columbus police force and the US Marine Corps Reserve. Today, he presents military-history lectures at the Grove City Library on topics ranging from Gettysburg to Guadalcanal.

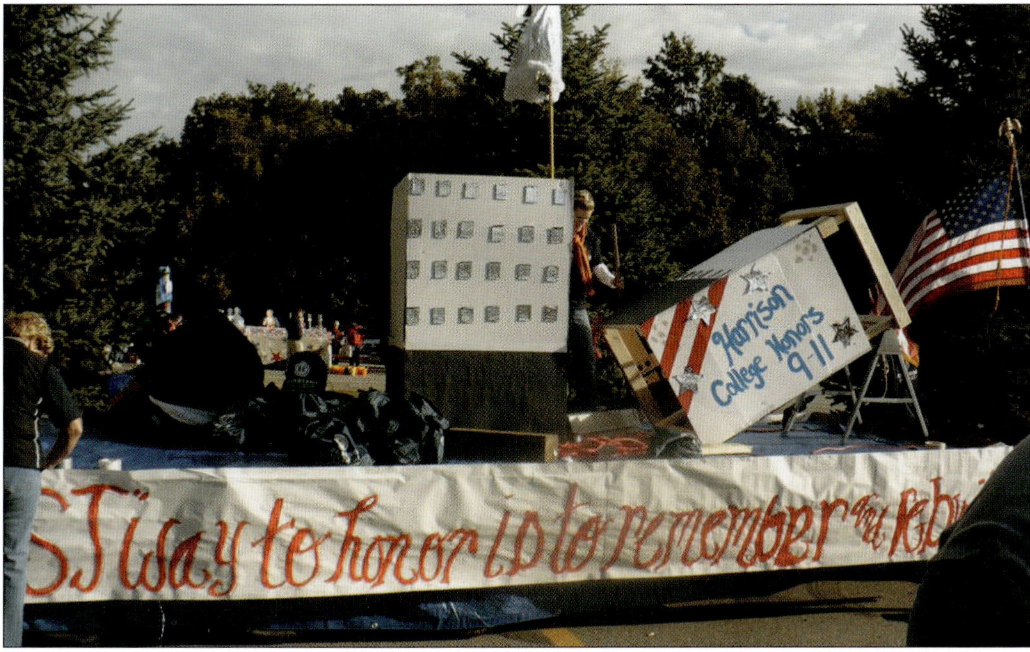

Harrison College's Arts in the Alley float honors the heroes of 9/11. The college started in Indiana in 1902 and in 2009 established a 20,000-square-foot branch campus in Grove City on Jackpot Road. The more than 300 students work toward degrees in business, criminal justice, and health sciences.

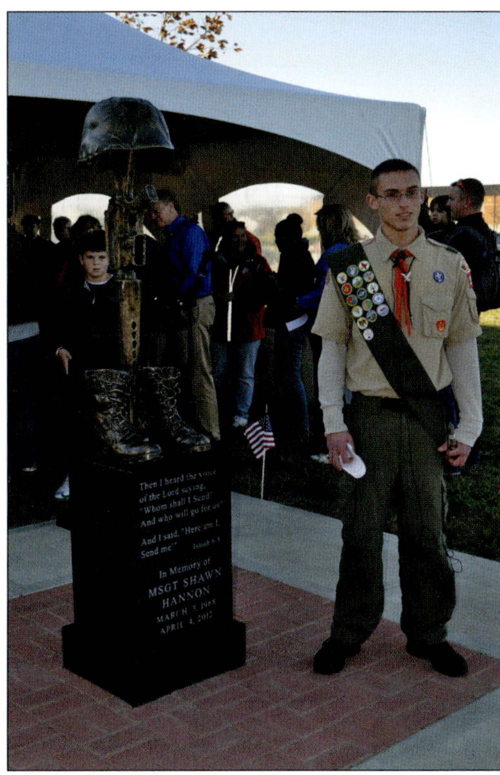

Brandon Weber of Troop No. 136 unveiled his Eagle Scout project honoring MSGT Shawn Hannon at Henceroth Park to a gathering of friends, family, and local officials. Master Sergeant Hannon, a 1986 Grove City High School graduate and chief legal officer at the Ohio Department of Veterans Services, was killed in 2012 by a suicide bomber in Afghanistan. As part of his project, Weber gathered donations and worked with city officials and the Hannon family to complete the battlefield cross statue.

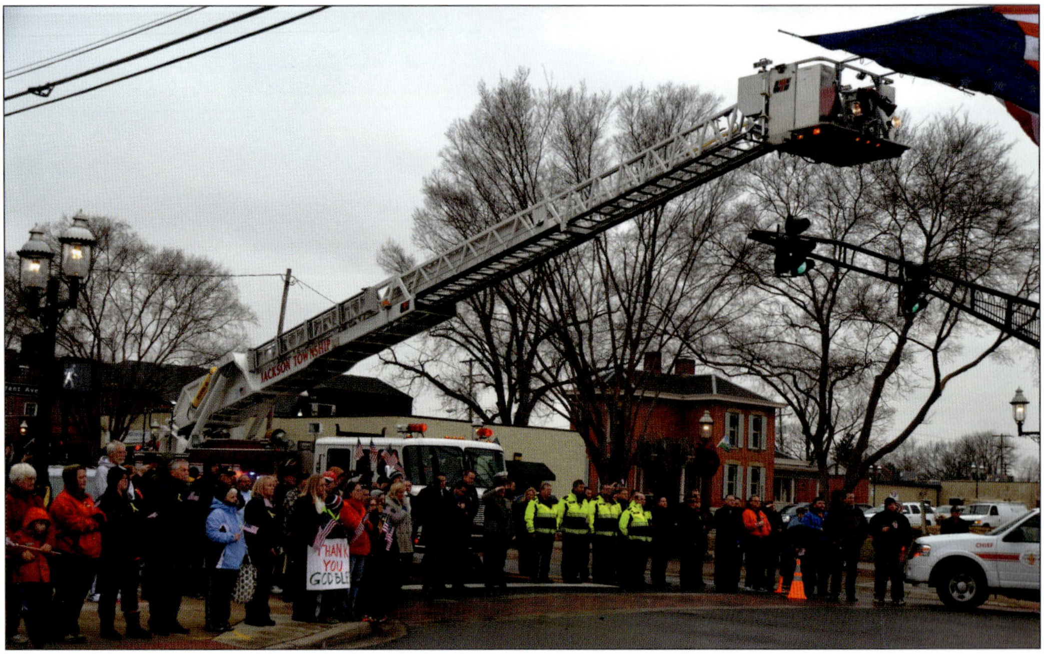

Along streets lined with American flags and yellow ribbons, mourners gathered to honor Army specialist Joey Riley, who was killed by a suicide bomber in Afghanistan in November 2014. A standout football player and team captain, Riley graduated from Grove City High School in 2005, enlisted in the Army in 2012, and served with the 82nd Airborne Division after graduating from Capital University.

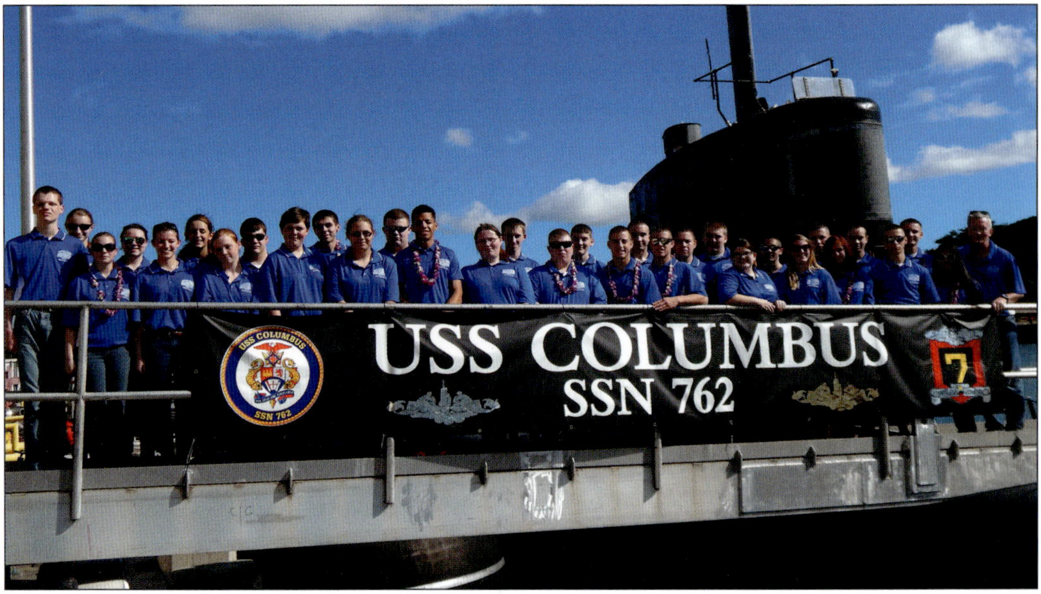

The Central Crossing High School Navy Junior ROTC was selected as the lone representative from Ohio invited to participate in the Pearl Harbor Memorial Parade in Hawaii in 2014. Here, the cadets and their commander (Ret.) Sgt. Maj. Don Bocook (far right) stand on the deck of the USS *Columbus*. The unit spent months working to raise money for the trip, and they have been invited back in 2016.

Six

Around Town

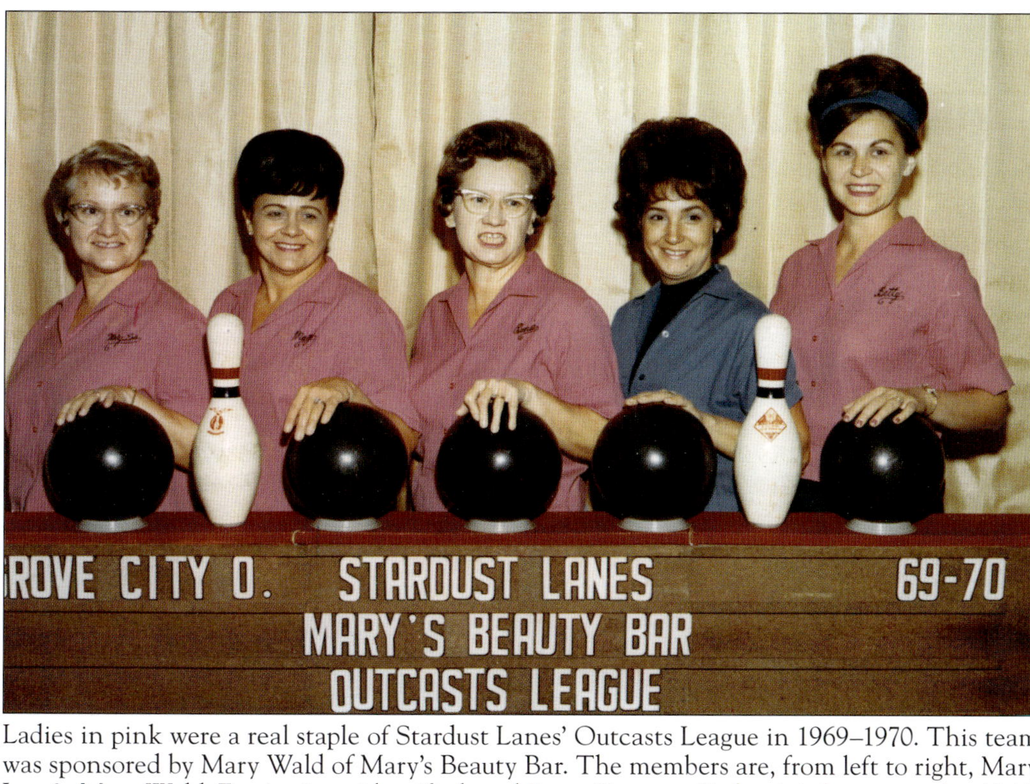

Ladies in pink were a real staple of Stardust Lanes' Outcasts League in 1969–1970. This team was sponsored by Mary Wald of Mary's Beauty Bar. The members are, from left to right, Mary Lou ? , Mary Wald, Eunice ? , unidentified, and Betty Grooms. Today, it is known as the AMC Stardust Lanes and has 24 lanes with 42-inch flat-screen televisions.

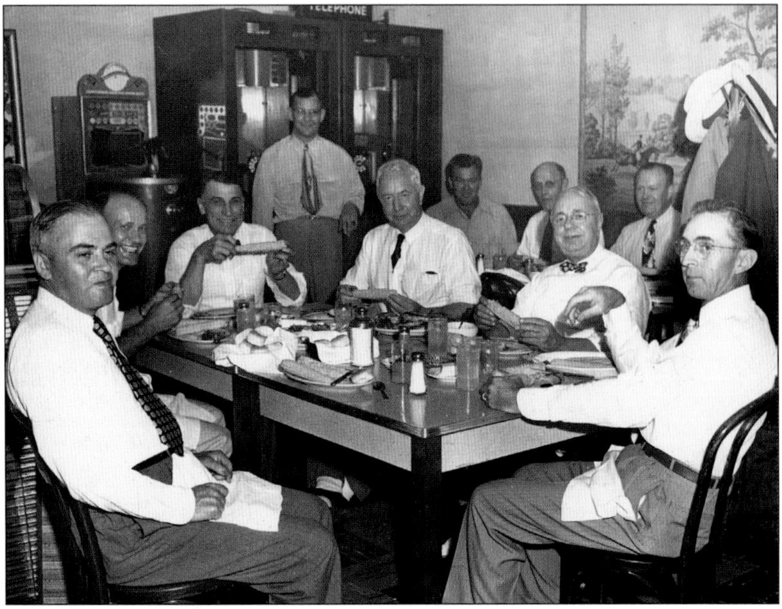

This corn dinner at Devault's Restaurant, which stood at the southeast corner of Broadway and Park Street, shows one of the many groups that met there for meetings and evening meals. Mayor Paul White, who headed city government from 1945 to 1955, presided over the group of businessmen. Note the two telephone booths in the back of the room.

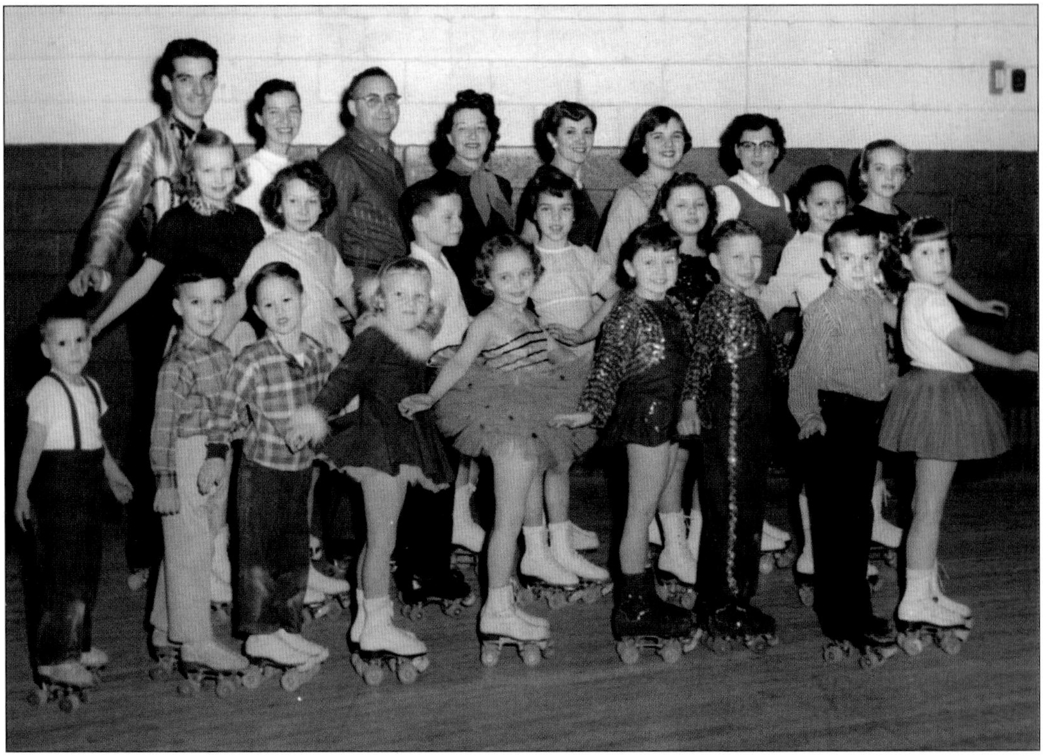

From 1956 to 1975, the Grove City Figure Skating Club performed in shows and competed in state, regional, and national competitions. Members from left to right are (first row) Mike Ruoff, Terry Seese, Greg King, unidentified, LaRae Rehl, Carolyn Henson, Richard Osterloh, Jim Lanman, and Nancy Ruoff; (second row) Sherry Landes, Linda Haughn, Gene Ruoff, Janet Seese, Phyllis Benjamin, and unidentified; (third row) Jack Gall, Betty Seese, Carl Osterloh, Gladys Gall, Isabel Rehl, Patty Jones, Ann Wells, and Sharon Boos.

This photograph, taken in 1962, shows how Grove City homemakers relaxed between their household and child-rearing duties in a time before there were coordinated play dates, Xboxes, and smartphones. This was the beginning of the development of the Monterey neighborhood on Security Drive. From left to right are unidentified, Jane Mixer, and Gay Weber.

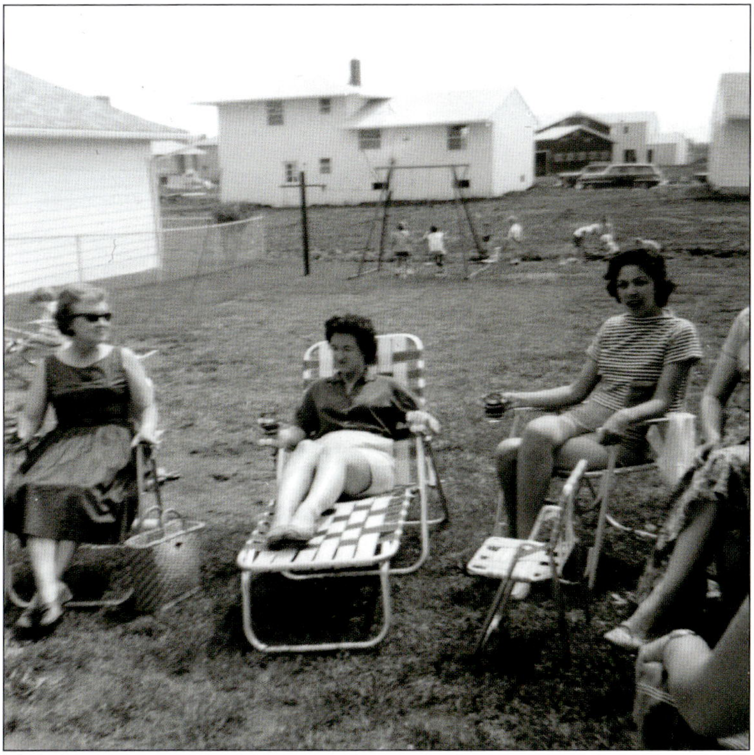

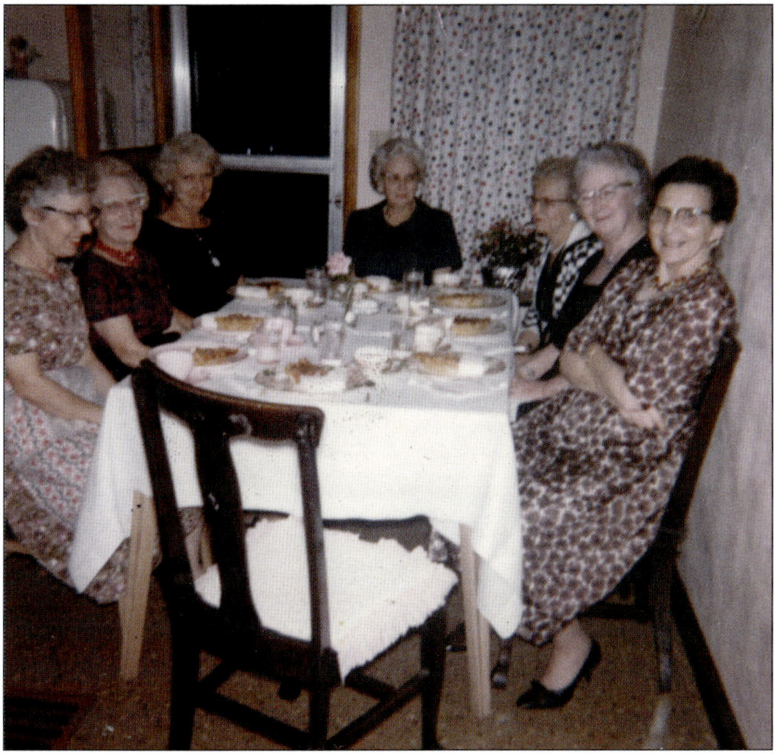

Gathering to discuss the news of the day has always been important to the citizens of Grove City. These women, all active in the PTA and other community activities, called themselves the Potluck Pals and met in each other's homes from the 1960s to the 1980s. They are, from left to right, unidentified, Lillian Metzger, Clara Fritz, Helen Arick, unidentified, Sarah Haines, and Eileen Simmons. The photographer was Mae Gibboney.

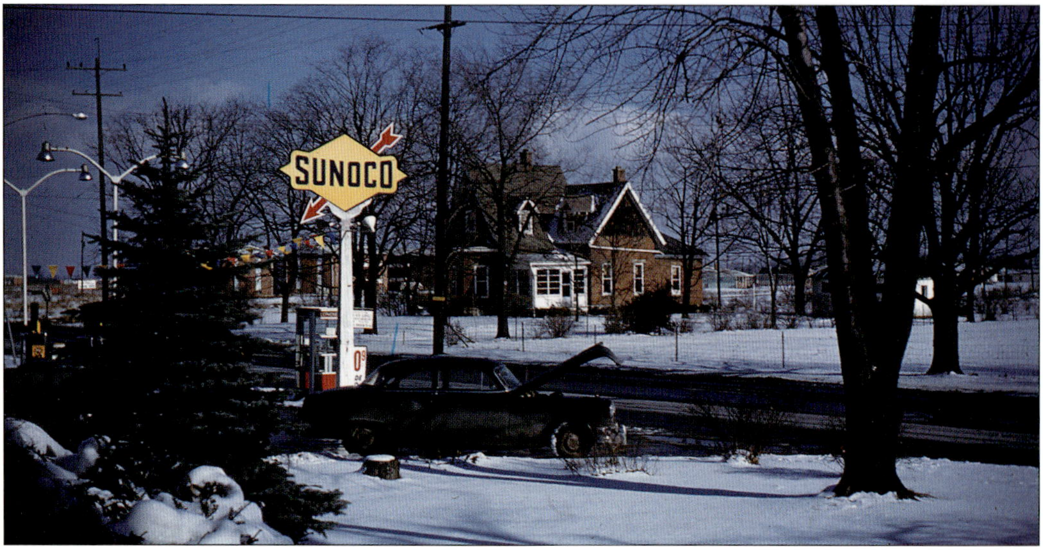

This photograph of Bethard's Service Station represents the area of north Broadway as it looked in the 1950s as growth was just beginning in that end of town. O.W. Bethard first built the Sunoco station and garage in 1935. His son V.K. Bethard took over management in later years.

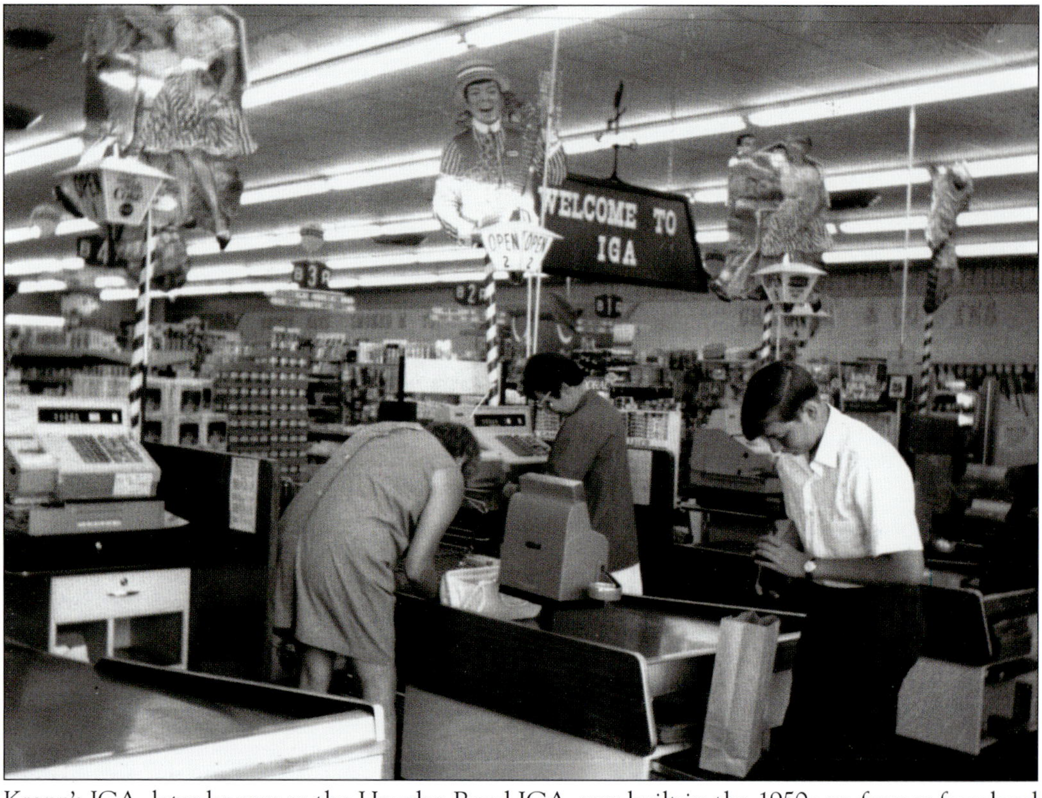

Kropp's IGA, later known as the Haughn Road IGA, was built in the 1950s on former farmland owned by the Kropp family. The store was best known for its butcher's counter. Today, the building is owned by South-Western City Schools and has been converted into a preschool center.

This entry into the 1968 Soapbox Derby was called the *Spirit of Grove City*. The racer is seen receiving its official city seal and safety inspection from Capt. Ray Ruoff. Two of the sponsors of the racer, Ron Barlett (left) of Robertshaw Controls and Galen Wade (right) of Surfin' Sam Shirts, are seen with Ruoff giving the car their final stamp of approval.

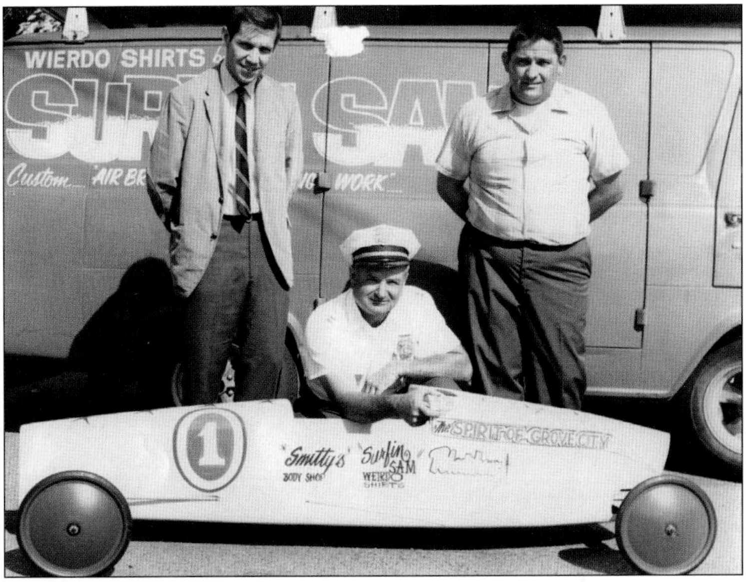

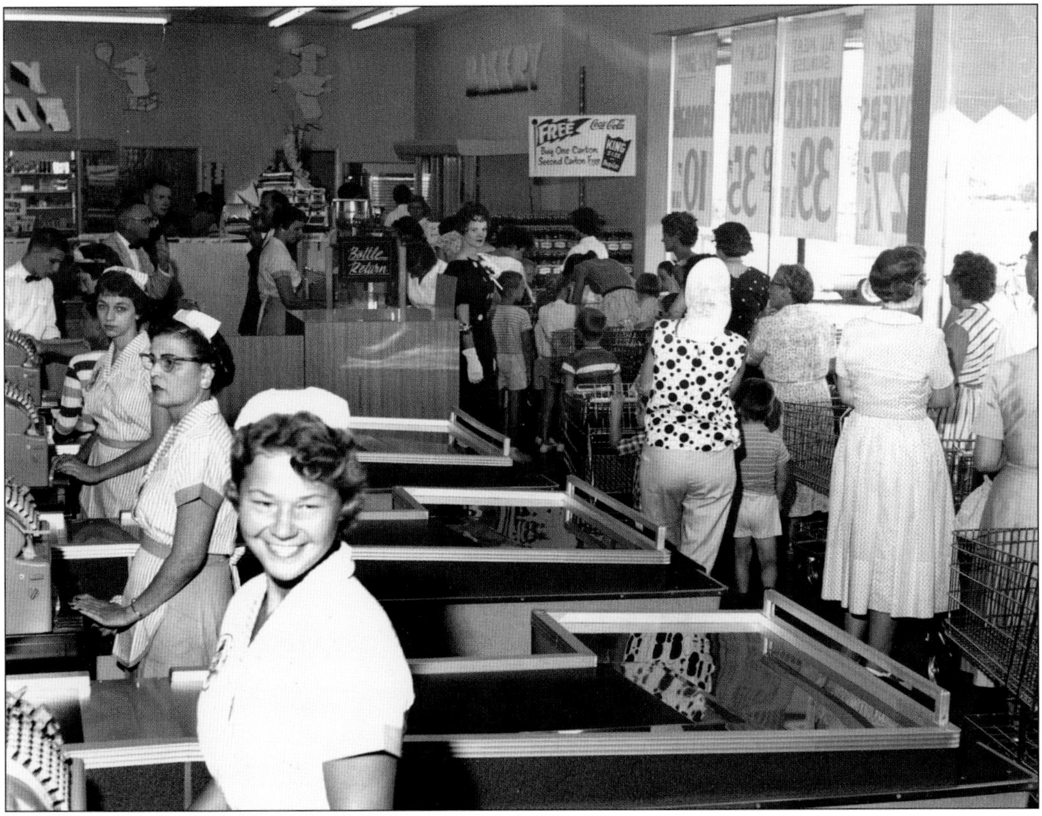

The Super Duper on Hoover Road at the High Meadow Shopping Center held its grand opening on October 13, 1960. Owner Howard Sigman greeted long lines of customers looking for what he called "a shopping paradise." Also located in the new shopping center were Sparkle Cleaners, Drustar Pharmacy, High Meadow Barber Shop, and a new Texaco gas station. Today, the old grocery is ASK Motorcycles.

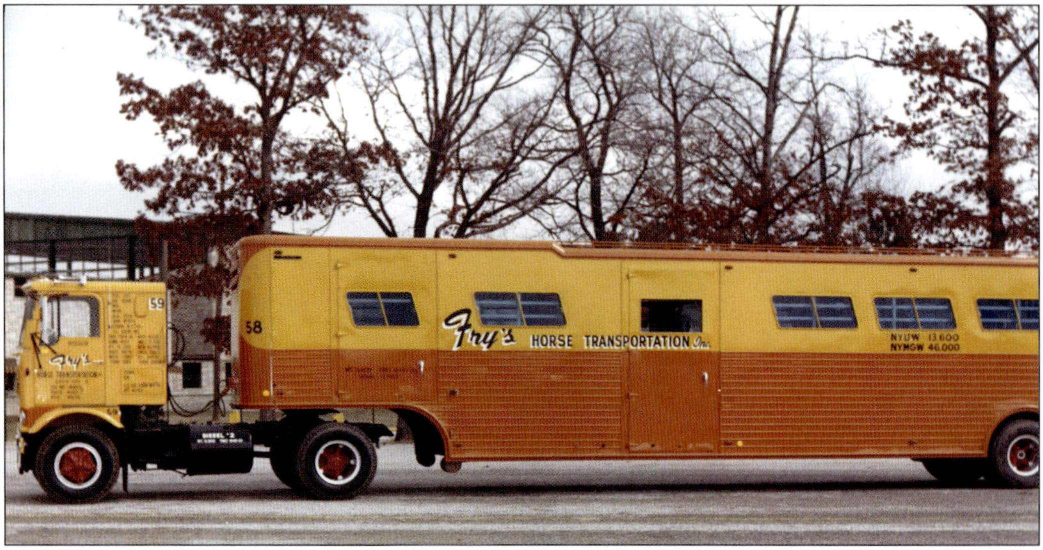

For three decades, Fry's Horse Transportation, at 3886 Elm Street, carried horses to and from Beulah Park, traveling as far as Florida. Founding owner Lawrence Fry passed the business on to this son W. Beale Fry and his grandson Jim. The vans were well known throughout town for their orange and yellow colors. The business was sold in 1980.

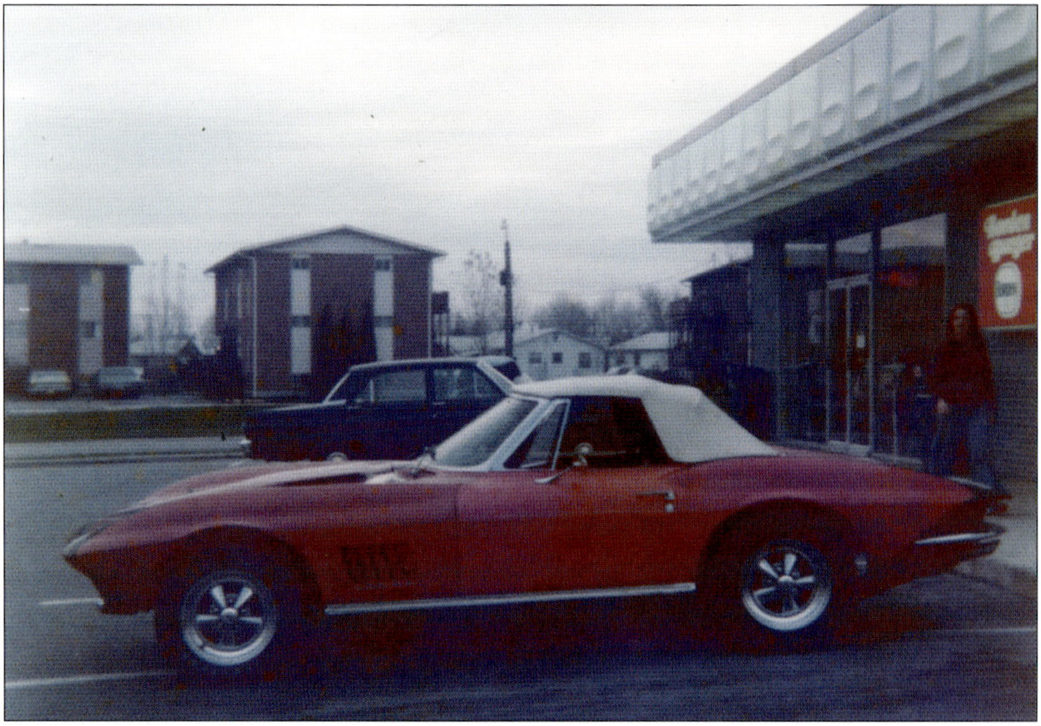

Mark Valentine's 1965 Corvette, sitting outside the Borden Burger on Southwest Boulevard in 1974, was one of the hottest cars in town. Borden had purchased the Burger Boy Food-O-Rama (BBF) chain in 1970 and continued to compete against McDonald's. Each store featured a "Whirling Satellite" and 15¢ hamburgers. BBF cofounder Milton Lustnauer and his wife, Jean, were well known in the area for their Green Gables restaurant at the Central Point Shopping Center.

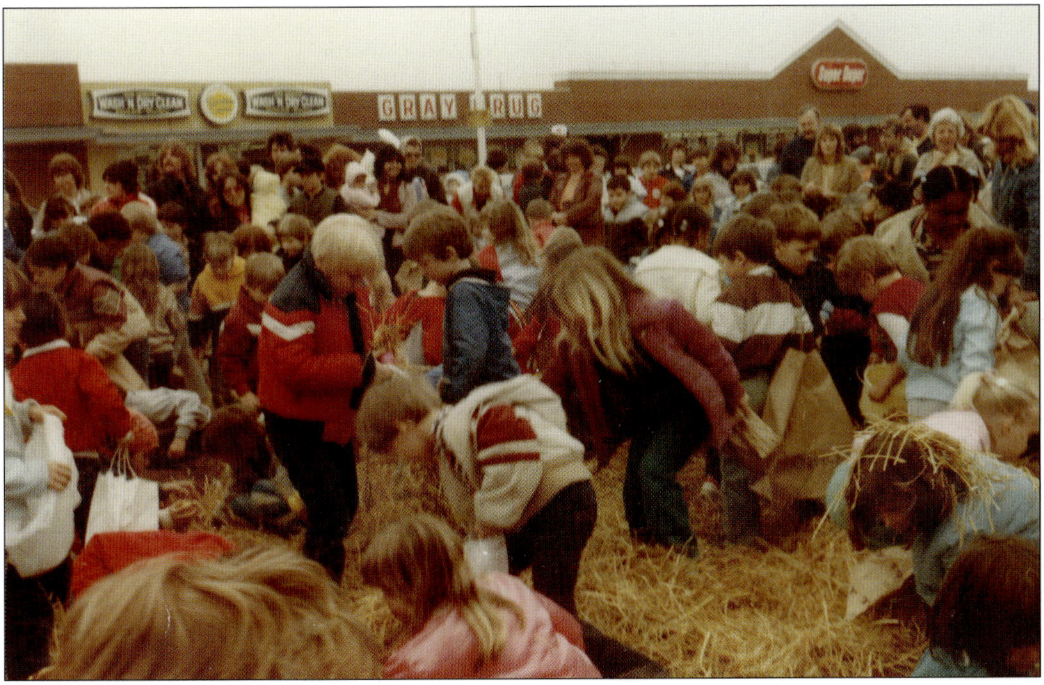

On April 21, 1984, the Broadway Merchants and the *Grove City Record* held their sixth annual Easter egg hunt in the field between Dairy Queen and Firestone on Southwest Boulevard. Today, the Grove City Church of the Nazarene hosts one of the city's largest egg hunts in the area.

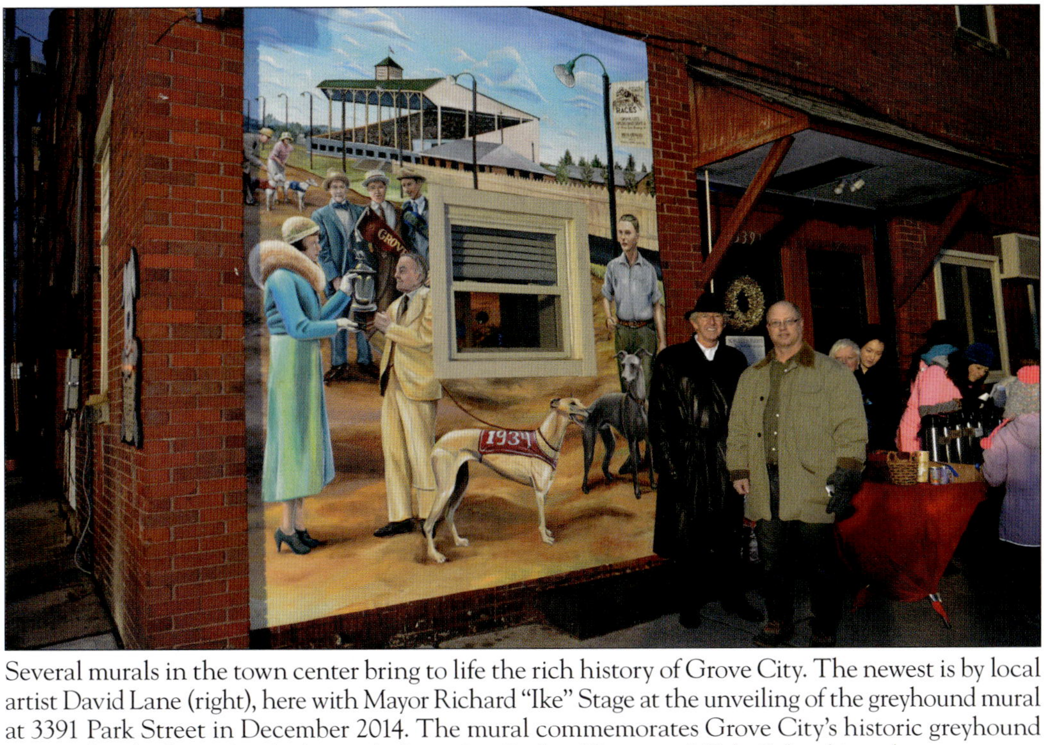

Several murals in the town center bring to life the rich history of Grove City. The newest is by local artist David Lane (right), here with Mayor Richard "Ike" Stage at the unveiling of the greyhound mural at 3391 Park Street in December 2014. The mural commemorates Grove City's historic greyhound racetrack, which used to be located where Our Lady of Perpetual Help School is today.

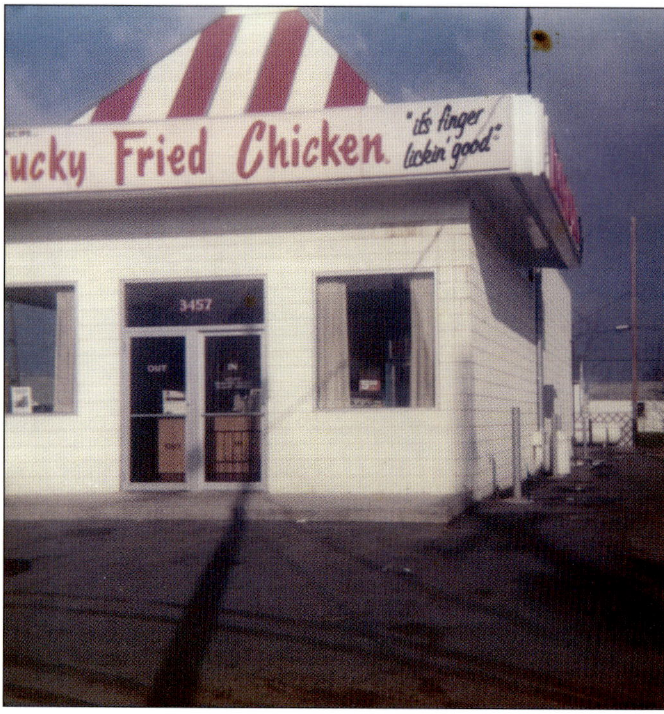

Kentucky Fried Chicken and its secret recipe arrived in Grove City in 1972 as one of the earliest fast-food restaurant chains. Unlike previous KFC restaurants that were converted from gas stations, this building was one of the company's first stand-alone designs. The starting pay was $1.60 per hour. Located on north Broadway, the site has more recently been home to a carpet store and a jujitsu gym.

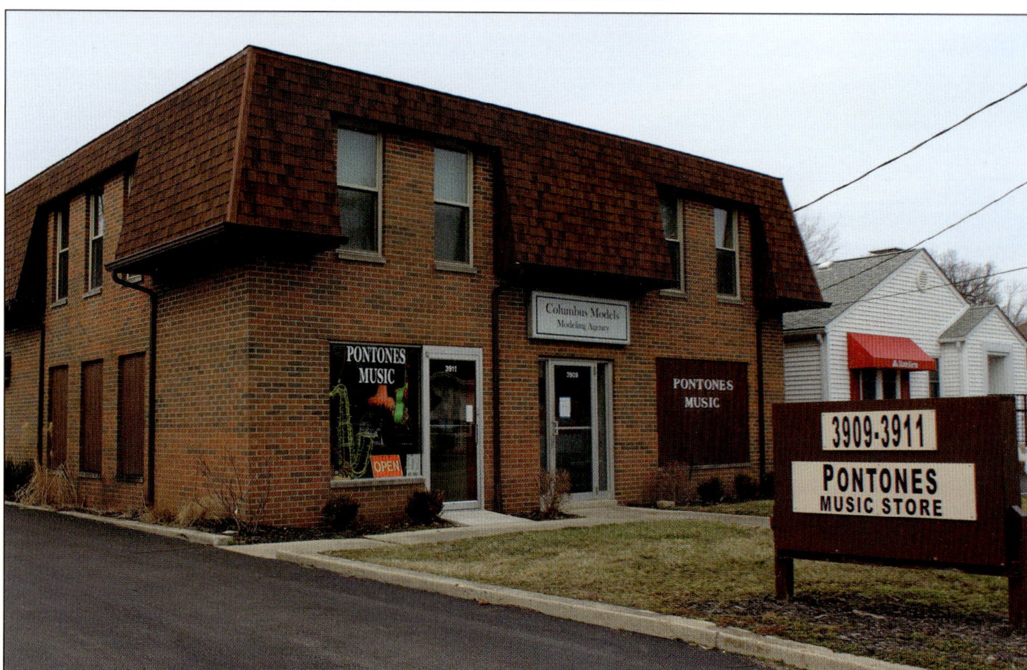

Leveraging his GI Bill to become an electrician, Jesus Pontones went to work in a music store repairing organs and other instruments. In 1968, he decided to open his own shop, where local students could take lessons and have their instruments fixed. His wife, Gena, continued the tradition before their daughter Maria and her friend Clara Jo Vance bought the town center business in 2003. They hold open jam sessions every Wednesday night.

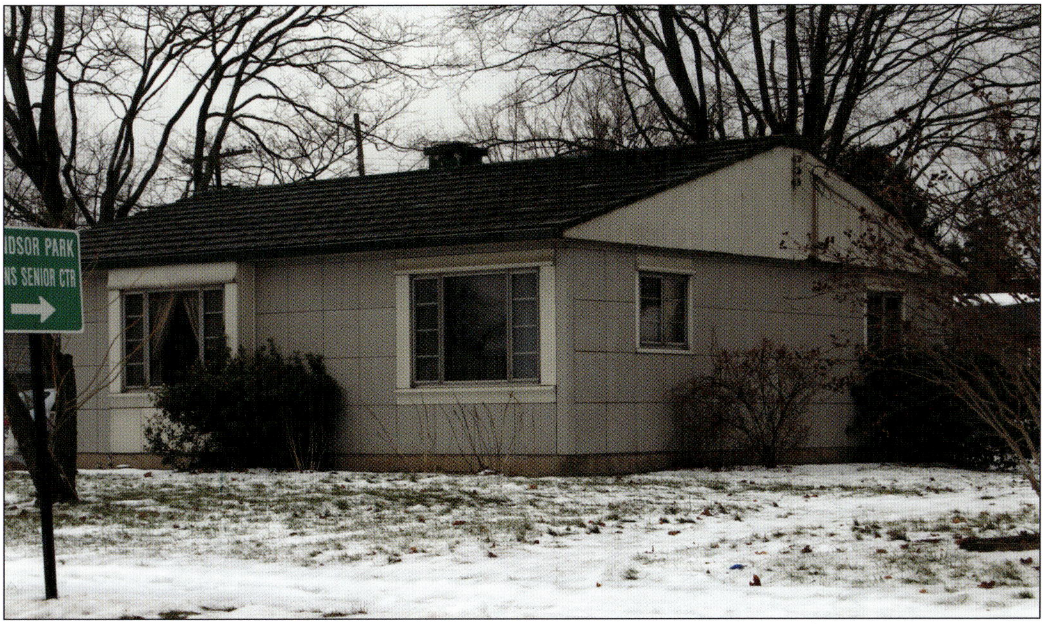

Mass-produced Lustron homes originated in one location: the former Curtiss Wright Navy dive-bomber factory in Columbus, Ohio. During the post–World War II years, Lustron manufactured the prefabricated steel buildings for the postwar suburban population who wanted low maintenance, durability, and affordability. The homes sold for approximately $8,500 to $9,500. This local Lustron house is located on Kingston Avenue.

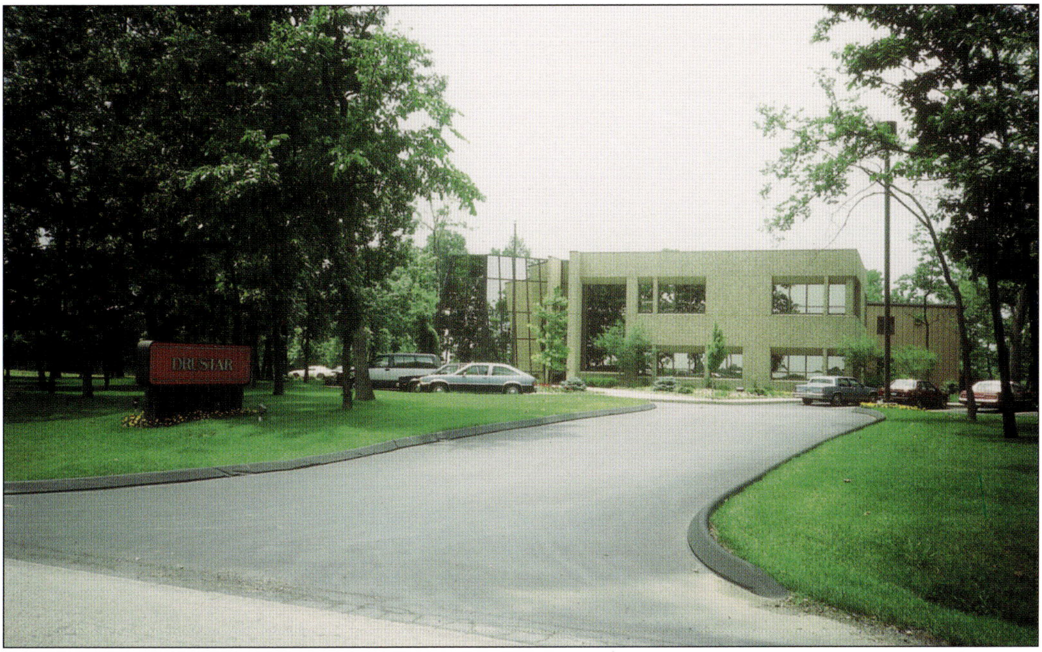

Drustar Unit Dose Systems, Inc., at 3805 Marlane Drive, was founded by Grove City inventor Kenneth Relyea in the 1970s using a new method for preparing and distributing individual-unit dose containers of pharmaceutical materials. After the business closed at that location, the complex was sold to South-Western City Schools and is now the district's central office.

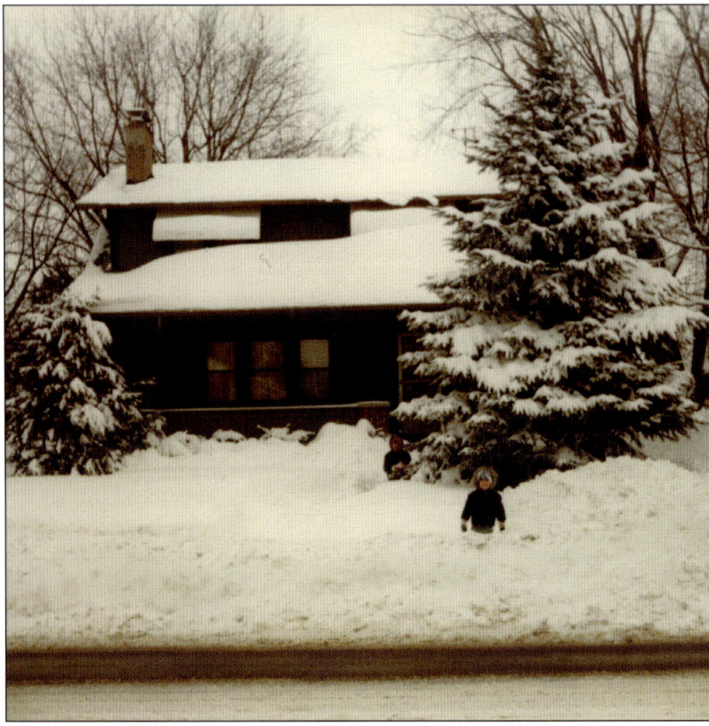

Residents in and around Grove City, including the Brace residence here, and throughout the Ohio Valley region dug out from under the great blizzard of 1978. Hurricane-force winds of up to 76 miles per hour, coupled with rapidly falling snow on January 26 and 27, made the winter storm system one of the fiercest in history. Several Grove City churches and the Grove City Municipal Building were turned into shelters for the city and neighboring communities.

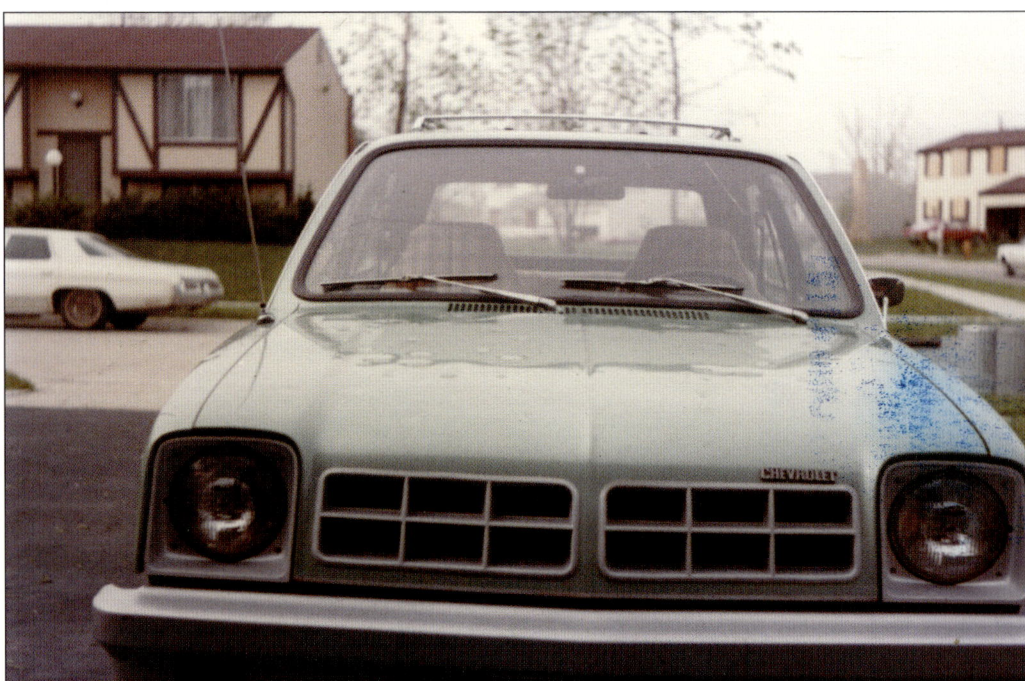

On May 11, 1980, a massive Mother's Day hailstorm sliced across Grove City, smashing windshields, shattering windows, and denting the sides of houses. Hailstones the size of baseballs (some as large a grapefruit) pulverized crops right into the ground. The estimated damage across southern Franklin County was $10 million. Automobiles like the one here had dozens of dents.

On June 7, 1996, about 3,000 people lined Broadway to watch the Olympic torch pass through Grove City. As one of only two central Ohio cities selected, Grove City was the halfway point in time (day 42 of 84) during the torch's travels. The route went from Los Angeles to Atlanta and included 56 continuous hours via Pony Express riders. Among those selected to carry the torch were students Jennifer Snyder, Justin Hoff, Jerry Huffman, Paula Bennett, teacher John Weddendorf, and Special Olympian Ryan Walker.

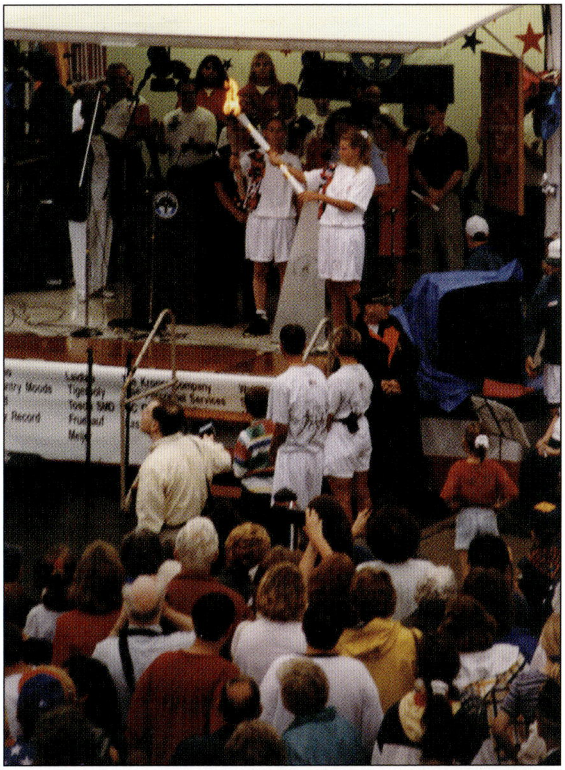

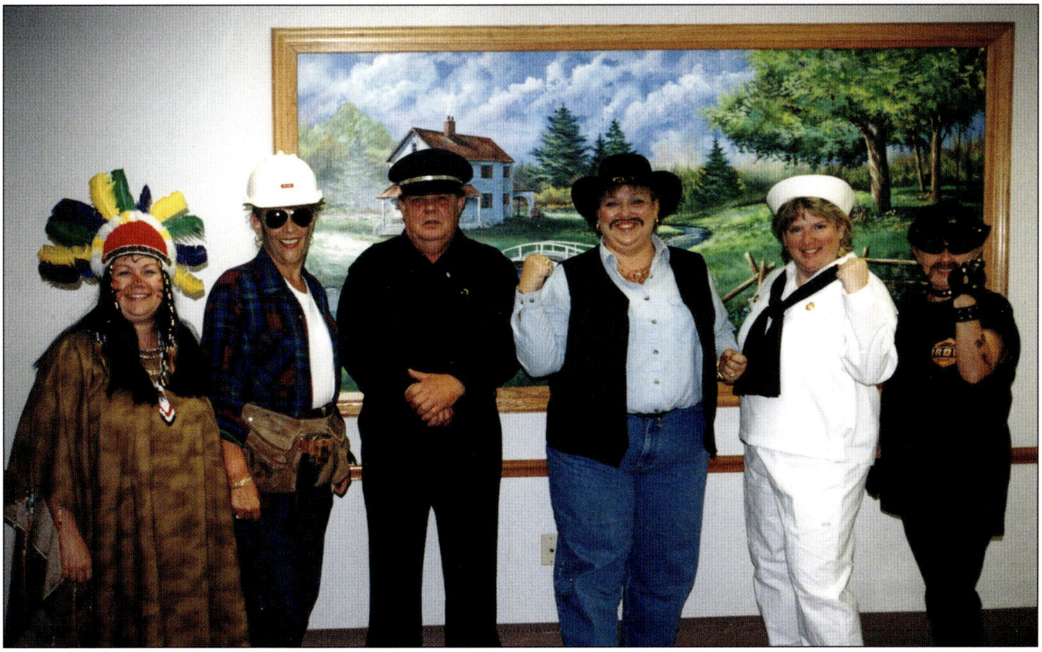

Pictured here is the parks and recreation staff entertaining the Evans Center seniors with a Halloween skit. In the late 1990s, the staff performed as the Village People. Pictured are Kim Crowe (Native American), Diane Mills (construction worker), Doug Longmire (police officer), Bev Longmire (cowboy), director Kim Conrad (sailor), and Karen Eaton (biker guy).

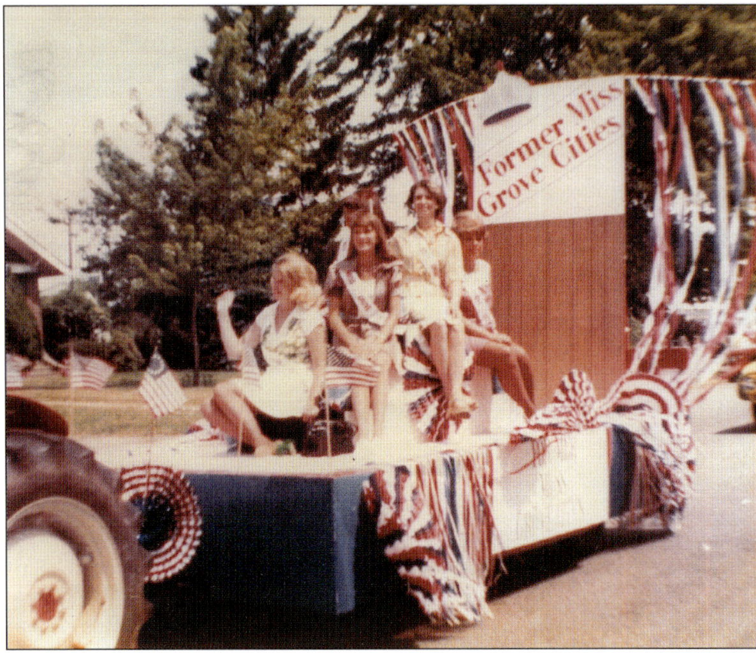

Before the Arts in the Alley parade became the annual community parade in the 1980s, the Grove City Fair Board organized a parade held every year on the Fourth of July. This float shows some of the former queens from the Miss Grove City pageant. Among those honored in 1975 were Betty Shoaf Baker, Sherry Johanneman, Beverly Russell Doyle, Jan Konkler, Robyn Rice, Donna Theado, Debbie McGongile, and Becky Murray.

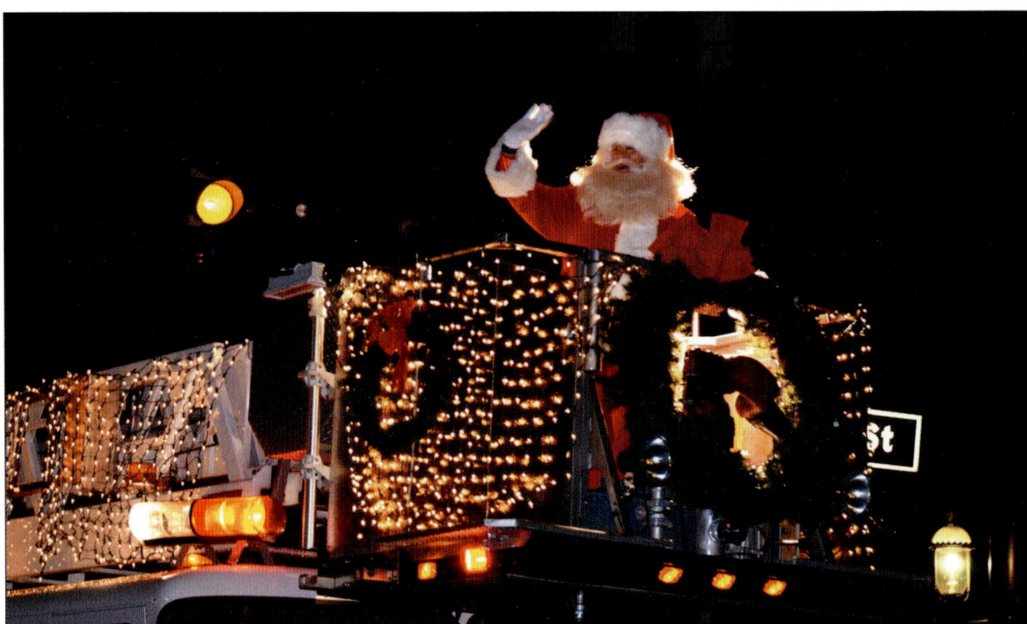

Santa Claus has ushered in the holiday season by announcing his presence in a December parade as far back as 1947. These days, Jolly Old Saint Nick takes center stage in the bucket of a Jackson Township Fire Department ladder truck adorned with festive lights. His annual arrival marks the beginning of the Christmas season in Grove City, along with the lighting of the community tree in the town center.

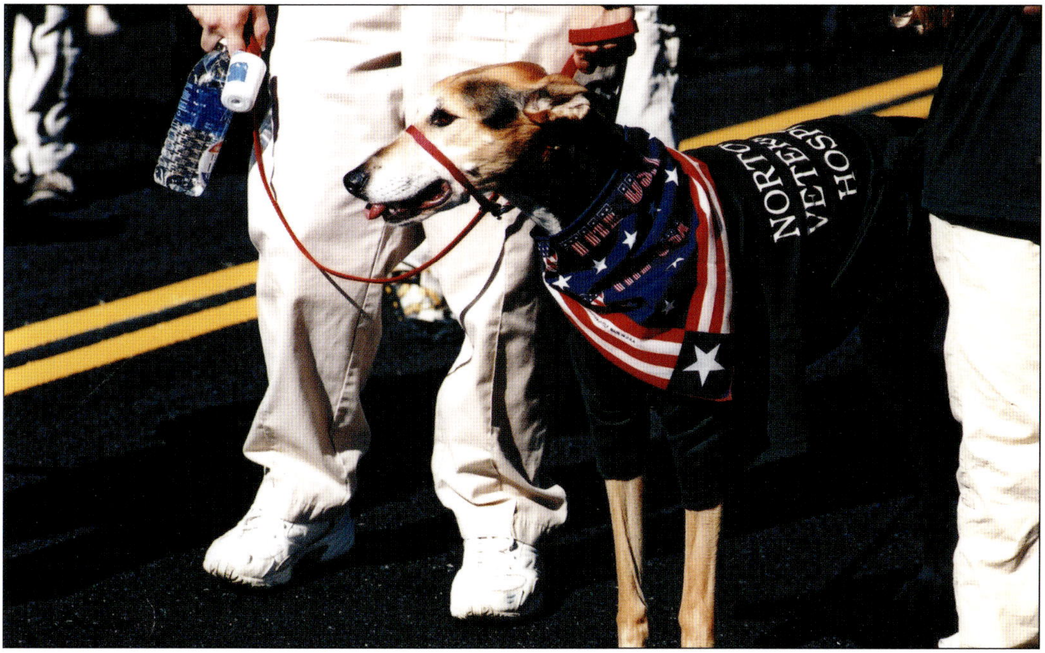

This photograph was taken at the Arts in the Alley parade. Lori Millard, a staffer at the Norton Road Veterinary Hospital, adopted a foster dog named Vegas. Veterinarian Beth Logan showcases foster dogs from Colony Cats and Dogs to march alongside friends and family in the parade. Usually, one or two canines get adopted every year after their exposure during the well-attended parade.

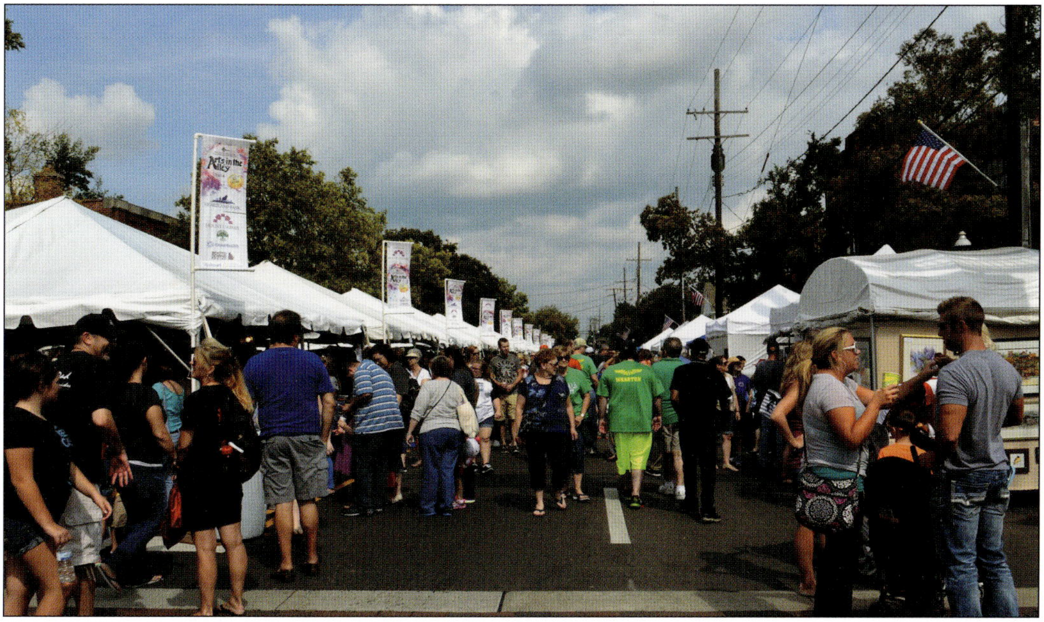

Arts in the Alley is Grove City's longest-running uninterrupted signature event. Sponsored by the Grove City Area Chamber of Commerce every third weekend in September, Arts in the Alley has grown from a few vendors along Broadway in 1979 to a two-day extravaganza complete with several juried art shows, vendors, music, and food along Broadway in town center. The community parade kicks off the much-anticipated weekend every year.

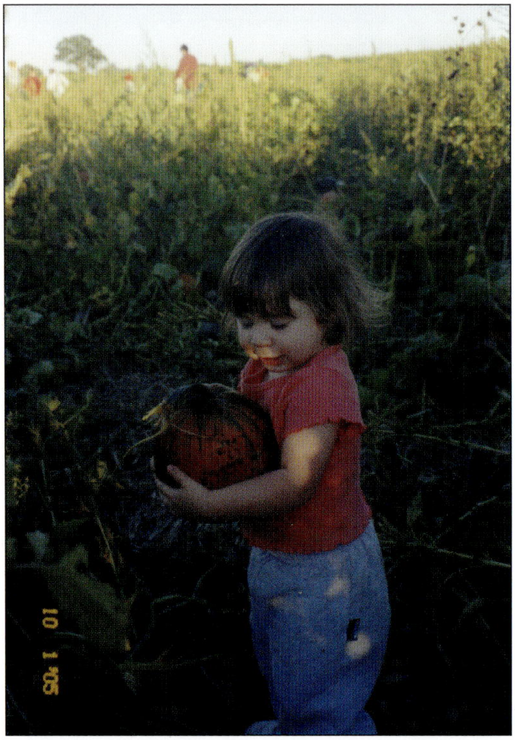

Circle S Farms had a modest start when Doug and Ethel Sullivan's children began selling sweet corn on the side of the road in the 1970s. This led to the school tour business in the early 1980s. While best known for their Fall Fun Days program that includes pumpkin picking, tractor rides, corn mazes, and barn slides, the family farm has also offered summer berry picking and locally produced jams. Pictured here is Francesca Lanese in 2005.

Trapper John's Canoe Livery is situated on the Big Darby National Scenic Creek. The livery has been around since about 1970 and been owned and operated by Jason Kaufman for more than 20 years. The livery has canoes, kayaks, tubes, and a campground in addition to access to 12 miles of stream to meander down. Pictured here is the parking lot of Trapper John's Canoe Livery.

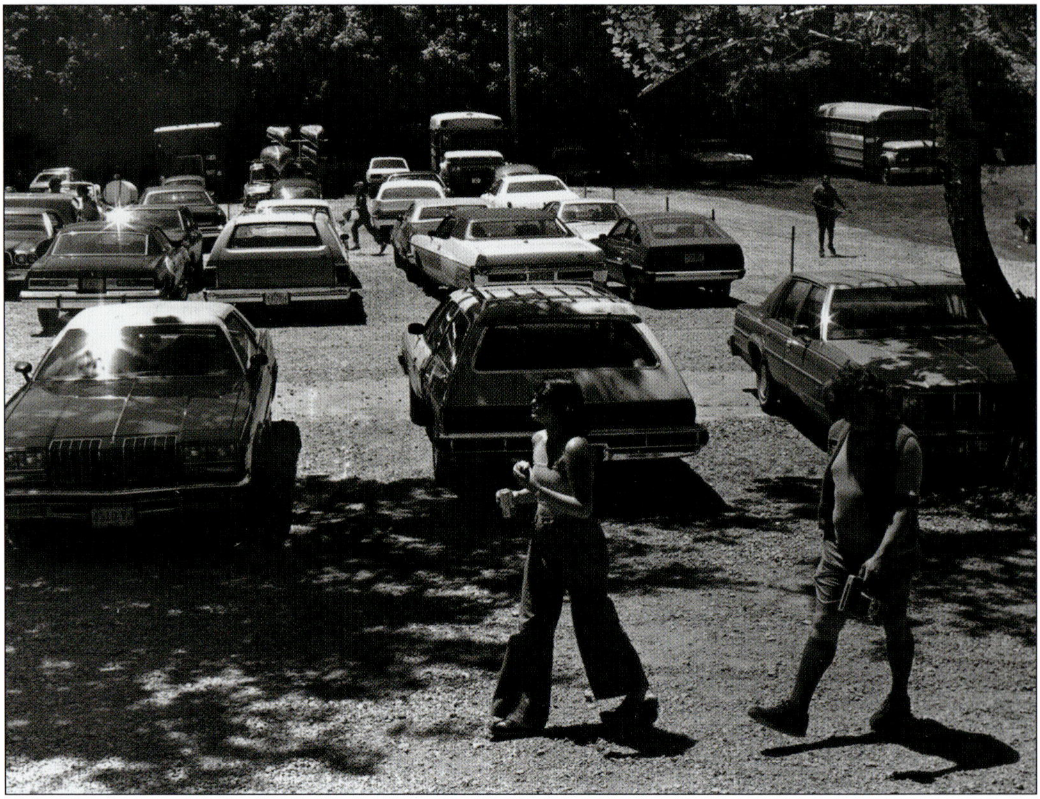

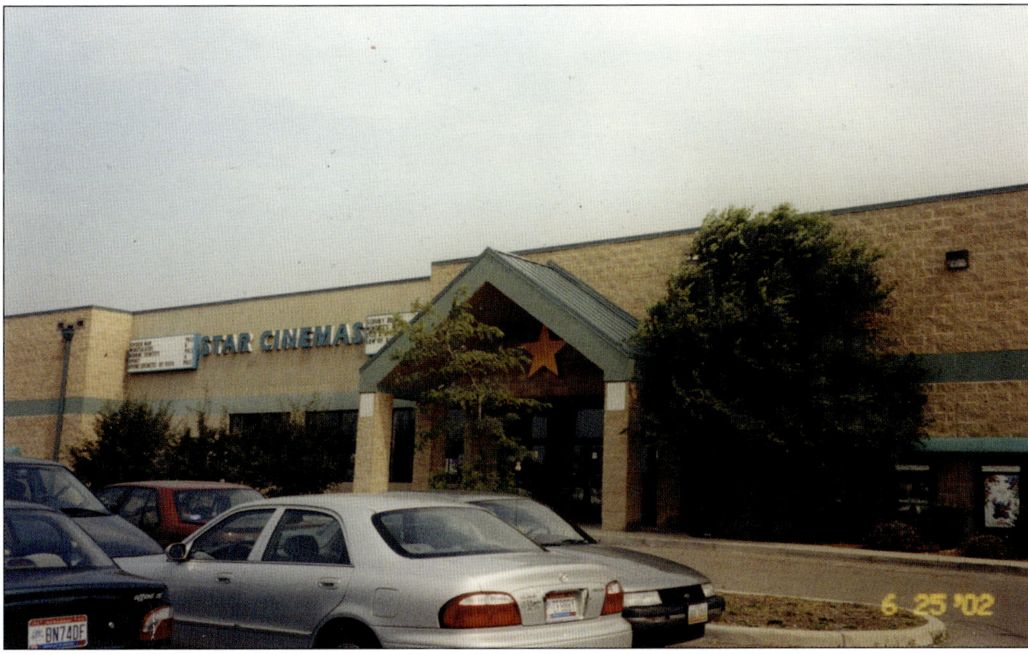

Star Cinema operated its first movie reel in 1996 in an eight-screen complex located on Stringtown Road. The tax-abated theater could not survive the onslaught of increased competition when several nearby theaters opened around the same time. The increasing competition and the cost-prohibitive move to digital projection equipment led to the theater's closing in the fall of 2014.

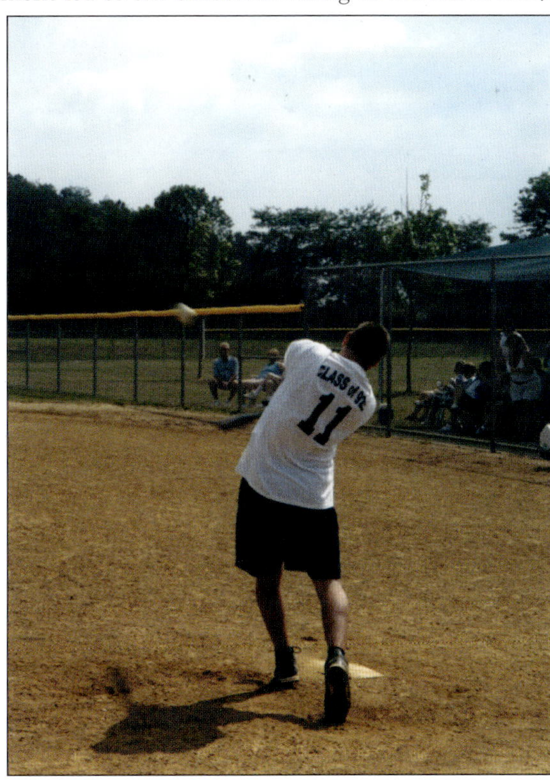

The Grove City High School Alumni Softball Tournament began in 1983 and is now billed as the "World's Largest High School Alumni Softball Tournament." Founder Steve Carr developed the double-elimination tournament and still remains at the helm after 32 years. Starting with just 10 teams in 1983, the alumni tournament has grown to 90 teams representing seven decades of Grove City High School graduates competing for seven division championships.

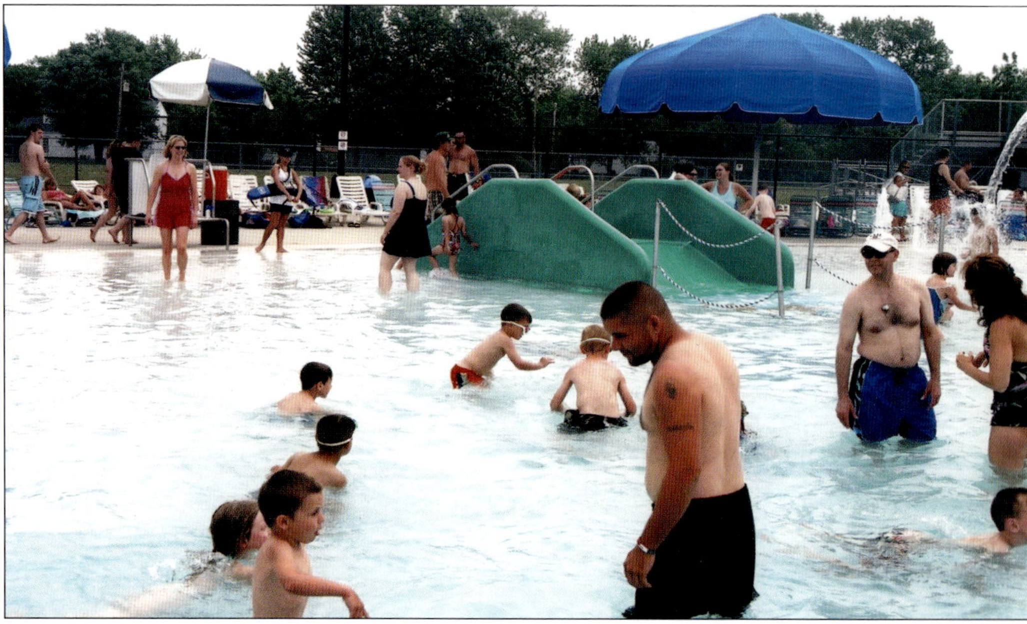

The Big Splash helped fill the hole left by the departure of the privately run Twin Towers Swim Club. Built in 1999, the publicly run pool offers a six-lane lap pool, a large body slide, award-winning aquatic climbing walls, and interactive water toys. The Big Splash hosts a variety of theme nights throughout the summer, including movie night when families can swim and watch flicks on the pool's big screen.

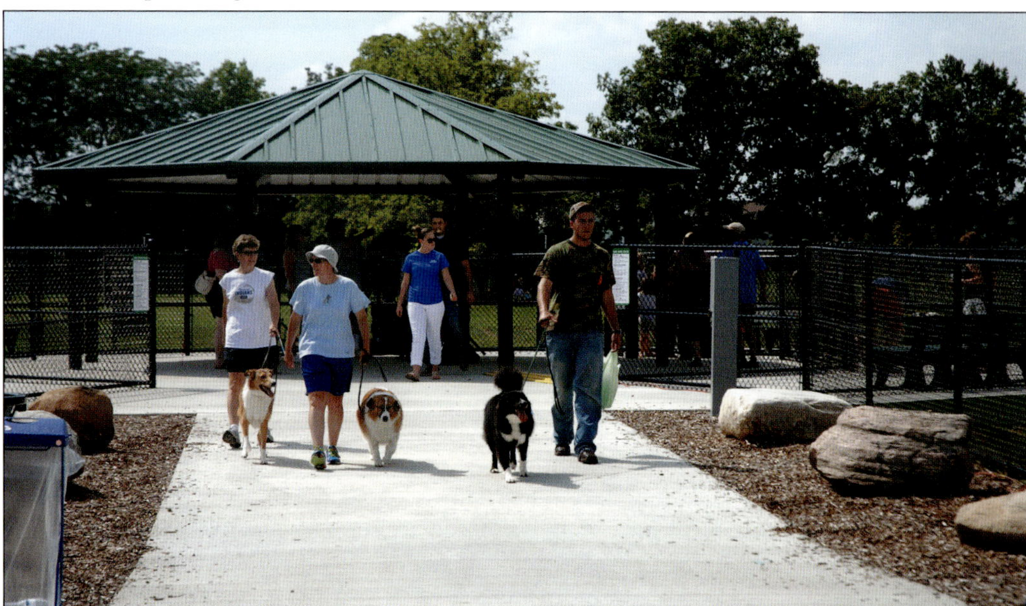

Part of a planned community park on Demorest Road, Grove City's dog park opened in the summer of 2014 to playful pups and their companions. The park has four fenced-in areas for off-leash dog play separated for large and small dogs. It is the first phase of a larger community park that will include a fishing pier, community garden, and walking trail. The park is named after the town's founder, William F. Breck.

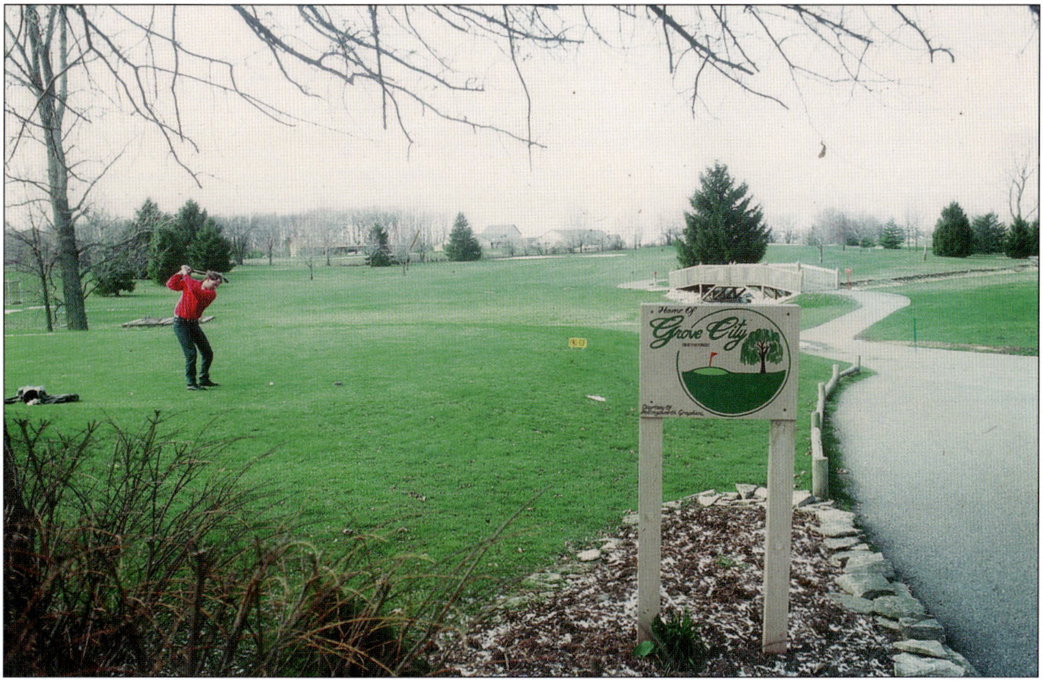

Before there was Pinnacle Golf Club, there was the Grove City Country Club, which opened for business in March 1972. The initial nine-hole course was a nod to the growing population of Grove City at the time. The name was eventually changed to Grovebrook Golf Club. The club closed in early 2005, and the new Mount Carmel Grove City medical complex now occupies the property.

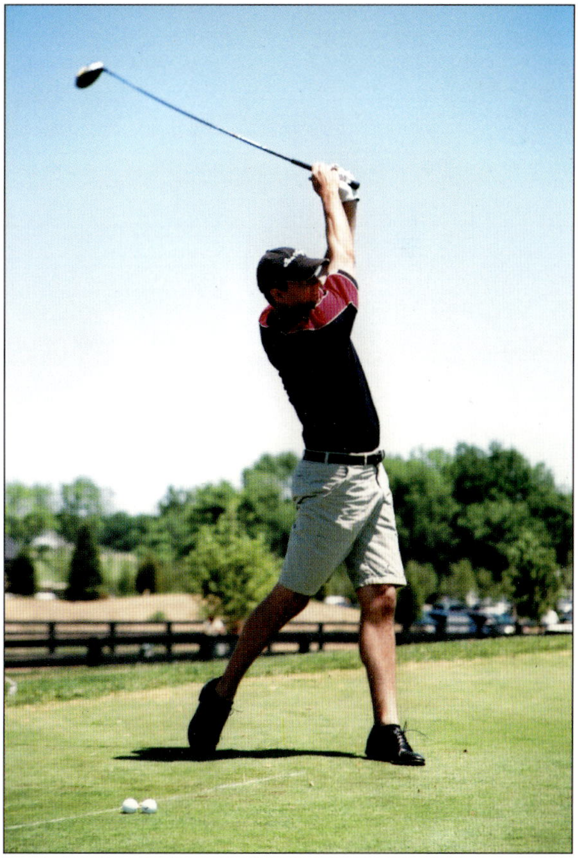

Years in the making, and the crown jewel in the Pinnacle development east of Buckeye Parkway, the Lanny Wadkins–designed 18-hole private Pinnacle Golf Club opened in 2006. It brought with it upscale housing, a fine-dining restaurant, and a banquet center located on former Eberhard family farmland. It is considered one of the premiere private golf clubs in all of central Ohio.

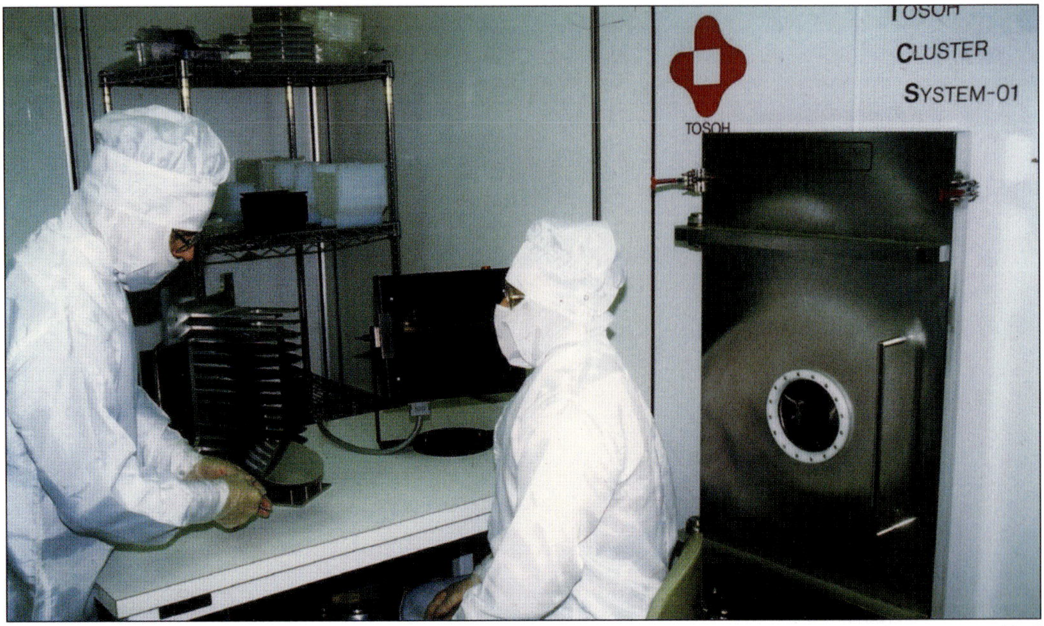

In the 1970s, two Battelle veterans, Neal Griesenauer and Leo Wenzinger, started a company called Specialty Metals and Alloys in Griesenauer's Borror Road home. In 1988, the much-expanded company became a wholly owned subsidiary of the Tokyo-based Tosoh Corporation. Tosoh SMD relocated to Gantz Road in 1991. Tosoh sells primarily to microchip manufacturers and has more than 100 patents. Tosoh chemists analyze every nonhazardous element on the periodic table.

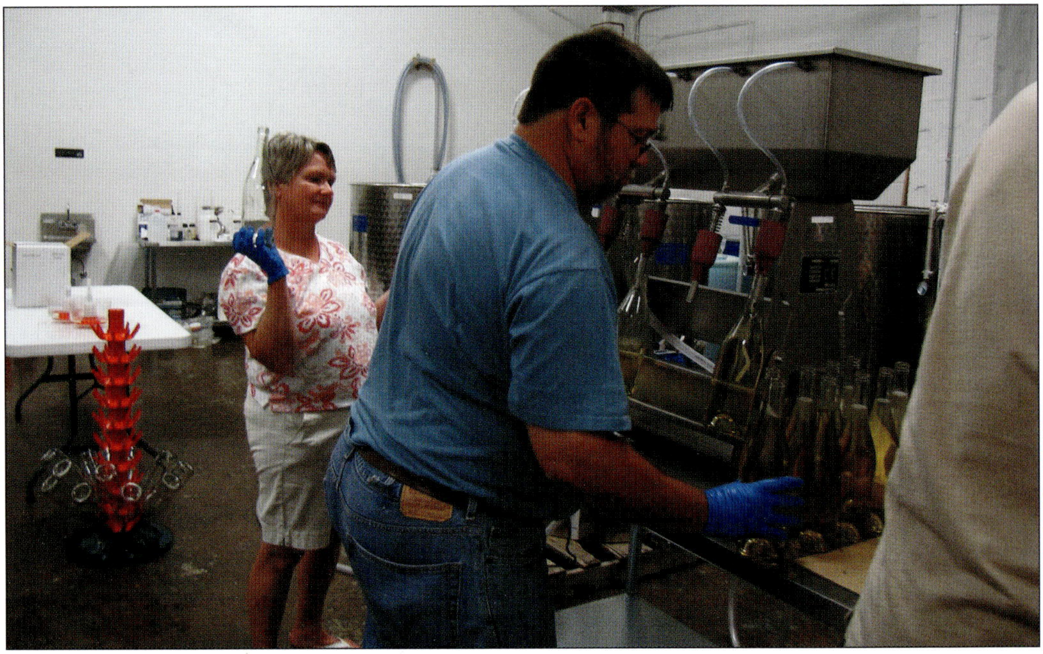

Diane and Dave Crosby opened Plum Run Winery in July 2012, naming it after their vineyard on their farm south of Grove City. It is the only vineyard in Franklin County. Pictured here are Nancy Snashall and Dave Crosby in the middle of the winemaking process. Located in the former Harley Motors building, the winery hosts many events, including a painting class and a spa night.

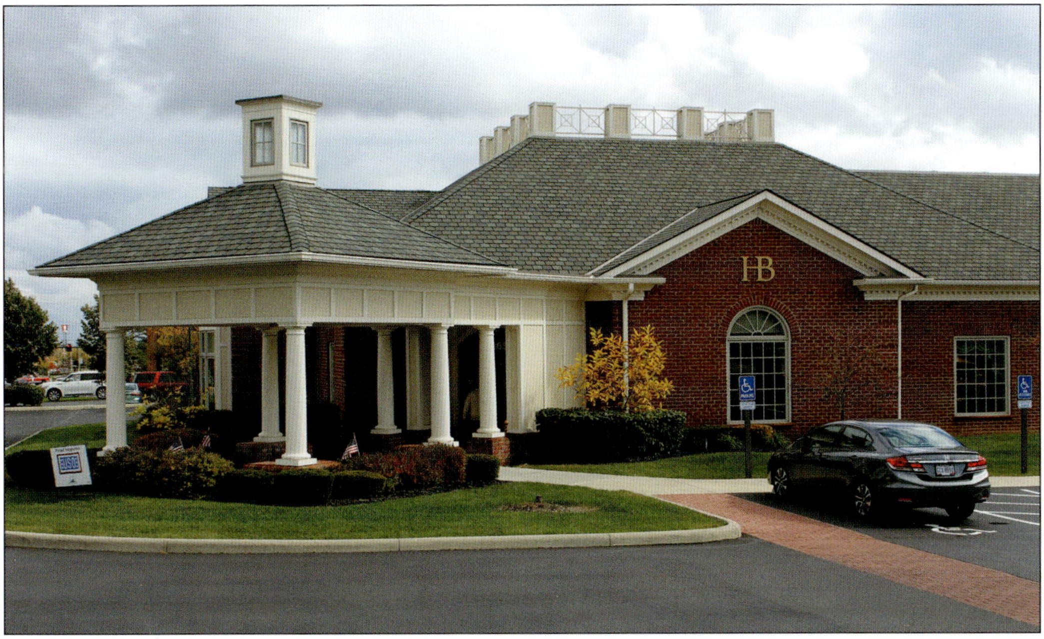

Grove City resident Tiney M. McComb founded the Heartland Bank Corp, later the Heartland Bank of Central Ohio, in 1988. McComb was very active in the community. He was a former Federal Reserve Bank of Cleveland board member. His son G. Scott McComb is chairman, president, and CEO of Heartland Bank, which has 14 locations.

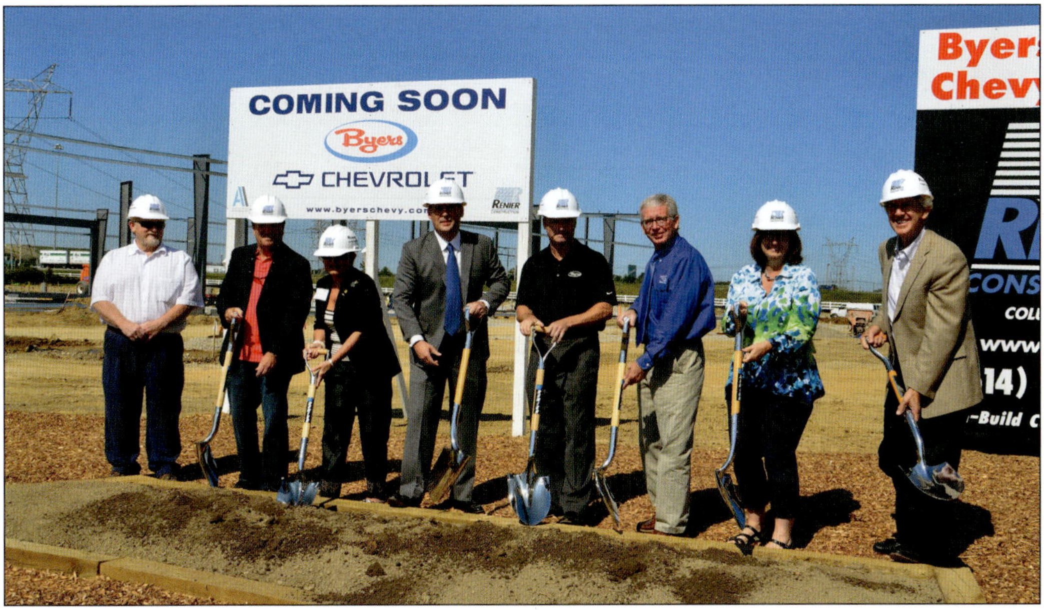

The arrival of the Byers Chevrolet dealership in 2014 heralded the return of a new car dealership to the city after the departure of Harley Motors from the town center in the 1970s. From left to right are Steve Bennett (councilman), David Burris (Jackson Township trustee), Maria Klemack-McGraw (councilwoman), George Kauffman (Byers vice president), Jeff Peters (general manager), Jim Rauck (Jackson Township trustee), Laura Lanese (councilwoman), and Mayor Ike Stage taking part in the ground-breaking ceremony.